HOW THE
POPE BECAME
INFALLIBLE

HOW THE POPE BECAME INFALLIBLE

Pius IX and the Politics of Persuasion

August Bernhard Hasler

Introduction by Hans Küng

Translated by Peter Heinegg

DOUBLEDAY & COMPANY, INC.
Garden City, New York   1981

This book was originally published in German under the title WIE DER
PAPST UNFEHLBAR WURDE: Macht und Ohnmacht eines Dogmas (©
1979 by R. Piper & Co. Verlag, München).

ISBN: 0-385-15851-3
Library of Congress Catalog Card Number 79–6851

Translation copyright © 1981 by Doubleday & Company, Inc.

"When papal infallibility was defined in 1870, the Church was anticipating on a higher level the historical decision which has now been made on a political level: a decision for authority and against discussion, for the pope and against the sovereignty of the Council, for the Führer and against the parliament." (Prelate Robert Grosche, September 1933)

Contents

HOW THE
POPE BECAME
INFALLIBLE

INTRODUCTION:
The Infallibility Debate—
Where Are We Now?

Can a great public question be laid to rest before it has found an answer? The old infallibility of kings, emperors, and tsars reigning by the grace of God has long since ceased to be an issue. And the newer infallibility of autocrats, dictators, duces, führers, and general secretaries reigning on their own has now become—after two world wars, Auschwitz, the Gulag Archipelago, democratization in Spain, and the first signs of a turning away from Mao in China—distinctly brittle. Of course, debate over infallible *parties* (and their current representatives) is still being stifled as usual, from Moscow to Havana, with every oppressive and repressive means available. And then, many people are asking in turn, what about the infallibility of *churches*, which, like certain political parties, "are always right"? What about the Church's representatives, past or present, who invoke the Holy Spirit to justify their decisions? Whatever other differences may separate the Catholic Church from totalitarian societies, this one at least is clear: In the wake of the Second Vatican Council it is simply impossible for the Church to bury the issue of infallibility.

On the occasion of the hundredth anniversary of papal infallibility (defined by the First Vatican Council in 1870), I tried to give a precise formulation to this widely discussed but vague question in my book *Infallible? An Inquiry* (1970). This was something like a parliamentary interpellation by His Majesty's loyal opposition in a free commonwealth. Religious authorities in Rome, with the help of bishops' conferences, were doing their best to mandate silence on this problem, which had suddenly sprung to life again, and to get rid of the whole thing once and for all. But, though condemned to death, the issue remained alive, and discussion among believers could not be throttled.

And surely, unprejudiced observers in Rome never imagined that in this day and age the Church could dispose of such an inquiry merely by repeating conciliar decrees whose infallibility had been dubious from the very beginning and which were once more being challenged. Well before the 1970s a similar line used to be taken by kings and generals, fathers, teachers and, often enough, professors trying to rescue their jeopardized infallibility: We are infallible because we have said that we are infallible!

But there was no avoiding the reply: With what right have you—and your forebears—said that you were infallible? And in the Church of all places. With what right do you lay claim to the infallibility of the Holy Spirit of God, which "blows where it wills," you who are men and not God? Doesn't "to err is human" hold true for you? Or has God anywhere ascribed to you his own infallibility? If so, that would have to be attested to in the most unambiguous language. People in the Bible (and in the Church of the New Testament, beginning with Peter, the "Rock") do not exactly convey an impression of infallibility. Peter was not the only one—Peter, whom the Lord once called "Satan," who denied the Lord three times, who, even after Easter, and above all in Antioch, proved to be quite fallible in his controversy with Paul—for whom the cock crowed. And thus, for many long decades nobody mentioned any infallibility of the bishop of Rome (nor, for the time being, of the ecumenical councils either). In fact, upon close inspection the historian must judge infallibility to be an innovation of the second millennium, and really only of the nineteenth century. So what is left of the argument that papal and conciliar infallibility are rooted in Scripture and old Catholic tradition?

Or may one not ask that question? Should even asking it be

a sin, and full-fledged inquiry a mortal sin? No, once the Vatican has gotten over its first (and understandable) shock, it can't seriously say things like that anymore. That would be a sign of fear, and would only provoke the child's question about the emperor's new clothes. No, a church that has nothing to fear from the truth, that has nothing more to fear than untruth, that claims to be the "pillar and foundation of the truth"—a church like that has an altogether vital interest in seeing that the truth is not stifled but continually "revealed" anew. Too much is at stake here to let silence become the long-term policy. For, after all, isn't the problem of infallibility now as ever the biggest obstacle to renewal within the Church? Isn't the doctrine of infallibility the most serious stumbling block on the road to ecumenical understanding? Isn't it the claim to infallibility which costs the Church its credibility and makes it seem so inept, despite all its unquestionably positive contributions and its still greater potential for good in today's society? Poverty and underdevelopment in the Third World, the population explosion, birth control, the encyclical *Humanae vitae*, the infallibility of traditional church doctrine—all these things are now so tightly connected that people who preach such loud sermons to outsiders actually ought to shout this message to those inside the Church instead of keeping silent on the whole business of infallibility.

Certainly anyone who has clearly and repeatedly said what needs to be said on this subject doesn't have constantly to start all over again. In the current overheated atmosphere, that might do more to hinder than help thoughtful self-criticism and practical planning (on both sides). But continual readiness to discuss the issues is just as imperative as thorough respect for the persons involved (though in any case there must be no compromise on essentials). This way we can be sure of reflecting on the problem in a spirit both critical and self-critical. But there can be no "truce" on such a fundamental matter—and there never has been one—not just because the authorities in Rome have yet to enter into any such "partnership" but also because in the long run unconvinced individuals would be obliging themselves to keep silent, which would go against their conscience, against the freedom of scholarly research, and against the true interests of the Church and its leadership.

The Catholic Church and its leaders, in fact, ought not to view questions and inquiry as an attack from outside but as help from within. For they themselves have the greatest interest of all in seeing

1) that the process of undoing the ideology of the absolutist-authoritarian magisterium, which began with John XXIII and Vatican II, be completed so as to create a genuine spiritual authority and to free the Church from the arrogance, coercion, and dishonesty of a curialist theology and administration;

2) that a conscious effort be made to exploit the new beginnings of Vatican II, which, under the inspiration of John XXIII, deliberately chose to forego infallible definitions, and in opposition to traditional dogmatism called for a new way of proclaiming the Christian message—and to some degree made such a proclamation itself; and

3) that the historicity of truth and of its formulations be given fresh recognition in the Church, thus making possible a better foundation for the Christian faith, furthering the modernization and renewal of the Catholic Church, and in all this helping the cause of Jesus Christ to make a new breakthrough in a "church" system which in many ways contradicts the message of him in whose name it speaks.

Fortunately, the latest phase of the infallibility debate—as early as 1973 there was uncontested evidence of progress here—has already clarified a good number of points:

I. *Justification for the inquiry:* The uncomfortable texts from Vatican I and II—on this point both the critical inquirers themselves and the Roman authorities agree—are to be taken literally. Their original meaning may not be softened or watered down, as Catholic theologians in recent days (for reasons which are transparent) have continually tried to do. Opportunistic reinterpretation, ultimately leading to outright denial of the text, is a common feature of all authoritarian systems, but it only obscures the problems, violates intellectual integrity, and delays a comprehensive solution. Of course, read in their original sense, knowing what we know today, the texts on infallibility pose a still greater challenge to every Catholic than they did one hundred years ago. But sticking one's head in the sand, theologically speaking, leads nowhere: An enlightened attitude here is as indispensable as it once was on the issue of Galileo. Catholic belief need not degenerate to the level of blind faith, where one believes only because the pastor says so. On this matter our examination must go beyond the (so-called "extraordinary") infallibility of the pope making dogmatic definitions ("how the pope became infallible"). A second question, much neglected by the anti-Infallibilist minority at Vatican I, is the (likewise "extraordinary") infallibility of definitions made by an ecumenical council. And a third is even more explosive: the (everyday, usual, "ordinary") infallibility of the entire episcopate all over the world. According to Vatican II, this body is also supposed to be infallible whenever pope and bishops concur in teaching that a specific theological or moral doctrine (e.g., the immorality of "artificial" contraception) is definitively binding. This question of doctrinal agreement between pope and bishops was a determining factor in the promulgation of *Humanae vitae*. Vatican II guaranteed the infallibility of such joint declarations ("Thus they proclaim in infallible fashion the teaching of Christ"), even in the absence of any explicit definition. This has proved to be the chemical agent that keeps the question of infallibility in constant ferment. Traditionally minded theologians often see this connection more clearly than the ones thought of as progressive. Such clarity, however, only throws into sharper relief the general perplexity vis-à-vis the infallibility of this "ordinary" magisterium.

II. *The contemporary Catholic consensus:* There is fundamental agreement on three important points:

A. The errors of the magisterium are a fact. Nowadays Catholic theologians concede with heretofore unwonted frankness that even the organs responsible for "infallible" doctrinal decisions can err, at least in principle (though perhaps not in

specific situations), and often have erred. "No one who observes
the history of the Church with any objectivity can deny that it
has often enough promulgated errors. This is true both of the
Church as a whole and of those church authorities which view
themselves as the source of infallible doctrinal decisions, namely,
the pope and the ecumenical councils, as well as the entire
episcopate in the daily exercise of proclaiming the faith—insofar
as it does this in a body." (O. Semmelroth)

B. Skepticism has been eating away at the concept and
practice of infallibility: Even some conservative theologians consider the notion misleading, in fact, largely incomprehensible in
today's world. One cannot help noticing that since the recent
debate on the issue began, the word "infallible" has largely
disappeared from theological and even official ecclesiastical terminology. Nobody wants infallible definitions anymore, neither
to foster piety nor to clarify complex contemporary problems. If
it hadn't already been defined, papal infallibility would certainly
not be defined today. The plausibility structures—the political,
social, cultural, and theological presuppositions—supporting the
Vatican definitions in the nineteenth century no longer exist. All
that remains for the Catholic people is the definition itself, and
neither the laity nor the theologians nor even the popes have a
very good idea of what to do with it. The "exaggerations" and
"misuse" of the papal magisterium over the past hundred years
are often bemoaned, but those who complain are less willing to
admit that such negative developments are not accidental but
built right into the structure of the Vatican dogmas. Still, there
is no longer any ignoring the pattern leading from Pius IX and
Vatican I through the campaign against modernism under Pius
X to the *Humani generis* purge under Pius XII. The era of the
Sodalitium Pianum (see Chapter 8) in nineteenth- and twentieth-century church history only ended with John XXIII.

C. Despite all its errors, the Church will remain preserved
in the truth: Even for conservatives who defend infallible pronouncements, the Church's indestructible link with the truth (indefectibility) is more basic than the infallibility of particular

statements. And now that no one can argue about the existence, in general, of errors by the magisterium, there is agreement, at least in principle, on the positive thesis that the Church will be preserved in the truth of the Gospel, for all its errors. But what this means concretely will have to be discussed later on.

III. *The decisive question:* Beyond this fundamental indefectibility, aren't there perhaps judgments, statements, definitions, and *credal propositions* which are not only de facto true (which no one denies) but *infallibly true?* That is, are there not certain officials or authoritative institutions which, owing to the special assistance of the Holy Spirit, in a certain specified situation find themselves a priori incapable of making a mistake? This is a clear and precise phrasing of the question in the wake of Vatican I, which taught that the repositories of authority (pope and bishops) were not continually infallible, but only in delivering themselves of carefully specified judgments, sentences, definitions, and "propositions." In the recent debate on infallibility, critics have taken direct aim at these infallible propositions, which are not only not false de facto but can in no way be false because of the help of the Holy Spirit (e.g., the Marian dogmas). And what was the result? Briefly put, to date not a single theologian and not a single official authority have managed to make a case for the possibility of such infallible credal propositions which, together with the authorities behind them, would be guaranteed by the Holy Spirit. The altogether exhaustive discussion we have had thus far shows that there are no solid grounds in Scripture or the body of Catholic tradition for accepting such infallibly true propositions or authorities. And to adduce as proof for them the very doctrinal texts from Vatican I and II that are in dispute is a transparent begging of the question. It only stands to reason that Vatican I and Vatican II never solved problems whose existence neither Council recognized.

IV. *Unexpected confirmation:* The newer (older, in point of fact) Catholic position on infallibility has been unexpectedly confirmed by Catholic scholars:

A. With regard to *Peter:* Recent exegetical studies by Catholics have elaborated on Peter's genuine but fallible authority, and the problems related to succession in the "Petrine service." The symbolic figure of Peter kept its importance for the Church in the generations that followed him, but there is little support in the New Testament and the first three centuries for any infallibility on his part (the biblical evidence characteristically combines Peter's positive *and* negative qualities at every turn), and still less for the infallibility of the bishops of Rome. The main proof text cited at Vatican I for papal infallibility, Luke 22:32 ("I have prayed for you that your faith may not fail") was never used even by medieval canonists to document this dogma—and rightly so. In this passage Jesus does not promise Peter freedom from error but the grace to persevere in the faith till the end. Still, the same medieval canonists applied this not to the Roman bishops but to the faith of the entire Church. To construe Luke 22:32 as referring to the infallibility of the bishop of Rome turns out to be an innovation with no textual basis.

B. With regard to the *ecumenical councils:* The first Ecumenical Council of Nicaea (325) got along without any claim to infallibility. Recent historical research has pointed out the way in which the leader of this Council, Athanasius, along with many Greek Fathers of the Church and Augustine as well, explained the true—but in no sense infallible—authority of a council: A council speaks the truth not because it was convoked in a juridically unobjectionable manner, not because a majority of the bishops in the world were in attendance, not because it was confirmed by any sort of human authority, not, in a word, because it was, from the start, incapable of being deceived; but because, in spite of new words it says nothing new, because it hands on the old tradition in new language, because it bears witness to the original message, because it breathes the air of Scripture, because it has the Gospel behind it. One must distinguish this classical Catholic notion of a council from, in the East, the later mystical or juridical *Byzantine* "conciliar revalorizations," and, in the West—especially with reference to the authority of the papacy—from the *Roman Catholic* versions. The latter began to take on a distinctly Roman character with the popes of the fifth century, became dominant after the reform of Gregory VII, and was finally made a dogma at the First Vatican Council.

C. With regard to the *origin of the Roman doctrine of infallibility:* The latest historical studies—this was perhaps the biggest surprise of the whole debate—have discovered the unorthodox origins of the Roman doctrine of infallibility at the end of the thirteenth century. Scholars have the American historian Brian Tierney to thank for the discovery that the doctrine did not slowly "develop" or "unfold," but rather was created in one stroke in the late 1200s. And the "inventors" of papal infallibility and irreformability (both go together from the very beginning) were not at all, as previously suspected, the orthodox papalist theologians and canonist-popes of the High Middle Ages but an eccentric Franciscan, Peter Olivi (d. 1298), repeatedly accused of heresy. At first no one took Olivi's notion seriously, and in 1324 it was condemned by John XXII as a work of the devil, the Father of Lies. Even the Reformation popes could not invoke any generally accepted concept of infallibility, and the Council of Trent, it is worth noting, likewise never defined the pope's infallibility. Intellectually speaking, it was the ideologues of the counterrevolution and the Restoration, de Lamennais and above all de Maistre, who were primarily responsible for Vatican I's definition of infallibility: The dogma was essentially a "new idea of the nineteenth century" (C. Langlois). The medieval canonists—and in those days the Church's teaching was their business—had never claimed that the Church needed an infallible head to preserve its faith. Instead they maintained that, however its head might err, the Church as a whole would never be led astray.

On the strength of the exegetical, historical, and systematic research conducted thus far, one point can hardly be disputed: More than was to be expected, the modern critical attack on the principles of infallibility has the backing of Scripture and the body of Catholic tradition. This fact has now been reconfirmed in many different ways by the new book of a Vatican insider: August Bernhard Hasler, Catholic theologian, historian, and for many years member of the staff of the Secretariat for Unity. I could not turn down the request of my fellow countryman for a word of introduction. What new material does his book bring to bear on the subject of infallibility?

1. *Hasler's book tells the story of how the definition of infallibility came about.* Anyone who has read Butler and Lang's history of the First Vatican Council or the Louvain Catholic historian Roger Aubert's studies of Pius IX and Vatican I knows in the main what awaits him. Hasler, to be sure, recounts the history of infallibility in a more systematic, detailed, graphic, and unsparing fashion than do either Aubert or Butler and Lang. This is not due to the historian who does the telling; it is the story he has to tell, one that is by and large simply a *chronique scandaleuse.* Hasler unfolds it before us without glossing over or hushing anything up, describing the manipulation of the debate over infallibility—how the definition was prepared for, promoted, and pushed through—and returning again and again to Pius IX. Finally we have a Catholic historian who gives truly serious attention to the losing side at the Council and to their arguments (which have been proved right many times over since then); who has exhaustively perused the diaries and notes—those still available, at any rate—of the anti-Infallibilist bishops and even of the most hard-line spokesmen *for* infallibility (often just as awkward as the first group for writers who stress the Council's harmoniousness); who deals with both parties without defusing, downplaying, or explaining away the conflict between them; and who thus, with an understandable one-sidedness, brings in new sources to correct and balance the previous one-sided historical accounts.

Where my *Infallible? An Inquiry* merely broke a taboo, Hasler seems to be digging into an open wound, which may be the reason why in a few cases Catholic critics reacted to his earlier scholarly study of Vatican I by maligning him instead of arguing with him. But all the various defense mechanisms, narrow-mindedness, repressions, anxieties, and ideological interests manifest in the writing of these critics only make it more difficult to argue the question rationally. For all the attention that Hasler devotes to the most pronounced tendencies,

developments, and structures of the age, he focuses especially on
the figure of Pius IX, analyzing him as one would other world-his-
torical personalities, from both the historical and psychological
point of view. This is appropriate for the narrative of a period
where no one played a more decisive role than this man: Without him Vatican I's dogma of infallibility would never have been
defined. (For fuller documentation of Hasler's account of Pius
IX and Vatican I, see his earlier scholarly study, *Pius IX* [*1846–
1878*], *Papal Infallibility, and the First Vatican Council: Dogmatization and Imposition of an Ideology*, on which this new book
is based.) In view of the superabundance of convergent testimony from participants and observers at Vatican I, one wonders:
Can all the suspicious facts reported here concerning the genesis
of the dogmatic definition and its triumph at the Council really
have no impact on the question of the *truth* of the definition?

2. *Hasler's book intensifies the inquiry into the legitimacy of
the definition of infallibility.* Reducing this book to a mere
popularized retelling of how this extraordinary late stage of
papal evolution occurred would be to belittle it. No, this is a
very concrete treatment of the fundamental questions as they
emerge from history itself. Almost all of them had already been
discussed during Vatican I or immediately after it, but later sank
out of sight, only to reappear with new explosive force in the
context of the recent debate over infallibility. Historians may
quarrel with Hasler over his evaluation of this or that source, the
way he incorporates specific details into his presentation, and
similar things. But one would have to trot through history wearing blinders if, after reviewing the quantity and quality of the
disquieting material Hasler has accumulated, one did not find
oneself asking questions akin to the following four:

A. Was Vatican I a *really free council?* Freedom is certainly
a very relative concept, historically speaking. But what if there
is evidence that a quite significant part of the Council did not
feel free? Anyone who tries to head off the question of freedom
at Vatican I by pointing out the lack of freedom of other councils (such as, say, Ephesus in 431) merely aggravates the problem. Non-Catholic church historiography unanimously contests

the freedom of Vatican I with respect to the infallibility debate (which is the only issue here). But recent Catholic writing on church history likewise concedes that conciliar freedom was sharply limited—though it generally dilutes this admission with the claim, more apologetic-dogmatic than historical, that there was enough freedom to insure the validity of the Council's decrees.

But even back in 1870 a large number of prominent participants and observers at Vatican I denied the presence of this necessary freedom, and hence this issue deserves to be looked into today. In point of fact, what sort of freedom could there be at a council where discussion had been prejudiced from the very start, where the agenda only allowed a limited freedom of speech and never when it counted, where the pope exercised a predominant influence from beginning to end—a pope whose own peculiar claim to power and sovereignty was the subject of the whole debate? So repressive were the agenda and official procedures; so one-sided and partisan were the selection of the main theological experts and the composition of both the conciliar commissions and the conciliar presidium; so numerous were the means of pressure (moral, psychological, church-political, newspaper campaigns, threatened withdrawal of financial support, harassment by the police) to which the bishops of the anti-Infallibilist minority *and* the Infallibilist majority were exposed; so varied were the forms of manipulation applied, at the pope's behest, to advance the definition before, during, and after the Council that we should not be surprised to see the old question of conciliar freedom, once pushed aside, now coming back, revived by the recent debate over infallibility. As painful and embarrassing as it may be to admit, this Council resembled a well-organized and manipulated totalitarian party congress rather than a free gathering of free Christian people.

B. Was Vatican I a *really ecumenical council?* Ecumenicity, too, is a historically relative concept, but this much is clear from church history: Not every council that claimed to be ecumenical has been accepted ("received") as ecumenical. And the fact that when its freedom is called into question, the ecumenicity of Vatican I also becomes problematical, ought not to prevent a new, objective investigation.

What the French bishop François Lecourtier wrote at the time is confirmed by similar testimony from countless bishops and council observers: "Our weakness at this moment comes neither from Scripture nor the tradition of the Fathers nor the witness of the General Councils nor the evidence of history. It comes from our lack of freedom, which is radical. An imposing minority, representing the faith of more than one hundred million Catholics, that is, almost half of the entire Church, is crushed beneath the yoke of a restrictive agenda, which contradicts conciliar traditions. It is crushed by commissions which have not been truly elected, and which dare to insert undebated paragraphs in the texts after debate has closed. It is crushed by the commission for postulates, which has been imposed upon it from above. It is crushed by the absolute absence of discussion, response, objections, and the opportunity to demand explanations; by newspapers which have been encouraged to hunt the bishops down and to incite the clergy against them; by the nuncios who bring on reinforcements when the newspapers no longer suffice to throw everything into confusion, and who try to promote the priests ahead of the bishops as witnesses to the faith, while reducing the true, divinely chosen witnesses to the level of delegates of the lower clergy, indeed to rebuke them if they do not act accordingly. The minority is crushed above all by the full weight of the supreme authority which oppresses it with the praise and encouragement it lavishes on the priests in the form of papal briefs. It is crushed by the displays of favor to Dom Guéranger, and of hostility to M. de Montalembert and others."

There is no getting around the questions which arise out of this situation: Did the other "half" of the Catholic Church get a sufficient chance to speak? Were not the representatives of this group in a hopeless position before they started, faced with the numerical superiority of the bishops from Italian cities and overmatched by the pope and the curial machine? Was the quantitative majority of this Council truly representative of the whole Catholic Church, not to mention the entire Christian ecumene?

And, at the very least, has the definition of infallibility been accepted ("received") by the whole Catholic Church?

The drama of Bishop Lecourtier—who ended up throwing his conciliar documents in the Tiber and leaving Rome prematurely, for which reason he was removed from office as bishop of Montpellier after the Council—is an example of the crisis of conscience that so many of the most prominent and best educated of the bishops went through. They, too, left Rome before the deciding vote was taken, and only endorsed the dogma after being subjected to indescribable pressure from the Vatican and from their own dioceses. They often gave their final consent only for the sake of church unity, acknowledging the definition in an attenuated sense and without any inner conviction. All the books put on the Index, the dismissals, the sanctions and excommunications, all the manipulative and repressive methods used by the Curia and the nuncios, the threats, surveillance, and denunciations, and, last of all, the Old Catholic schism and the "interior emigration" of so many Catholics, especially theologians and educated people: All this makes it seem perfectly justified to ask whether the definition of infallibility passed by this Council ever got anything like a free "reception."

C. Were *the sacrifices* worth it? The definition of infallibility marked the apogee of the Roman system, particularly as it had developed after the Gregorian reform in the eleventh century. Infallibility performed the function of a metadogma, shielding and insuring all the other dogmas (and the innumerable doctrines and practices bound up with them). With infallibility—and the infallible aura of the "ordinary," day-to-day magisterium is often more important than the relatively rare infallible definitions—the faithful seemed to have been given a superhuman protection and security, which made them forget all fear of human uncertainty, as well as freedom and the risk that faith entails. In this sense the dogma of infallibility has undoubtedly integrated the lives of believers and unburdened their minds, and most effectively furthered the unity, uniformity, and power of Roman Catholicism. This was fitting for a Church which, as time went on, increasingly came to look upon itself as a "bulwark" (Cardinal Ottaviani's *il baluardo*) against evil in this world. What could be better for legitimizing, stabilizing, and immunizing this system against criticism than the dogma of the infallibility of its highest representative(s)? The only question remaining was whether the dogma of infallibility itself was actually legitimized, stabilized, and immunized: whether its own truth was secure.

Up until Pius XII the system seemed intact. Only under John XXIII did the energies which had been forcibly repressed and dammed up for so long come bursting forth, leading in a relatively short time (to the surprise of the greater part of mankind) to a new attitude on the part of the Catholic Church towards itself, the other Christian churches, the Jews, world religions, and modern society in general. Things tabooed under Pius IX (such as religious freedom and tolerance, ecumenism and human rights) were now loudly praised as Catholic teaching. By the time Vatican II was under way, infallibility, which had been used for an entire century to defend traditional positions on every trend in modern life, already seemed to many people, in Rome and elsewhere, badly shaken and in danger of collapse.

But, as Catholics realized with fresh clarity after John XXIII and Vatican II, what sacrifices it had cost to achieve the old authority, continuity, and infallibility! John XXIII had named some previously condemned theologians as official conciliar experts, which gave many council fathers pause. Even the more traditional theologians later wondered whether Vatican I's definition of infallibility might not have been, after all, something like the "gigantic disaster" Hans Urs von Balthasar said it was. Had the Old Catholic schism and the emigration inward of so many educated people, who no longer felt at home in an authoritarian and often totalitarian church, really been necessary? Had the demoting of bishops to lackeys of Rome, the purges of theologians under Pius IX, Pius X (*Pascendi gregis* and the antimodernism campaign), Pius XII (*Humani generis* and the condemnation of the worker-priests), and even Paul VI (*Humanae vitae*) really been worth it? And all the bans on speaking and writing, the advance censorship and autocensorship, the denunciations and prohibition of books, the excommunications and suspensions, the restricted access to archives, the dictation of policy on church personnel, the Curia, and the episcopate along party lines, and, lastly, along with all this, the self-imposed isolation of the "prisoner in the Vatican" (a prisoner in more than one way)—had it been worth it? Was Ignaz von Döllinger altogether wrong when he wrote to the archbishop of Munich in 1887 that the papal dogmas had come into being thanks to force and coercion, and that they should also have to be continually paid for with force and coercion?

There is no dodging the fact that in the Catholic world church history, exegesis, dogmatics, moral theology, and catechesis have all had to pay a high price since Vatican I for this infallibility, which allowed for no genuine corrections and revisions, but at best "interpretations" and adaptations. It brought on a continual conflict with history and the modern world which profoundly shook the credibility of the Catholic Church; a continual defensiveness towards new information and experiences, towards all scientific criticism, towards all possible enemies, real or imagined. And it created a gap between the Church and modern science, between theology and historical research, but increasingly, too, within theology itself between dogmatic history and dogmatics, and exegesis and dogmatics. Enormous sacrifices were also indirectly demanded of the "little people"—in the interests of authority, continuity, and doctrinal infallibility. The ban on contraception is only a particularly striking example of all the burdens placed on the individual conscience by the teaching presented as de facto infallible in catechisms, confessionals, religious instruction, and sermons. The exodus of countless intellectuals, the inner alienation of many believers, the lack of creative people and initiatives in the Church, the processes of repression, the symptomatic hardening and stiffening, the psychic disturbances, the loss of touch with reality, the mighty religious machine whose operations very often conceal the absence of inner life . . . There is no point in prolonging the list of complaints, but the question suggests itself irresistibly: Was all that necessary? What good did it do?

D. *Will Pius IX be canonized?* Right now powerful reactionary forces in Rome are once again pressing for the canonization of the "infallible teacher of the faith." The motives for this are transparently ideological and political, to support Pius IX and Vatican I and to oppose John XXIII and Vatican II, and hence to oppose any overtures by the Catholic Church to the rest of Christianity and the modern world. However, the negative judgments of Pius IX by his contemporaries, both bishops and others, are so numerous and carry so much weight that only with difficulty could they be made to square with the requirements for canonization. Catholic saints are supposed to exhibit a "heroic degree" not just of the theological virtues (faith, hope, and charity) but also of the four cardinal virtues (prudence, justice, fortitude, and temperance). Pius IX had a sense of divine mission which he carried to extremes; he engaged in doubledealing; he was mentally disturbed; and he misused his office. These negative qualities cannot be changed around into positive ones by appealing to the allegedly providential, unique ecclesiastical vocation of this pope. And then, in addition to Pius IX's notoriously weak theological training, there are his anti-Semitic, antiecumenical, and generally antidemocratic attitudes. A saint for the twentieth century? Discussion here ought to concentrate less on hypothetical or speculative matters (the effects of the pope's epilepsy, whether Cardinal Guidi was Pius IX's illegitimate son, and so forth) than on the undeniable facts which stand in the way of a canonization. These facts naturally make it advisable to suspend the proceedings as soon as possible. Otherwise the problems involved in such canonizations (especially when popes canonize their papal predecessors) will only become even more obvious.

The whole issue of Pius IX and Vatican I gives a particular urgency to the demands by church historians for broad access to the Vatican archives. Of what use was the much-heralded announcement that the Vatican's secret archives would be opened up for the entire pontificate of Pius IX (and now for the pontificate of his successor, Leo XIII, as well), when the archival material from Vatican I, along with other important documents, is still being withheld from researchers as much as ever? As long as the most significant archives remain closed (those belonging to the Congregation for Extraordinary Church

Affairs and the Congregation of the Faith, formerly called the Holy Office and before that known as both the Holy Inquisition and the Congregation of the Index), one can only speak of conditional accessibility. Leo XIII, who opened the Vatican's secret archives for the first time, said the Church had nothing to fear from the truth. If this is so, why does the policy of suppressing it go on?

The questions which grow out of Hasler's historical study are, unmistakably, highly troublesome ones. But even someone who would answer them differently from Hasler will admit that they are all, without exception, questions which may, indeed, which must, be asked for the sake of truth and of the Church's credibility. Anyone who finds this scandalous ought to recognize where the scandal is—in reality—and not accuse the man who simply reports about it, and who has the right to a free, unbiased, critical discussion of his findings.

With the critical destruction of Infallibilist myths and the historical reconstruction of Vatican I finally out of the way, the first half of the theological business at hand has been taken care of. But no less momentous than the question of "how the pope became infallible" is another one: "How can the pope (once more) be pope without infallibility?" Here are some thoughts on that subject as I framed them in connection with the infallibility debate back in 1973.

How could the pope "function" without infallible doctrinal definitions? As a matter of fact, we have in our time come to know two possibilities here. There was a pope—Pius XII—who, not quite a century after Vatican I, felt he had to lay claim to the full power which the Council had ascribed to the popes but which they had never used. He did this in order to proclaim an infallible doctrinal definition, a new dogma on Mary, *urbi et orbi*. Yet none of his other pronouncements were ever so controverted, throughout the Christian world and even in the Catholic Church, as this "infallible" definition. Pius XII had high hopes then that the dogma would foster devotion to Mary among Catholics and help to convert the world—hopes which, thirty years later, we can only judge to have been intemperate.

The fact that Vatican II dissociated itself from Mariolatry has made the questionableness of that definition still more apparent.

The other example: The next pope, John XXIII, had, from the start, no ambition whatever of proclaiming an infallible definition. On the contrary, he continually stressed in the most varied ways his own humanity, his limitations, and now and again even his fallibility. He lacked the aura of infallibility. And yet none of the popes in this century had as great an influence on the course of Catholic history and of Christianity itself as this pope who put no stock in infallibility. Pope John and Vatican II ushered in a new era of church history. Without any infallible proclamations he succeeded in getting the Church to listen to the gospel of Jesus Christ once more. This is what gave him the authority he had both inside and outside the Catholic Church, in a way that would have been unthinkable back in the days of his predecessor. In any event, with all his weaknesses and mistakes —his approach was more spontaneous than planned, more sketchy than programmatic—he demonstrated in rough outline how the pope could be pope without claiming infallibility: no jealous insistence on full power and prerogatives, no exercise of authority after the fashion of the ancien régime, but an authority of service, in the spirit of the New Testament, with a view to the needs of today—fraternal partnership and cooperation, dialogue, consultation and collaboration, above all, with the bishops and theologians of the entire Church, participation in the decision-making process of everyone affected by it, and an invitation to share responsibility. In other words, even when teaching and proclaiming the faith, the pope is most emphatically to see his function as *in* the Church, *with* the Church, *for* the Church, but not *over* or *outside* the Church.

On the other hand, this does not exclude the possibility of a pope's taking a decisive stand *against* something or, under certain circumstances, having a duty to take a stand. There was no need of any sort of infallible definition in the face of the blitzkrieg in Poland or the mass murder of the Jews: A clear, understandable statement from the "Deputy" truly reflecting the Christian message would have been enough. It is remarkable how seldom the popes have spoken "infallibly" in modern times just when countless millions of people would have expected them to. Conversely, in spite of all his fallibility, the pope can (together with the rest of the bishops) serve the community of the Church, promote its unity, inspire the missionary work of the Church in the world, and intensify his efforts for peace and justice, disarmament, human rights, the social liberation of nations and races, and the disadvantaged everywhere. Without making any claim to infallibility, he can let the voice of the Good Shepherd ring out time and again in the Christian ecumene and far beyond it through his life and work. He would then become a source of inspiration in the spirit of Jesus Christ and a leader in Christian renewal, and Rome would become a rendezvous for conversation and candid, friendly cooperation.

It follows from all this that the pope can indeed function without infallible doctrinal definitions. He can, in fact, *better* fulfill his obligations in the Church and the world such as they are today without such definitions. To raise doubts, then, about the infallibility of papal pronouncements is not to call the papacy itself into question. This point must be stressed as firmly as possible to correct the continual errors, distortions, and insinuations one hears on this topic. Many aspects of the Petrine office *have* become dubious, most notably the medieval and modern forms of absolutism, which have been retained right up to the present. The papacy has a future only if it is understood in the light of the Petrine symbolism found in the New Testament. The exegetical and scholarly grounds for a *historical* succession of the bishops of Rome have also become questionable. But the papacy will have kept its real meaning if it functions as a *practical succession* of servants to the entire Church: a primacy of service in the full biblical sense.

Such a primacy of service, as we saw it, at least sketched out if not completed, in the figure of John XXIII, offers the Catholic Church and the whole Christian world a great *opportunity*. A primacy based on service would be more than a "primacy of honor." The latter would be unforgivable in a church that aimed to serve mankind; it would, in its very passivity, be of no help to anyone. A primacy of service would also be more than a "primacy of jurisdiction": Seen purely in terms of power and authority, that would be a fundamental misunderstanding of the ideal, and if taken literally would leave out the most important thing of all, namely, service. The papacy, as the Bible would have it, can only be a "pastoral primacy": a service of ministry to the entire Church. This sort of papacy is fully supported by the New Testament, despite all the problems of historical succession which have not yet been cleared up and probably never will be. This sort of papacy could greatly benefit all of the modern Christian world.

I bring this up partly by way of answering Hasler's question about my own position: Yes, the Catholic Church once was and might once more become a community "without strictly authoritarian management (as in the magisterium's official monopoly on interpreting Scripture and Tradition)." Free, unbiased scientific research, which obviously includes critical historical examination of the New Testament (see *On Being a Christian*) as well as critical reflection on the relationship between faith and understanding (see *Does God Exist?*), does not lead to the self-destruction of the Church but to its renewal. In the context of this Introduction, I would rather not go any further into the basic theological issue of the Church's indefectibility in the truth —which is admittedly a matter of faith. Instead I refer the reader to my brief "theological meditation" entitled *The Church— Maintained in the Truth?*, which is coming out just now.

There is one last question left: Can a Catholic theologian who criticizes infallibility *remain a Catholic?* Superficial observers sometimes miss the point that excommunication, suspension, or loss of one's teaching post are still real possibilities. They are, wherever they prove effective, still in use. Even Catholic theologians with economic and legal security would find such forms of condemnation difficult to bear. This again is naturally something which only someone who values his membership in a specific community of believers can really understand.

Thus far the recent debate over infallibility has not been marked by excommunications, suspensions, or professors losing their jobs, and such things are not likely to occur in the future. This is not only because, as Hasler argues, individual theologians critical of Rome have so much popularity, influence, and power that they could not be punished; but because people throughout the Catholic world and even in Rome have recognized that the facts at issue and the questions being asked are complex and difficult. The number of doubters is too high. Opinion polls, were they taken, might well show that in many countries only a minority of Catholics believe in papal infallibility. And so the previous attempt to brand the critics of infallibility before all the world as un-Catholic proved to be a failure. The same thing happened with the critics of the Papal States, who were threatened with excommunication but who have finally been vindicated—many of them, of course, only after their death.

We have to make a distinction here. "Un-Catholic" does not mean someone who turns against the *Roman system,* that is, Roman Catholicism, which achieved a position of dominance in doctrine, ethics, and church government in the eleventh century, and which has been continually accused of overcentralization, absolutism, triumphalism, and imperialism, both at Vatican II and in the postconciliar period, by bishops, theologians, and laymen. From the standpoint of the Gospel, there is no reason to reject the notion of a unique role—in connection with Peter and the great Roman tradition—for the pope as servant ministering to souls. But that absolutist curial system which views the free community of the Catholic faith as a religious version of the Roman Empire violates the spirit of the Gospel and is chiefly responsible for the schism with the Eastern Church, for the Protestant Reformation, and for the petrifaction of the Catholic Church.

"Un-Catholic" refers to anyone who voluntarily turns his back on the Catholic (or whole, universal, all-encompassing) Church. Or, more precisely, anyone who abandons the dogged continuity of belief and of communion in that belief (catholicity in time), which has persisted through all the Church's failures; anyone who gives up on the universality of belief and of communion in that belief (catholicity in space), which embraces all different groups; anyone, then, who falls prey to a "Protestant" radicalism and particularism, which has nothing to do with genuine evangelical radicalness and orientation to local communities. Today, more clearly than ever before, the question poses itself: Does not the infallibility of doctrinal propositions (like the

Papal States in the last century) belong more to the curialist system than to the Catholic Church, as it has understood itself from the very first?

The author of this new book on infallibility should realize, though, that any Catholic theologian who tries to make distinctions in his critique of the Church has chosen a narrow and dangerous path, and he is likely to be the target of invective from two opposing sides. This sort of theology, which subjects everything to critical scrutiny, will undoubtedly be abused by the benighted guardians of the faith. Because these people (for reasons one can partly comprehend) would prefer not to have theologians saying their piece in a new fashion. The Church, after all, might lose some of its teaching authority if anyone thinks or speaks about God and the Church except along lines that have been sanctioned by ecclesiastical tradition and officialdom.

A theology that continually presses forward through and beyond all its negative criticism to positive answers will doubtless be attacked by both conservatives *and* pseudoenlightened despisers of religious belief. Because these people (again for reasons one can partly comprehend) would prefer not to have theologians saying anything at all about God and still less about the Church in the world of today. In their dreary one-dimensional manner they have yet to notice that it is precisely the enlightened individual nowadays who can think and speak in a new, different, and better way about God and even about the Church.

Anyone choosing this intermediate critical path will quite likely be taken by the first group for an unchurched heretic and by the second for an ecclesiastical conformist. Both groups say the same thing, the first out of pastoral concern, the second out of cynical provocation: Be consistent. Either come over to our side or the other; there's no partial identity. Isn't there? As if, when you detect serious flaws and abuses in a democratic state, you must, for consistency's sake, either acquiesce in them completely or leave the country. But this is not the case. True consistency is not artificial rigidity—that would be false consistency. There is a course that avoids uncritical accommodation and hypercritical sectarianism, even if it is hard to hold to and exposed to misunderstanding from both sides: loyalty based on a sense of obligation to the Church, but always a critical loyalty, manifested in loyal criticism. That way his duty to the Church and to its message does no more harm to the critical theologian than duty to a state and its constitution does to a critical jurist. Loyalty and criticism, duty and freedom, sympathy and open-mindedness, faith and understanding are complementary, not mutually exclusive.

In hopes of reaching a fair resolution of the controversy over infallibility, the French theologian Yves Congar has called for a "re-reception" of Vatican I's papal doctrines. More than anyone else it was Congar who laid the groundwork for the modern understanding of the Church characteristic of Vatican II. Historical studies (Aubert, Torrell, Schatz), historical-theological analyses (Thils, Dejaifve, Pottmeyer), radical questions (Küng), then the fact of Vatican II itself, the revival of local and particular churches and, lastly, the revived appreciation of the principles of Eastern ecclesiology—all this, Congar maintains, has made more people realize how trapped in its own time Vatican I was. It also impels us "with our Catholic loyalty" to "re-receive" the Vatican dogmas, and especially the dogma of papal infallibility. Taking into consideration an authentic conception of the magisterium, the best exegetical, historical, and theological studies of the past few decades, the ecumenical contacts (made in such a changed environment) with the theology and concrete existence of the local churches, Congar thinks Catholics should get together with the other Christian churches to re-examine and reformulate the dogmas first defined by Vatican I in 1870 and subsequently accepted by the rest of the Church under the conditions prevalent during that epoch. Hasler believes that such a "re-reception" would, in fact, boil down to a revision of the decrees of Vatican I, which would in turn provide the Catholic Church and its theologians, and all of the ecumene, too, with a way out of a position which has become indefensible and a way into a new future.

Let me take Congar's suggestion and make it more concrete, not to stir up another round of arguments over infallibility but to put an end to the old one:

Now that there is a new pope, why not have a fresh investigation into the problem of infallibility from the exegetical, historical, and theological point of view, judging the matter with objectivity, scientific integrity, fairness, and justice?

Why not set up an *ecumenical commission* to deal with this issue (as was done before with birth control) made up of internationally recognized experts from the various disciplines (exegesis, history of dogma, systematic theology, and relevant nontheological fields)?

In carrying out this investigation, why not put more emphasis than before on the positive, constructive side of the question and less on the negative, critical side? Why not ask whether the notion that *the Church will remain in the truth despite all errors* doesn't have a more solid foundation in the Christian message and the great Catholic tradition than does infallibility, and whether this wouldn't make for a better life in the Church today?

One application of this idea: Pope Paul's rejection of every form of contraception was based on the Roman concept of the authority, continuity, universality, and therefore de facto infallibility and irreversibility of traditional doctrine. Since that time Rome seems to have come to an impasse on this question, as it has on some others. *Non possumus* (we cannot) is still the response today, as it once was to the demand that the Church relinquish the Papal States. The only way to solve the problem of contraception is to solve the problem of infallibility. The Church's leadership is all too often satisfied with admonishing everybody. In this case it could, in an act of humility and self-criticism, lend the world some active help by courageously revising the doctrine of the supposed immorality of all (!) contraception. This teaching, which forms the basis of *Humanae vitae*, has laid a heavy burden on the conscience of innumerable people, even in industrially developed countries with declining birthrates. But for the people in many underdeveloped countries, especially in Latin America, it constitutes a source of incalculable harm, a crime in which the Church has implicated itself. High birthrates are linked in a cause-effect relationship with poverty, illiteracy, unemployment, malnutrition, and disease. In the last two decades most of the gains (by no means insignificant) in food production among Third World nations were wiped out by population growth.

Pope John Paul II has just come back from Latin America with a store of new experiences. While he was there he spoke out clearly against poverty, underdevelopment, and the misery endured by children. He has also indicated a desire to work for greater ecumenical understanding. Is it hoping for too much, then, to expect him to take a decisive step towards clearing up this vexing question of infallibility—in an atmosphere of mutual trust, free research, and fair-minded discussion?

Tübingen, February 1979

Hans Küng
Director of the Institute
for Ecumenical Research,
University of Tübingen

FOREWORD
to the First Edition

Paul VI laid aside his tiara. Both his successors, John Paul I and John Paul II, dispensed with the throne and crown. But the popes' claim to infallibility has remained, and hence so has their position of power. For power was the issue in 1870, when the First Vatican Council ascribed to the pope inerrancy in matters of faith and morals, together with direct sovereignty over the entire Church.

Discussion of the dogma of infallibility has been going on now for several years, with theological and philosophical arguments getting most of the attention. Until very recently there had been no historical study of the way the solemn definition of papal infallibility came about and why this happened precisely in 1870.

In the late summer of 1977 I published a two-volume work dealing with these problems.[1] Not only did it evoke a wide response, but some of the more heated reactions to it showed how important the pope's supreme authority was and is to many people and, on the other hand, how historical research can make tempers flare when it touches on one of Catholicism's sore points without glossing it over or explaining it away. And so in this book I would like to make the most important findings of my investigation available to a broader reading public, presenting these results within a historical framework that stretches from Jesus to the pontificate of Paul VI. Anyone, of course, who wishes to explore this question thoroughly, in all its complex detail, will have to consult both volumes of the earlier version. That edition also contains all the references for material cited here, except for a few new items, which I annotate. I have not given references for the quotations carried over from the longer version so as to keep the critical apparatus down to reasonable limits.

This book was supposed to appear (in German) in the fall of 1978, put out by a well-known Catholic press. For reason of church politics, however, the publisher withdrew from his contract on short notice. I should therefore like to thank Mr. Klaus Piper all the more for taking my manuscript. It is a pleasure to recall my collaboration with R. Piper & Co., especially with Mrs. Renate Böhme and Dr. Klaus Stadler. I thank Professor Georg Denzler for his help in reading galley proofs.

The opening up of numerous archives and the publication of several historical studies have altered our idea of the events which led to the dogma of infallibility.[2] Only when as many people as possible take note of these new and still widely ignored discoveries can the papal claims of infallibility have a fair public trial. It is the author's opinion, naturally, that these claims constitute, even today, one of the grave problems facing the Church and society. The Vatican dogma is not merely one of the greatest obstacles in the path to Christian unity, it also blocks reform within the Church and, generally speaking, supports the spirit of authoritarianism in the community at large.

Rome/Munich, November 1978   August Bernhard Hasler

FOREWORD
to the Second Edition

Hardly anyone thought it could still happen, but it has: Papal Rome is once again branding as heretics those unwilling to believe in its infallibility. Of late, events have been following each other in rapid succession. On December 18, 1979, Professor Hans Küng was stripped of his ecclesiastical teaching privileges. In the future he can "neither be considered a Catholic teacher nor engage in teaching as such." A final "attempt at reconciliation" between Küng and the bishop of Rottenburg, Georg Moser, on December 30, 1979, proved to be a failure. The Congregation of the Faith justified its action on the express grounds that in the introduction to this book and in another piece Küng had disputed the pope's infallible magisterium.

Rome has spoken out in condemnation without advancing even a single argument on the matter at issue. This is all the more incomprehensible and regrettable in that those of us who have challenged infallibility have always called for a fair and open discussion of this doctrine, which has crumbled in the wake of recent scholarly studies. Innumerable Catholics now find that they can no longer accept the dogma of infallibility. For this reason arguments about it must go on—and they will.

Once more it has become evident that the doctrine of the infallible pope is no mere harmless leftover from the past, as some would like to believe. No, the Roman Curia is not simply adhering to it as firmly as ever, and using it to prop up its system, but ruthlessly hounding the dogma's opponents as well. This just heightens the need to show that Rome's pretensions are standing on feet of clay. And only if we realize this and act accordingly can the Church become truly Christian again.

For the second edition some corrections have been made, along with additions to the notes giving a listing of reviews of my book, *Pius IX (1846–1878), Papal Infallibility, and the First Vatican Council,* which have appeared since the spring of 1979.

St. Gall, January 1980   August Bernhard Hasler

1

From Rabbi Jesus
to the Infallible Pope

Christianity will soon be two thousand years old. Over the course of this long time it has split up into a host of different churches, denominations, and sects. All of them appeal to Jesus as their teacher and master, but among these many confessions the Roman Catholic Church occupies an altogether singular position owing to its size as well as to its antiquity and its remarkable claims. It views itself as the only true church. Its leader, the pope, styles himself *vicarius Christi,* the deputy of Christ. He maintains that he has the exclusive right to leadership of the entire Church, and that he is incapable of error when he makes *ex cathedra* decisions on matters of faith and morals.

What sort of path led from Jesus, the Jewish rabbi, to this infallible papal king in Rome? Is it simply the well-worn historical path of institutionalization, something that was necessary to carry on Jesus' original ideas? Or does it represent an aberration, a perversion of the original Christian message, a betrayal of the thoughts and goals of its founder? In this regard, let us briefly consider a few crucial moments in history.

Jesus Becomes a
Universal Teacher

Jesus himself never spoke of his infallibility, and yet he ar-
rives on the scene with an astonishing air of authority. True
enough, he inserts himself into the tradition of the Old Testament, the Torah, and the Midrashim (the law of the Jews and
commentaries by their teachers), but he also keeps his distance
from it. Alongside his fidelity to the Law goes his unmistakable
cry, "But I say to you . . ."

He proclaims the Kingdom of God which has dawned on us,
provided we open ourselves up to the grace offered by God, our
loving Father in heaven. These are some great, fundamental,
and yet simple truths, and Jesus will brook no doubts about
them. He even claims they are "infallible"—in the same way that
every religious prophet is convinced of the irreversible truth of
his preaching. Of course, Jesus also believed that the end of the
world was imminent, and in that he was mistaken.

Jesus did not demand the acceptance of any systematic doctrine. He was not concerned with abstract theses but with trust
in God and right living. His counsels were always very general.
He said nothing about vast areas of life, about politics, art, or
the relations between the sexes. But Jesus the religious charismatic gave freedom broad scope not simply by his silence:
Above and beyond that he just wasn't interested in setting rigid
limits.

As anyone can see, this powerful religious awakening is
quite different from the doctrinal system of the nineteenth- and
twentieth-century Catholic Church. There everything is covered
by the institutional insurance of laws and dogmas, and the infallibility of the papal magisterium offers a final, unsurpassable
guarantee of security. How did this come about? The roots of
this situation go a long way down.

The shocking, unexpected death of Jesus put the community
of his disciples to a hard and critical test. The Master had come
to a miserable end on the cross. No provisions had been made
for the survival of a group of people united in his name. No one

could say that Jesus founded a church. He had proclaimed the Kingdom of God to the whole nation of Israel; he had never wanted to establish a separate community.

But his frightened and discouraged disciples found a new solidarity through faith in his glorious resurrection. In this process, however, a decisive change took place. Now it was not Jesus' message but Jesus the messenger the person himself, who became the focal point for his disciples. In Jesus they saw the fulfillment of the promise which the scriptures of the Old Covenant had spoken of. In his death and resurrection God's act of salvation had been made visible, a concrete model for all men and women. Jesus had said nothing about this. On the other hand, the early Christian community confessed that Jesus was the *Kyrios*, the Lord. It thereby raised him to the sphere of divinity and made him the universal teacher of humanity.

Before long, various constructions began to form around the core of this primitive *kerygma*. Confessions of faith and hymns were written; there was teaching and preaching. And with that the Church began to prescribe a certain body of doctrine. We see the first signs ushering in dogma and the magisterium.

Sacred Books

By the time a second generation of Christians had arisen, a need was felt to fix the message of Christianity in writing. Next to the letters of the Apostle Paul came the accounts by the Evangelists, along with further epistles from various authors. Around 100 A.D. the canon of Old Testament scriptures was drawn up, and Christians, too, adopted it as *their* holy book. The first canon of Christian scriptures, the Muratori fragment, lay just a hundred years ahead. By the end of the fourth century the canon of the New Testament had been definitively spelled out. Now the Christians had their own Sacred Book.

The decisive criteria for inclusion in the canon were liturgical use and authorship (in most cases only putative) by one of the apostles. Holy Writ was held to be inspired by God, composed under his direction, and therefore incontrovertible evidence of the truths of religion. The holy, infallible Book joined the infallible religious Teacher, and so all was complete.

Jesus' Deputies

But we are anticipating the course of history. The canon would not have been possible without some authority to select from various sacred writings and to lay down arbitrary limits. And this church authority was slow to develop. At first untrammeled charisma was the rule, and the community lived in the belief that its Lord, Jesus Christ, was leading it through his Spirit. The critical thing was to proclaim Jesus as the Lord, and not to legitimize the power of one's office.

It is easy to see why this situation couldn't last. Every individual Christian, every community could appeal to the guidance of the Spirit. But who was to judge among differing opinions? A solution to this predicament became increasingly urgent as Christian thought underwent the influence of the surrounding Hellenistic world, where philosophical speculation played a much larger role than in Judaism. Gradually a change took place: The notion that Jesus himself led the Church by means of his Spirit gave way to the view that he had appointed his disciples as apostles, or *deputies*, and entrusted them with the leadership of the Church. They, in turn, no longer based their legitimacy on the message they proclaimed but on their mandate from Jesus. Thus the norm for doctrinal correctness shifted from the content of the teaching to the validity of the teacher's office.

This development was further spurred by the struggle against heresy. Where, people kept asking, can we find the true teaching? St. Irenaeus of Lyon (d. ca. 202 A.D.) was one of the first to come to grips with this question. He advised the faithful to adhere to the churches which had been founded by an apostle. Among others, he had the church of Rome especially in mind. As a matter of fact, however, it was not Apostolic origins but political position that determined who got authority in the Church. Constantinople is the most eloquent example of this. The community there had no ties with any of the apostles. (St.

Andrew would later be called on to remedy this defect.) Nevertheless, as the new capital of the Eastern Roman Empire, the city soon acceded to the second highest place in Christendom.

The Turning Point: Constantine and the Merger of Church and State

The reconciliation of the Roman Empire with Christianity under Constantine the Great (ca. 280–337) and the establishment of Christianity as the state religion altered the nature of churchly offices. A church hierarchy grew up that corresponded to the state's. Church officials received numerous privileges, some of them rising to the rank of senators. Civil and religious laws were now often identical. Canon law entered upon a boom period. After the partial breakdown of the Roman Empire, high church officials also took over political functions.

The most important consequence of all this was the creation of two classes within the Church: those who held office and those who didn't—lay people. The former, the masters, were to teach, to take action. The latter were looked upon as uneducated and were supposed to be passive and obedient.

Throughout all these centuries, however, nobody dreamed of an infallible magisterium in the Church—despite the positive abundance of religious controversies. Once Christianity became the state religion, deviations from orthodoxy threatened both the unity of the empire and of the Church. And it was the emperor who had the greatest interest in settling doctrinal disputes. He convoked ecumenical councils and largely dictated their results. With time, the decisions of some councils took on an obligatory character. But as yet no one said anything about infallibility. If anybody was infallible it was the emperor.

Legal Thinking in the Second Millennium

From the fourth century on, the bishops of Rome repeatedly

tried to spread the idea that their decrees were irrevocable and universally binding. They began to invoke biblical passages like Matt. 16:18 ("And I tell you, you are Peter, and on this rock I will build my church, and the powers of death shall not prevail against it") and Luke 22:32 ("I have prayed for you that your faith may not fail; and when you have turned again, strengthen your brethren"). They failed to impose this view in the West, and in the East they met bitter, determined opposition. But in the first millennium the popes themselves still weren't talking about their own infallibility, probably because all through Christianity's first thousand years content was more important than form, right teaching more critical than legal authority.

Then gradually the emphases began to shift. In the eleventh century, above all in the pontificate of Gregory VII (1073–85), juridical thinking began to sweep through the Church like a mighty river. From now on the canonists, the teachers of canon law, would have an enormous impact on Catholic life. New questions emerged: Who has the highest teaching authority in the Church? Who has the last word?

John XXII: The Doctrine of
Infallibility Is the
Work of the Devil

Interestingly enough, the Franciscan priest Peter Olivi (1248/9–98) was the first to attribute infallibility to the pope—from something less than the purest motives. In the year 1279 Pope Nicholas III (1277–80) had decided in favor of the Franciscans in the controversy over poverty by holding that communal renunciation of property was a possible way to salvation. One year later Peter Olivi tried to render this papal decision irreversible when he asserted that the pope was an unerring standard for all Catholics on questions of faith and morals. A good forty years after that, Pope John XXII (1316–34) came to a different decision on the matter of poverty. The Franciscans appealed to the contrary "irreversible" declaration of his predecessor, Nicholas III. But John XXII didn't want to hear about his own infallibility. He viewed it as an improper restriction of his rights as a sovereign, and in the bull *Qui quorundam* (1324) condemned the Franciscan doctrine of papal infallibility as the work of the devil.

The pope's objection may strike us today as grotesque, but the point was well taken: Infallibility always constitutes a limit to the power of an individual pope, who is bound by the infallible declarations of his predecessors. For the time being, the bishops of Rome had no interest in this theory. Discussion of the issue faded away for centuries.

The papacy, of course, had entirely different things to worry about. Schism after schism shook the unity of Western Christianity. Pope rose up against pope, and the papacy itself could find no way out of this cul-de-sac. Only the Council of Constance (1414–18), convened by the German emperor, managed to save the situation. All three popes, who were busy attacking and excommunicating one another, were deposed, and the Council elected a new pope. Is it any wonder that the papacy fell into discredit? That many people once again took the council for the supreme authority in the Church? Soon the notion sprang up that the council was the final, infallible court of appeal. The French theologian Jean Charlier Gerson (1363–1429) was the first to speak of the council as the norm of faith and incapable of error. Cardinal Nicholas of Cusa (1401–64), in describing the council, used the term "infallible."

Thus, in the late Middle Ages there was a conspicuous trend to look for an infallible authority, whether it be pope or council, to buttress the great edifice of the Catholic system. Its original religious power had been lost, and yet the entire social structure still rested on religion as much as ever. Behind the perfectly intact facade doubts and uncertainty began to spread. Signs of disintegration became apparent in philosophy and theology. The old spontaneity and unquestioning naturalness of the faith were largely gone. The quest for infallibility looks like a desperate attempt to recover a lost sense of security.

The endeavor to shore up doctrinal structures was unusually momentous because religion still played such a unique part in most people's lives. Their personal happiness depended on it, first of all in this world, and still more in the next. The great majority of the population had neither the skill nor the desire to

judge questions of faith: They wanted to rely on authorized
teachers. This only heightened the power and influence of the
religious elite, which held the fate of so many in its hand. This
arrangement thoroughly suited the mutual interest of both
groups. Only those who could offer certainty in matters of salvation would be of any use to the people of that time. And so it
didn't sound like blasphemy when men of the Church appeared,
claiming they had been given all power in heaven as well as on
earth (Boniface VIII).

*Infallibility
as a Weapon Against
the Protestants*

But, as we have already indicated, there were many other
forces at work in the bosom of the Church. They burst forth
abruptly into the light of day in 1517, when the Augustinian
monk Martin Luther (1483–1546) launched the Reformation
with his theses on indulgences. This powerful movement was, in
the first instance, a protest against church authority and its
mediating position between God and man. Faith alone, grace
alone, the Bible alone, Christ alone, God alone! Here lay the
last, absolute authority, and not in historically circumscribed,
concrete individuals and institutions. For religious thought this
was no mere shifting of emphasis, it was a revolutionary up-
heaval.

In what remained of the Catholic Church, the Reformation
caused the pendulum to swing to the other side. The more Protestants contested the authority of Church and pope, the more
Catholics stressed it. In their embattled resistance to the reform movement, the popes recalled the doctrine of infallibility.
For the moment, however, they had no notion of formally declaring it a dogma: The tenets of conciliarism were still too
influential. All throughout the national churches opposition to
the central power in Rome was stirring. At the Council of Trent
(1545–63) the definition of papal primacy ran aground on the
rock of resistance from the bishops, especially the French. Nonetheless, from this time onwards the popes flirted continually with

the thought of their own infallibility. They were supported by the Italians and Jesuit theologians. Cardinals Robert Bellarmine (1542–1621) and Caesar Baronius (1538–1607) stood in the front lines of the battle for papal privileges. Still, they failed to carry the day.

In the eighteenth century the Enlightenment brought another decisive setback. Suffragan Bishop Johann Nikolaus von Hontheim (1701–90)—he had written a famous book against the claims advanced by Rome under the pseudonym "Febronius"— reported that in all of Austria, from the year 1769 on, by order of the Empress Maria Theresa (1717–80), infallibility was attributed only to the Church as a whole. A glance at manuals of theology and canon law from the period confirms this fact. By the beginning of the nineteenth century papal infallibility was still generally rejected, except in much of Italy and Spain.

The French Revolution Changes the Climate of Opinion

This state of affairs, however, underwent a change, and more than anything else the papacy had the much-abused French Revolution to thank for it. The Revolution destroyed centuries-old patterns of church government in the leading European countries. For a while even the papacy seemed to be facing extinction. But the ecclesiastical vacuum thus created soon provided the Roman pontiff with quite unexpected possibilities for extending his powers. This was particularly evident in the concordat signed by Napoleon (1769–1821) and Pius VII (1800–23). The pope succeeded in forcing the retirement of bishops installed in office during the Revolution. He came to an agreement with Napoleon on new appointments for the vacant episcopal chairs and on the reorganization of the whole French church. In so doing he not only demonstrated the extent of his power, he also struck Gallicanism a mortal blow. Thus ended the school of thought that had set the tone for the church in France from the fifteenth to the nineteenth century. It had championed relative independence from Rome, had taught the superiority of the councils over the pope, and held that infallible decisions were contingent upon the consent of the entire Church.

The papacy no longer had the look of a force that could be ignored, or even of a foreign power—it was now an important partner in the battle for the interests of the (French) church. Through the concordat with Napoleon, Pius VII won over the lower clergy, in particular, to his side. The abolition of benefices and the terms of the Napoleonic laws concerning the church ("Organic Articles") left pastors at the mercy of their bishops. Hence they sought protection from Rome, preferring a single faraway despot to a hundred in the neighborhood.

In Germany, too, the Napoleonic secularization made necessary a new order of things, and this led to closer ties between local churches and Rome. Plans for the creation of a church for the Austrian Empire collapsed at the Council of Vienna (1814–15) under the opposition of the pope's agent, Cardinal Ercole Consalvi (1757–1824), and of most of the German states. And so separate agreements had to be concluded in Rome, by means of which the Curia strengthened its position and gained greater influence in the nomination of bishops. But Catholics also often looked to Rome for support, for a counterweight to the frequently oppressive national churches. In this way they promoted the growth of a centralized Church governed by the Curia. State churches and the papal system were each predicated upon the other.

Obviously the Church could carry out its new centralizing policy much more easily in regions of the "Diaspora"—Holland, England, and America—as well as in the mission countries. And, needless to say, such alterations in its structure only took effect with the passage of time. Gallican and episcopalist tendencies were still widely prevalent. In France moderate Gallican principles continued to predominate even after 1815, although the destruction of the old theological faculties and the resultant decline of historical training robbed Gallicanism of the soil which had nurtured it.

Of course, no one could overlook the great spiritual turnabout which followed the French Revolution. The Revolution had discredited the rationality so glorified by the Enlightenment: It was only too evident what horrors could be perpetrated in its name. The Enlightenment was no longer fashionable; people were looking for new forms of authority. They found them, for the most part, in tradition, including Catholic tradition. Above all in France there were signs of a new trend towards the Catholic Church.

The French writer François René Vicomte de Chateaubriand (1768–1848) praised the beauty of Catholic dogmas, rites, and sacraments. Christianity, he thought, corresponds to the feelings, to fantasy, to the heart. For Count Louis de Bonald (1754–1840) man can only reach the truth by way of tradition. Therefore Bonald finds external authority critically important: "The evidence of authority must replace the authority of evidence." The Savoyard Count Joseph de Maistre (1753–1821) gave the most concrete expression to such postulates: He called for an infallible pope. De Maistre did this for political and social-psychological reasons. The infallible authority of the legitimate representative of sovereign monarchy would make society invulnerable to any renewed revolutionary assaults. De Maistre had no interest in a biblical or historical basis for his ideas. In the face of such negligence, Rome was slow in warming to de Maistre's book *On the Pope*. De Maistre's thought first began to take hold in church circles, especially among French Catholics, due to the influence of Félicité Robert de Lamennais (1782–1854).

Similar movements took shape in German-speaking countries, most notably in the Viennese circle of Klemens Maria Hofbauer (1751–1820) and Friedrich Schlegel (1772–1829), as well as in Munich and Münster. The Mainz school, led by the Jesuits and their disciples, also exerted a great deal of influence with its journal *Der Katholik*.

Ultramontane Offensive

This Ultramontane movement—as it is widely called on account of its orientation towards Rome, *ultra montes* (on the other side of the mountains)—advocated a centralized, authoritarian system of church government. It sought to extend the pope's prerogatives as far as possible. To this end Ultramontanism applied modern methods for organizing and swaying the masses (Catholic associations, annual Catholic "days"). This policy did not, however, spring from any fundamental democratic conviction but simply served to achieve the Church's aims.

At first Rome took a rather dim view of de Maistre's notions. But starting with Pope Gregory XVI (1831–46), the Curia began to lend them strong encouragement—and actively to direct them towards its own goals. While still an unknown Camaldolese monk named Mauro Capellani, Gregory XVI had written a book, in the middle of the chaotic Napoleonic period, entitled *The Triumph of the Holy See and the Church over the Attacks of the Innovators*. In it he defended the thesis that as a true monarch the pope was also necessarily infallible. Otherwise he wouldn't be able to exercise his functions. The book had already been long forgotten, but the advancement of its author to the papacy sent its stock way up, and it was adroitly employed in the Ultramontane campaign.

Gregory XVI also helped the new intransigent movement in other ways. In the encyclical *Mirari vos* he condemned the ideas

Papal blessing in St. Peter's Square, 1869

of liberalism. He viewed freedom of conscience as "a false and absurd concept," indeed a mad delusion (*delirium*). Freedom of the press, to his mind, could never be sufficiently abhorred and anathematized. In the Church itself he took good care that only men "of sound principles" got ahead.

What Gregory XVI had begun, his successor, Pius IX (1846–78), carried on in a much more thoroughgoing manner. One can only call it a massive Ultramontane offensive based on a systematic plan. Horrified at the revolution of 1848, Pius IX envisioned the Church as under siege from all sides. And so he and his sympathizers wished to erect a barrier against the dangers of secularization, against liberalism, rationalism, and naturalism: the infallible authority of the pope.

Wherever possible, Pius IX named only Ultramontane priests as bishops. In keeping with the old Roman maxim "divide and conquer," he forbade the formation of national bishops' conferences. The bishops were to have as little contact as possible with each other, but were instead to cultivate all the more their connection with Rome. For this reason Pius IX introduced the obligation of regular visits to the Holy See. At bottom, the idea was to eliminate the bishops' independence as much as possible. The bishops had to administer their dioceses in strict subordination to the pope. In carefully gradated fashion, various curial measures were brought into play to attain this end: praise, blame, coercion, condemnation. With their many informants scattered far and wide, the nuncios lent significant help. Again, as far as possible, theology and catechesis were brought into line with a centralized standard. Episcopalist manuals had to be rewritten, or they were put on the Index of Forbidden Books or even burned in the style of an auto-da-fé. The intransigent curial party forced the acceptance of papal infallibility in many catechisms.

It became increasingly clear that Pius IX was consciously promoting the doctrine of papal infallibility. Directly or indirectly, Rome saw to it that the pope's authority got a fair share of the limelight at the many provincial councils held during the pontificate of Pius IX. But only in exceptional cases did these councils expressly attribute infallibility to the pope. Nevertheless, the documents they issued were later quoted with eager frequency at Vatican I as proof of infallibility. Often enough they had been drawn up with this very purpose in mind.

As early as 1854 Pius IX ventured a test of strength. On his

Pius IX with a snuffbox

own authority he elevated the doctrine of Mary's Immaculate Conception—the belief that the mother of Jesus was born without any stain of original sin—to the status of dogma. At the solemn ceremony of definition, Cardinal Vincenzo Macchi, dean of the Sacred College, spoke about the supreme, infallible judgment of His Holiness. In response to a previous inquiry, 90 percent of the bishops had, in fact, endorsed the doctrine. But the pope thought a discussion of it would be too risky because of the negative votes (coming mostly from the German-speaking world)—and so he forbade it. Theologians such as Ignaz von Döllinger said nothing, even though they could see many historical difficulties with the definition. Since the dogma had already been promulgated, they were afraid of being trapped in a hopeless situation.

With the dogmatization of the Immaculate Conception, Pius IX had de facto demonstrated his own infallibility. Since practically no one protested, he could proceed on the assumption that the Church would also accept his advancing further in this area.

Pius IX proclaims the new dogma of Mary's Immaculate Conception

He was not satisfied with a factual recognition of his infallible magisterium; he wanted it to be expressly declared, if possible through a solemn acclamation by the bishops with no prior discussion. When the episcopal assembly in Rome disappointed him on this score in 1862, Pius IX pinned all his hopes on the next great gathering of bishops for the centenary celebration of the Apostle-Princes Peter and Paul in June 1867. An appropriate address had already been prepared, but owing to indiscretion word of the pope's intentions got around. Bishop Félix Dupanloup, a member of the editorial commission for the address to the bishops, put a stop to the whole business. As early as April 1867 Bishop Wilhelm Emmanuel Freiherr von Ketteler of Mainz had implored Dupanloup to do everything to block a definition of infallibility. Ketteler himself had little desire to travel to Rome just to enhance the papal pomp.

This was no isolated case. For some time now the pope's wishes had been running into bitter resistance, not only from some of the bishops but also from a great many professors. In Germany, above all, most theologians opposed the centralization of the Church and the accompanying increase in papal power in the name of history and the historical sciences. The leader of this group was Ignaz von Döllinger, the church historian from Munich.

In France, particularly around the theological faculty of the Sorbonne in Paris, a strong party grew up in opposition to the papal campaign. Even many Ultramontanes were disillusioned when they realized that the papolatry so much in vogue then had nothing to do with Christianity. Count Charles Forbes René de Montalembert, who had deserved so well in the struggle to win greater freedom for the Church, spoke of the idol which lay theologians (he was thinking especially of the editor in chief of *L'Univers,* Louis Veuillot) had set up in the Vatican, and to which they were willing to sacrifice justice and truth, rationality and history.

The Ultramontanes were not content to supply Pius IX with titles like "King," "Pope-King," "Sovereign," or "Caesar." They went beyond "exalted king," "most beloved of kings," "most glorious prince," "most exalted regent," "supreme ruler of the world," and even "king of kings."[3] They applied to Pius IX hymns which

The various regions of the earth pay homage to Pius IX, who has surpassed St. Peter in the number of years spent on the papal throne

the Roman breviary addressed to God himself—to voice still more clearly their belief that Pius IX was God's representative on earth. One enthusiast called the pope the "vice-God of humanity." Such excesses were not limited to a handful of overexcited Catholics with no public responsibility. Even the semi-official Vatican journal *La Civiltà Cattolica* took the liberty of writing, "When the pope meditates, it is God who thinks in him." Bishop Berteaud of Tulle described the pope as "the word (of God) made flesh, living on in our midst." And the suffragan bishop of Geneva, Gaspare Mermillod, did not hesitate to speak of a threefold incarnation of the Son of God: in the Virgin's womb, in the Eucharist, and in the old man of the Vatican.[4]

Thus the Ultramontanes practically identified the pope with Christ, had him assume the place of Christ. Scriptural texts referring to Jesus were applied to the pope. He was called "redeemer." He hung on the cross as Christ did, and so forth.[5] From there it was only a short step to raise the pope, as it were, to the sphere of divinity.[6] St. John Bosco talked about the pope as "God on earth" and further asserted: "Jesus has placed the pope higher than the prophets, than the precursor John the Baptist, than the angels. Jesus has put the pope on the same level as God."[7]

Logically enough, Pius IX was also considered to be full of miraculous power. Many people, including the vicar-general of Nimes, Emmanuel d'Alzon, dispatched items from Pius IX's laundry to heal the sick. Others, like Léon Dupont, the "holy man of Tours," sent out the pope's hair clippings for the same reason.[8] Even in his lifetime Pio Nono had the reputation of working miracles, often merely by giving his blessing.[9] One of the leading Infallibilists, Archbishop Victor Dechamps of Mechlin, was convinced that the Holy Father's benediction could have the effect of "a stroke of Providence."

But despite such extravagances—they shed some extra light on the struggle for papal infallibility—and despite intensive preparation for the dogmatization, on the eve of Vatican I, which was scheduled to convene in the right aisle of St. Peter's on December 8, 1869, the Infallibilists had by no means won the game. Considerable resistance was already afoot. As Rome's intentions became more and more evident, the prime minister and foreign secretary of Bavaria, Prince Chlodwig von Hohenlohe-Schillingsfürst, sent a circular dispatch to the governments of Europe, probing the possibility of joint consultation in view of the threatened definition of infallibility. But Hohenlohe's inquiry evoked little response from the various powers.

The agitation among Catholics, however, was much greater, especially in Germany. Many lay people, in petitions to their bishops (the address of the Coblenz laity, the Bonn address, report of the Catholic members of the Customs Parliament) came out against the proposed new dogma. In the world of the written word, too, the battle raged back and forth. At this juncture fourteen of the twenty members of the German Bishops' Conference assembled in Fulda directed a confidential memorandum (dated September 4, 1869) to the pope, letting him know that a definition of papal infallibility held extreme dangers for Germany and was therefore inadvisable at the present time.

Nonetheless, they calmed the faithful with a special pastoral letter assuring them that "a general council can absolutely never pronounce a new doctrine which is not contained in Sacred Scripture or Apostolic tradition . . . A general council can never proclaim doctrines that contradict the fundamental principles of justice, the rights of the state and its authorities, that contradict civilization, the true interests of science, or lawful

Pius IX inaugurates the First Vatican Council

freedom and the welfare of nations."

In other countries, too, especially France, there was substantial opposition. And once the controversial question was aired in public discussion there would be much stiffer resistance to reckon with. So the battle had in no way been decided. The Infallibilists would have to go to a great deal of trouble if they wanted to carry the day. Up till now they had relied little on the persuasive force of their arguments, preferring other methods to reach their goals. This would not change during the Council.

Waiting for
Nineteen Centuries?

Why was papal infallibility made a dogma precisely in 1870? The question may at first seem rather unusual to people who have assumed all along that the dogma was much older than a hundred years. It may also disturb those who have always thought that the pope has been considered infallible by common consent for centuries now, and who like to view the dogma of infallibility merely as the climax of an age-old development. Such forgetfulness of history is due in no small degree to the hierarchy itself. The facts speak a different language.

It is by no means obvious or easy to explain why a definition came about as late as 1870. By that time many historical studies had shown what a shaky foundation the papal claims were resting on. Much more was known than had been before. The projection of a supremely powerful pope back into the early Christian period had been made possible thanks largely to proven forgeries. In 1870 anyone who still claimed that papal infallibility had always been Catholic teaching was far behind the scholarly consensus of the period.

Some writers see an explanation for the dogma in the downfall of the Papal States. The pope, they suggest, extended his spiritual jurisdiction as compensation for the loss of his secular

Christ entreats the pope: "My kingdom is not of this world!"

power. But this reading doesn't fit the facts. At the time when the First Vatican Council was convened, neither the pope nor the Curia had in any sense resigned themselves to losing the greater part of the Papal States. On the contrary, they looked upon the assembly of bishops as a means of recovering the lost territories. The definition of infallibility was designed to enhance the pope's prestige, and a major result of that would be to strengthen the declaration that secular power was absolutely necessary for the exercise of the papal office. A text saying just that was ready at hand, to be passed at the Council.

A more plausible explanation of the definition is that the Infallibilist party, together with the pope, was hoping to use it to change the whole climate of opinion in society. The principle of authority, they thought, would counteract the principles of the French Revolution—the cause of all the contemporary social unrest. They also wanted to employ the infallible pope to contain the forces of unbridled journalism. But then in the end worldly interests got involved with this dream of a "renewed" society. Along with the pope, other Italian princes also had hopes of seeing the "Italian revolution" break down, thus enabling them to return to their lands.

But, of course, these enthusiastic expectations—shared by only a few—cannot explain how it was possible, in 1870, to impose a dogma which encroached so radically upon the rights of bishops and met with such grave historical and theological objections on their part. The pope himself was a momentous factor in the whole process. The definition of infallibility would have been unthinkable without the personality of Pius IX.

2

Manipulating the Infallibility Debate

Manipulation? Wasn't the overwhelming majority of the bishops in favor of the dogma of infallibility right from the start? Many readers will ask that question, and in so doing they merely echo the usual accounts of Vatican I. But the facts were otherwise.

The Wait-and-See Attitude of the Curia and the Majority of Bishops

Reservations and outright resistance to the new dogma were much more widespread than is commonly believed. They could be seen even within the ranks of the Roman Curia. On December 6, 1864, Pius IX polled the cardinals of the Congregation of Rites concerning his plan for the Council. Only one of the fifteen cardinals recommended defining papal infallibility. Of the thirty-two bishops consulted (most of them Ultramontanes), a total of seven were for the definition.

At this stage fear of the uncertainties of the coming Council doubtlessly played a crucial role, just as it did almost a hundred years later, before the start of Vatican II. And then, to make things worse, to raise such a ticklish question in front of a group

like that! "What!" "Call a council?" said Cardinal Giovanni
Battista Pitra to Bishop Charles Colet of Luçon, "But the French
and German theologians will wreak havoc on our congregation."
The number two man in the Vatican, Secretary of State Cardinal
Giacomo Antonelli, had similar worries. More than anyone else
it was Pius IX who wanted the Council.

The Romans have always been highly pragmatic. Only if we
keep this in mind can we understand their maneuverings on infallibility. As time passed, all the members of the Curia naturally
realized that Pius IX was driving towards the definition of infallibility. Common sense forbade any open resistance to this effort.
But even people in the Curia had lingering theological or historical misgivings. There can be no doubt, for instance, that despite
their occasional vacillation Cardinals Filippo Maria Guidi and
Gustav Adolf von Hohenlohe-Schillingsfürst opposed the dogma
on theological grounds. According to reports, other cardinals
shared Guidi's second thoughts: Antonio Maria Panebianco,
Giuseppe Berardi, Angelo Quaglia, Camillo Di Pietro, Pietro De

Pius IX and the College of Cardinals

Silvestri, and Domenico Carafa. Cardinal Antonelli was against the definition of infallibility for political reasons.

Among the curial archbishops, the papal almoner, François Xavier de Mérode, the pope's court preacher, Luigi Puecher-Passavalli, and the professor of church history, Vincenzo Tizzani, were unequivocal opponents of the new dogma. Guglielmo Audisio, lecturer in law at the University of Rome and canon of St. Peter's, took an equally clear-cut position.

When the definition of infallibility ran into unexpectedly stiff resistance at the Council, uncertainties within the Curia became more evident. Many members began to fear a schism. The anxiety became so widespread that the Spanish chargé d'affaires, José Fernández Ximenes, and the fanatically bellicose Ultramontane founder of the Assumptionists, Emmanuel d'Alzon, reached the same conclusion: The Romans didn't want infallibility defined as dogma. According to Ximenes, many curial prelates were saying quite openly: "The pope has decided upon it (the definition), and there's no way to counter his authority. Now it's a question of directing into the right channels what we can't prevent."

Ximenes had the impression that the Roman prelates would only have opposed the pope and risked his wrath if some extreme danger had arisen. But the occasional flickering threats of a schism were never serious enough to startle the Curia out of its lethargy.

Still, fear of a schism made itself felt all the way up to the Council leadership. Cardinals Luigi Bilio, Filippo De Angelis, and Antonio De Luca—three of the five Council presidents—were touched by it. "Towards the end of Holy Week," wrote Bishop Senestrey, "when everything seemed secure, the bishop of Regensburg (Senestrey himself) went to cardinal Bilio to request a session of the Congregation of the Faith on Easter Monday or Tuesday, so that discussion of the schema could begin. But what a change had taken place! The cardinal is anxious, alarmed, full of scruples. He hesitates, is afraid, scarcely dares to take another step. 'But Monsignore'—these were his words—'we're talking about a definition, about obligating the faithful to believe? What will happen? We'll have a schism—I can't get a good night's sleep anymore. Don't be in such a hurry! We *still*

Secretary of State Cardinal
Giacomo Antonelli

Emmanuel d'Alzon, founder of
the Assumptionists

have two months! etc.' The bishop of Regensburg left him with the words, 'Eminence, leave it to the Congregation. The Holy Spirit will take care of the rest!'"[10] Such painful hesitation clearly shows that the Curia cannot be considered the motivating force behind the crusade for infallibility.

Infallibilists
on the Attack

It was, above all, the pope himself who wanted the dogma. On his side stood a small but unshakably resolute band of some 50 episcopal companions-in-arms. On the other side were about 130 opponents of the definition and five hundred bishops who were at first undecided and indifferent. Of course, the 50 bishops were not alone. Their strength lay in the fact that they had the backing of the pope. But they could also count on the energetic

Ignatius von Senestrey,
bishop of Regensburg

support of a great number of Jesuits, especially from *La Civiltà Cattolica*, the semiofficial organ of the Vatican.

To understand the Infallibilist plan of action one must keep in mind their point of departure. On the eve of the Council the Jesuits began to unfold a series of far-reaching measures to pave the way to victory for the dogma the pope wanted so badly. Their chief tools were the pulpit, the confessional, the press, and the religious associations. But the actual authors of this campaign wanted to stay in the background. They wished to avoid the impression that all the orders were coming from Rome. Their first task, then, was to find bishops who would stand up unconditionally for the cause. The Jesuits of *La Civiltà Cattolica* thought up an unusual but effective scheme: In the summer of 1867 they spread about the idea that bishops and priests should take a vow to fight for the dogmatization of papal infallibility *usque ad effusionem sanguinis,* "to the point of bloodshed." And, in fact, on June 29, 1867, Archbishop Henry Edward Manning of Westminster and Bishop Ignatius von Senestrey indicated their willingness to shed theirs. They later formed part of the hard-core group of Infallibilists who pushed the dogma through.

On September 8, 1868, Pius IX promulgated the bull *Aeterni Patris,* convoking the council. He made no mention in the bull of defining papal infallibility. The call for that was supposed to come spontaneously from the bishops and the laity.

On February 6, 1869, *La Civiltà Cattolica* once again took the initiative on this issue. It published a report from the office of the Secretary of State in Paris claiming that France's real Catholics wanted papal infallibility to be declared a dogma and hoped that such a definition would occur by unanimous acclamation of the council fathers. Readers quite rightly read between the lines of this article, which relayed the wishes of the pope and the Ultramontanes. The Jesuits were acting not on their own but with the full consent of the pope and his Secretary of State, Cardinal Antonelli, which did not prevent either of them from pleading ignorance to the diplomats who came to complain. Pius IX added the further excuse that he, too, unfortunately had to tolerate freedom of the press in the Papal States.

The article in *La Civiltà Cattolica* was just the first shot. Now the bishops and priests had to be mobilized. Under the

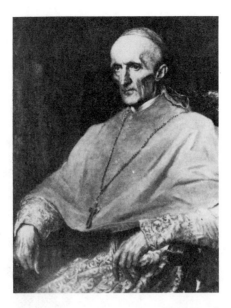

Henry Edward Manning, archbishop of
Westminster

leadership of Archbishops Manning of London and Victor Dechamps of Mechlin, a "true crusade" commenced in the Ultramontane papers of England, France, and Italy. As early as
November 22, 1869, Manning could write Louis Veuillot, "We
have made a good beginning, then, in this battle. But the final
blow is up to Providence."

The key method employed by the bishops was the pastoral
letter. Claude Plantier, Henry Edward Manning, and Victor
Dechamps entered the lists for papal infallibility with particular
zeal in this regard. Dechamps' pastoral letter was the result of a
secret agreement with the pope and Cardinal August Graf von
Reisach. (He was named a president of the Council but died
shortly before it opened.) Pius IX later publicly thanked Dechamps for the service he had rendered. He praised him for per-
suading not just the pious but even the rationalists of the truth
of papal infallibility. And he had an Italian translation of
Dechamps' letter printed up at his own expense. The other
pastoral letters may well have been written on order from Rome.

Bishops opposed to papal infallibility hesitated a long time

Victor Dechamps, arch-
bishop of Mechlin

before openly joining battle. Anyone who, like Félix Dupanloup
or Wilhelm Emmanuel Freiherr von Ketteler, so much as questioned the appropriateness of a definition at that time would for-
feit the pope's favor.

Another well-thought-out technique for swaying the masses
was the petition movement. The Infallibilists got the clergy and
laity to send special petitions to Pius IX calling for the dogmatization of papal infallibility. They directed the whole operation
from Rome, using as their mainstays the Ultramontane newspapers *L'Univers* and *L'Unità Cattolica*. The nuncios, too,
proffered their services. The pope wasn't stingy with praise, and
his praise worked as incentive for more petitions. Most of these
papal bulls (thanking Pius IX's supporters) were published
posthaste. If the petitions didn't come of their own accord,
Rome gave them a helping hand. If, as often happened, they did
not come pouring in voluntarily at the first summons, Ultramontane activists would have to draw them up. Sometimes they
were requisitioned directly from the bishops in certain dioceses.

The Infallibilists had yet another, secondary aim in view

with their petition movement. They especially liked to carry on their activities in dioceses belonging to the opponents of infallibility. That way they could put pressure on the bishops in the minority. Pius IX answered the petitions from such dioceses in predictable fashion, even when they preferred charges against their own bishops. The extreme harshness of this indirect mode of reprimanding people scarcely troubled the pope.

Pius IX also intervened in the literary battle for papal infallibility. Anyone who defended it with his pen could count on a brief from the Vatican full of thanks and praise. Among theological authors Benedictine Abbot Prosper Guéranger took first prize. On March 12, 1870, the pope sent his best known letter of this sort. In it he not only lauded Guéranger but launched a violent attack on the opponents of infallibility. He reproached them for perversity, foolishness, unreasonableness, and the greatest impudence. Guéranger, he said, had done a most useful job for the Church by refuting their works and exposing their tricks, seductions, and dissembling arts.

Journalists who enlisted in the campaign for infallibility also received letters of recognition from the pope. Notable among this group was Louis Veuillot, editor in chief of the most important Ultramontane newspaper, *L'Univers*. On the second day after his arrival in Rome, the pope welcomed him with the words, "You have fought the good fight in this matter as in all others." Among the other journalists, William George Ward, publisher of the *Dublin Review,* and Herbert Vaughan, editor of *The Tablet,* deserve special mention. Ward, in particular, has caught posterity's attention by wishing he could read a new infallible declaration by the pope in *The Times* every morning at breakfast.

Help from the
Curial Machine

Conversely, writings critical of papal infallibility were the target of the pope's displeasure. The most dangerous attack on infallibility, *The Pope and the Council,* by Johann Joseph Ignaz von Döllinger, professor of church history in Munich (published

Louis Veuillot, editor in
chief of *L'Univers*

under the pseudonym "Janus"), was put on the Index of Forbidden Books on November 26, 1869—*quocumque idiomate*, "in whatever language" it might appear, as the decree particularly stressed. The Orientalist and theologian Peter Le Page Renouf fared no better. At the suggestion of John Henry (later Cardinal) Newman, he had written a study of Pope Honorius I (625–38), who was condemned as a heretic by the Sixth Ecumenical Council (678–87). Le Page Renouf came to the conclusion that Honorius I had actually advocated heresy. On December 14, 1868, his book, *The Condemnation of Pope Honorius*, was placed on the Index. Bishop Henri Maret, dean of the theological faculty of the Sorbonne and author of a book dealing with the Council and the issue of infallibility, escaped the same fate only because a long line of French bishops and the French authorities in Rome stood up for him.

Even writers who published well-meaning and less controversial articles discussing the coming Council—people like Georg Carl Mayer, canon of the Bamberg cathedral, or his colleague Johann Spörlein, or Professor Friedrich Michelis from Braunsberg—might find their names on the Index. In Germany, works by the philosopher Jakob Frohschammer and the church historian Aloys Pichler were officially banned; in France, Gallicanist books by André Dupin, the writings of Jean Baptiste Bordas-Demoulin on church reform, and the history of France by Henri Bordier and Édouard Charton.

Episcopal sanctions were leveled against the *Letters* by the philosopher and theologian Alphonse Gratry, a member of the Académie Française. In them he had defended Bishop Félix Dupanloup against Archbishop Victor Dechamps. The bishop of Strassburg, Andreas Raess, forbade his clergy to read them, and many of his fellow bishops followed suit. These moves may not have been initiated by the pope, but at the least he approved of them.

With members of religious orders and congregations other methods were available to restore the proper spirit. Consider, for example, the case of the Franciscan Alois Matthias Hötzl, lecturer in philosophy and theology at Munich. When he wrote in defense of Döllinger, he was summoned to Rome by the general of his order. Even before this, the nuncio to Munich, Pier Francesco Meglia, had recommended to the Curia that Hötzl be dismissed from his teaching post. Once in Rome, Hötzl was condemned to compulsory spiritual exercises in a monastery on the Palatine. The sentence was only lightened on account of King Ludwig II of Bavaria's personal interest in the whole affair. On several occasions he ordered the Bavarian ambassador in Rome to intervene for Hötzl. But even so, Hötzl was not allowed to leave Rome before recanting his views and submitting in advance to the decisions of the Council. If this was the lot of foreign professors, their Roman colleagues had it even worse. Anyone who didn't toe the mark was threatened with dismissal.

All these tactics were part of the broad strategic preparations for the dogmatization of papal infallibility. They were not aimed, in the first instance, at the council fathers, but they nonetheless affected them. Above all, they were a way of bringing some extremely unpleasant pressure to bear on the representatives of the conciliar opposition.

*Infallibilists as a
Pressure Group
at the Council*

But let us return to the Council itself. The Infallibilists saw
clearly that infallibility would only be declared a dogma if they
controlled the key positions of power. Readers may be familiar
with the Council minority's defensive campaign and their international meetings. But long before the minority began to organize, the majority had formed an international committee which
included, among others, Archbishops and Bishops Henry Edward Manning, Ignatius von Senestrey, Victor Dechamps, Gaspare Mermillod, Nikolaus Adames, and Étienne Marilley. By
November 1869 a well-thought-out, concrete plan of action was
in the works. On December 6, 1869, the members met for the
first time in the residence of the bishop of Regensburg at No. 13
Via Gregoriana. Later they would meet in the Villa Caserta,
Roman headquarters of the Redemptorists. Their goal was to get
a firm grip on the Council bureaucracy and the Church's news
media. As a matter of fact, these goals would largely be met
with the help of the pope, most of the Curia, and the Jesuits.
With regard to methods, the group was not overly particular.
The international committee of the Infallibilists operated like a
pressure group. For the sake of winning votes, it did not flinch
from intrigues, promises, and threats.

In Rome itself the Infallibilist party had already handled
the preliminary business in its own fashion. The Council's preparatory commissions were securely in hand. The Infallibilist,
pro-Roman element was everywhere predominant. Of the 96
consulting positions, 59 went to Italians and 37 to other nation-
alities. But then 6 of these foreigners—7 if the Jesuit Fr.
Clemens Schrader is counted—were active in the Roman Curia.
Of the 59 Italians mentioned, all but 4 worked somewhere in the
Roman bureaucracy.

Half of the consultants on the most important commission,
which dealt with theology and dogma, came from the Congregations of the Holy Inquisition and the Index. The advice of
Cardinal Giuseppe Bizzarri that the Holy Office must form the
core of the commission entrusted with doctrinal matters had

Cardinal Giuseppe Bizzarri, one of the
presidents of the Council

been fully carried out. Eleven members of this commission went
beyond the call of duty: They took a vow to fight for papal infallibility, and in a special petition called for the definition of
the new dogma. The gross imbalance in this commission stirred
up protests. In particular, the cardinal of Prague, Friedrich von
Schwarzenberg, intervened with the Secretary of State, Cardinal
Antonelli. Thereupon several theologians were brought in from
the outside—Joseph Karl Hefele, for instance, professor at
Tübingen and later bishop of Rottenburg. Professor Ignaz von
Döllinger was *not* called in. Rome pleaded in excuse that
Döllinger wasn't ready to cooperate with his colleagues. In point
of fact, his nomination as a consultant had been blocked by Cardinal Karl August Graf von Reisach. The handful of non-Roman
consultants brought in left the basic situation unchanged. Hefele
repeatedly wrote to friends in Germany that foreign consultants
had only been called in to keep up a show of impartiality before
the world. To his colleague at Tübingen, Professor Johann Kuhn,
Hefele confided on December 27, 1868: "The longer I stay here,

Joseph Karl Hefele,
bishop of Rottenburg

the more clearly I see the duplicity behind my appointment as a
consultor concilii. That was just Rome's way of hoodwinking the
public with the appearance of neutrality. In reality I have no
idea what I'm supposed to be doing here. I've learned practically nothing about the theological questions the Council will be
engaged with. The only job I've been assigned is to excerpt the
ceremonial portions from the Acts of the Council of Trent. Is
that anything to be proud of? The second-best chaplain at the
Anima (the German seminary in Rome) could have handled it. I
think the sly Jesuits are laughing up their sleeve at the way the
Tübingen professor has been so neatly paralyzed."

Actually, that was just the role which Bishop Wilhelm Emmanuel Freiherr von Ketteler had wanted Hefele to play when
he proposed him as a consultant, along with Professors Johann
Baptist Alzog (Freiburg) and Franz Xaver Dieringer (Bonn),
to Munich Nuncio Pier Francesco Meglia. Hefele's nomination,
he claimed, would neither help nor hinder the cause, but it
would shut up all the apostles of German scientific progress.
"Take comfort," the German curial Cardinal Gustav von Hohenlohe remarked to Hefele, "there are more than a few cardinals

who've been given precious little to do with the Council because they don't belong to the party."

Thus, the theological-dogmatic commission could work out, discuss, and give its blessing to various proposals for the definition of papal infallibility without having to face any opposition. The definition, in other words, was decided on before the Council even met. "Everything is in readiness here for the proclamation of papal infallibility," Lord Acton wrote to the Prime Minister of Great Britain, William Ewart Gladstone, on November 24, 1869, "and the plan of operation has already been agreed on in a way that reveals a careful study of Sarpi's history of the Council of Trent."

The fact of these intense preparations, however, did not prevent Theodor Granderath, the official historian of Vatican I (he had access to all the conciliar archives back in the 1890s), from writing: "From the first moment it met until it dissolved, the general Council was occupied almost exclusively with an issue which had never appeared in any of the numerous preliminary proposals, an issue which no one in Rome had wanted to lay before the council fathers for debate. Today one point stands clear and beyond all doubt: The matter of infallibility was brought into the Council's deliberations from the *outside*."

Walling Up the Doors to the Secret Papal Archives

"Everything here," wrote Odo Russell, English chargé d'affaires to the Holy See, in a letter to London in January 1869, "is arranged and organized in such a way that foreign bishops find it quite impossible to express their own opinions freely. They will be unpleasantly surprised to find themselves forced to sanction something which they actually wished to condemn." The Infallibilists, in fact, would not quite achieve this goal later on, but they could nonetheless take credit for some very substantial successes.

Even before the bishops had convened in Rome, on November 27, 1869, the pope issued the procedural rules for the Coun-

Fr. Augustin Theiner,
prefect of the secret
papal archives

cil. This was contrary to the usage of earlier councils. At the
Fifth Lateran Council (1512–17) such rules of procedure had
only been submitted to the bishops for adoption, and at Trent
(1545–63) the bishops themselves had decided on the order of
business. The arrangements at Trent allowed for much more
freedom than the program Pius IX imposed on the council
fathers. For this reason the Vatican kept it strictly under wraps.
Despite this, the Oratorian priest Fr. Augustin Theiner, prefect
of the secret papal archives, let some of his friends take a look
at the agenda—which was the main reason why he was fired.
In a furious scene on June 5, 1870, Pius IX made him get down
on his knees and then told him he had been relieved of his
job. The pope ordered Theiner to surrender his keys and had
his direct access to the archives (from his room in the Tower
of the Four Winds) walled up—"out of fear I might have been
able to have the keys copied," as Theiner wrote on November 29,
1872, to Professor Johann Friedrich in Munich.

In his agenda for the First Vatican Council, the pope laid a
heavy burden of regimentation on all future debate. There was
to be no discussion in small groups, speeches at the Council
could not be printed, and the bishops were forbidden, under
pain of mortal sin, to say anything about what took place in the

great hall of the Council. This obsessive secretiveness made it largely impossible for theologians to play any part in the Council. Still worse, on the strength of the rules of procedure the pope, practically speaking, decided all by himself what the Council would take up. The commission assigned to make suggestions for the Council's program was named exclusively by the pope. Hefele had proposed a commission chosen partly by the pope, partly by the Council, but to no avail.

The bishops of the minority did not fail to protest—restrainedly in public, vehemently in private. The Roman Archbishop Vincenzo Tizzani spoke of inquisitorial practices. Archbishop Georges Darboy of Paris called it the grave of the bishops. In his eyes it would have been better if they had been told to stay home. For Bishop Henri Maret the rules of procedure had already made the pope's superiority over the Council a *fait accompli*. Many bishops wondered what they could do against the pope's command. "All this is completely new for an ecumenical council," Tizzani observed to Darboy, "but in Rome one may not say a word about it."

On February 20, 1870, the agenda was further tightened. Additional amendments to it restricted discussion even more and made cloture possible on the motion of only ten council fathers. Moreover, on questions of dogma all decisions were to be by majority vote. The bishops of the minority saw these supplemental regulations as a threat to destroy the Council's freedom and thus its ecumenicity. Bishop Joseph Georg Strossmayer of Diakovar in Croatia put it most clearly. He decried the new provisions as the "grave mound of the Council."

The stipulation of majority rule on dogmatic issues was, in fact, a fatal blow to the minority. For a long time many of its members refused to believe that anyone would dare to override a significant opposition. They therefore tried, in various position papers, to point up the necessity of moral unanimity in conciliar decisions on dogma. But the Infallibilists could never go along with this: The definition they wanted would never have come about. The pope himself got involved in the heated war of words over this controversial point and directed *La Civiltà Cattolica* to write articles against the minority.

Manipulating Elections

The Infallibilists had their biggest trump cards in hand even before the Council opened, thanks to their advance work and the imposition of the agenda. But there still remained a great deal to be done. It had not taken any great skill to pack the preparatory commissions with men "of sound principles." It was more difficult, however, to do this with the conciliar commissions since these were to be elected by all the bishops. The Infallibilists had declared their intention of not letting a single opponent of infallibility on any of the commissions. How could that be accomplished? The Infallibilist-Curial party at first attempted to rush through the elections as quickly as possible before the bishops had gotten acquainted with each other. Strossmayer and other bishops who wanted the elections postponed for precisely this reason were cut short.

When the bishops took matters into their own hands and began to organize caucuses, the Infallibilists managed, by and large, to neutralize these gatherings. The Curia spread the word that the pope wanted no meetings of more than fifteen to twenty bishops. Secretary of State Cardinal Giacomo Antonelli justified this prohibition, noting that each nationality had to give way before the ecumenicity of the Council.

The French were talked into this and dutifully broke up into two groups. When the leaders of these groups, Cardinal Jacques Mathieu and Cardinal Henri de Bonnechose, nevertheless agreed to propose joint candidates for election, their choices were boycotted by the Infallibilist side. In any case, any candidates nominated by the French who were opponents of infallibility never made it to the final balloting.

The best thing the Infallibilists came up with to manipulate the elections was, however, the notion of surrounding their own ticket with the aura of the highest official approbation. Here, too, they found the pope's confederates ready to help. Judging from information supplied by Senestrey, no one can doubt that the Infallibilist slate was submitted to the pope himself for confirmation. And then there was the massive support provided by key agents of the Curia. Cardinal De Angelis, later first president of the Council, organized the entire electoral strategy, to-

Cardinal Filippo De
Angelis, first president
of the Council

gether with Archbishop Manning and Bishop Senestrey. "Cardinal De Angelis' house," wrote Senestrey, "was the information center." Thus, they managed to clothe the roster of Infallibilist candidates with an official air of authority. The only people on it were those considered to be backers of the pope's interests, and it was made clear to the bishops that this was the preferred ticket. Most of them voted accordingly. And thus all the conciliar commissions dropped into the pocket of the Infallibilists. The most important commission, on theology and dogma, had only a single foe of infallibility on it, Primate Johannes Simor of Hungary. The Infallibilists had mistaken him for one of their own.

Practitioners of this biased electoral strategy could not and would not accept the idea that individual countries and dissenting opinions should be given proportional representation. Thus, for example, while the bulk of the bishops from Germany objected to making papal infallibility a dogma of faith, the two Germans sitting on the theological-dogmatic commission, Bishops Ignatius von Senestrey (Regensburg) and Konrad Martin (Paderborn), were both deeply committed Infallibilists.

"The elections are dishonest," Archbishop Georges Darboy of Paris wrote in his diary on December 20, 1870. And Félix

Dupanloup spoke to the Secretary of State, Cardinal Giacomo Antonelli, of "the utter worthlessness of these elections." But the Infallibilists rejoiced in the knowledge that with the successful outcome of the elections they now had the Council in their control. "The majority has made up the four leading commissions in the Council, and it will make up the rest as well," wrote Louis Veuillot. And Bishop Louis Pie remarked, "All these elections are to be viewed as the musical signature of the Council. They announce what will be the dominant note."

Collecting Signatures   •
for Infallibility

Once the elections were won, the Infallibilists had to smooth the way for adoption of the infallibility schema in the program of the Council. In the process, they wanted to avoid, as much as possible, any impression that the pope was behind this. On the contrary, the Infallibilists tried to get the bishops to promote the definition of infallibility of their own accord.

To achieve this, the leaders of the group had an inspiration: They thought of secretly collecting signatures calling for a definition of infallibility. As in the manipulation of elections, the chief actors preferred to work underground. The coordinator of the whole operation was the Jesuit priest Fr. Matteo Liberatore, an editor of *La Civiltà Cattolica* and Archbishop Manning's conciliar theologian. The ultimate source of protection, though, was Pius IX himself. For the carrying out of this undertaking, which was not without its risks, Bishop Ignatius von Senestrey offered to "sacrifice" himself. Later, when the job was done, Senestrey wrote in his diary: "And so the work which seemed 'inopportune' to many and unwise to most was completed. As a matter of fact, the archbishop of Westminster said in a private conversation with the bishop of Regensburg, as they discussed submitting the petition, gathering signatures, and procedures in general: 'What it comes down to is that one of us has to commit a very great folly.' To which the bishop of Regensburg replied, 'I shall gladly take that folly upon myself.' For nobody could say

Matteo Liberatore, S.J., member of the editorial staff of *La Civiltà Cattolica;* one of the chief manipulators in the campaign for papal infallibility

with any certainty whether we could gather together a sufficient number of council fathers who dared to sign. Nobody, except the archbishop of Westminster, was willing to play the leader, although a great many people ardently wished to see the matter brought before the Council."[11]

After the petition had been drawn up by several Infallibilist theologians, Senestrey wrote down, without prior consultation, the names of fifteen of his episcopal colleagues who, he assumed, would subscribe to it. In two cases he was deceived. Bishops Johann Baptist Zwerger of Seckau and Philipp Krementz of Ermland demanded that Senestrey immediately remove their names. Armed with these sham signatures, Senestrey and his helpers went out looking for more names. As soon as a large enough number of backers had been found, the petition was reprinted. Within fourteen days Senestrey repeated this process five times.

Father Liberatore recommended to Senestrey and his adjutants the stratagem of getting the presidents of the various Church provinces to sign. Once they did, moral pressure could be applied to their subordinates. And the larger the total of names, the more the collection of signatures would take care of itself. Soon it took courage *not* to sign, especially since nobody had any doubt where the pope stood on the matter. The pressure was felt, in particular, by bishops financially dependent on the Vatican. With the infallibility petition the bishops "had a knife at their jugular," as the Benedictine Simplicio Pappalettere put it in a letter dated February 17, 1870, to Giuseppe Colucci, prefect of Caserta.

Thus, before any discussion even began, the bishops were already committed to a course which the majority of them, at bottom, did not want to take. The Infallibilist leaders looked on them as a sluggish, amorphous mass, and as such despised them. Bishop Ignatius von Senestrey especially distinguished himself in this regard. He also considered the extraconciliar campaign far more important than what went on at the Council. Some who put their names down could make the excuse that the petition did not, after all, ask for very much. In point of fact, it avoided the term "infallibility" and gave the impression of being quite moderate. But all that was calculated: Later, harsher specifications had already been planned in advance.

The whole business amounted to a clear manipulation of the Council. An unmistakable sign of this was the strict secrecy of the operation, thanks to which the minority was taken by surprise. Within a short time the Infallibilists had managed to win over more than four hundred votes to their side. The opposition could only garner 137 signatures petitioning against the definition of infallibility. Infallibilist leaders such as Manning and Senestrey later defended the measures they had taken by pleading the maneuvers of the minority. But, in fact, the Infallibilists had begun collecting signatures long before their opponents. And then, what was the need for all the secrecy? In any case, the covert campaign paid off. On February 9, 1870, the commission for the program of the Council (*deputatio pro postulatis*), named by the pope, decided to recommend the issue of infallibility for discussion.

*Running Short
of Time*

That was a big step but not the final one. The Council had solemnly opened on December 8, 1869, and had begun by discussing a document on the Catholic faith. Then it scrutinized brief proposals dealing with the position of bishops and priests as well as with a common catechism. The question of infallibility was now on everyone's lips, but it did not immediately come up on the agenda for tactical reasons. Hence, to many observers the deliberations on faith appeared to be a mere preliminary. Others were unhappy because they felt there were more burning questions to debate. For instance, Augustin Vérot, bishop of Savannah and the *enfant terrible* of the Council, considered the condemnation of German idealists and rationalists mere hairsplitting. He would have much rather had a declaration by the Council that Negroes, too, had souls—an understandable concern for a bishop from a country where civil war had raged until recently over the question of slavery.[12]

But the Council leadership had other matters on its mind. After the constitution on the Catholic faith had been passed, the schedule called for discussion of a major schema concerning the Church. Only after this, logically speaking, would papal infallibility come up. But if this order were followed, the definition of

Augustin Vérot, bishop
of Savannah

Cardinal Antonio De
Luca, one of the
presidents of the Council

infallibility would fade into the dim distance. In view of the un-
settled political picture, that was dangerous. It was critical,
therefore, to fight to give the infallibility question preferential
treatment.

So the Infallibilists resorted to a tried and true method:
They started up several petition drives for the immediate discussion of infallibility. Once again they had the complete backing
of the pope. Indeed, in contrast with the beginning of the Council, as time went on the pope increasingly abandoned his reserve
and seized the initiative. He urged Gaspare Mermillod and other
bishops, along with their confidants, such as the vicar-general of
Nimes, Emmanuel d'Alzon, to press the issue of infallibility with
the council fathers. By the first months of the new year (1870)
rumors were already spreading of the imminent outbreak of war
between France and Germany. This would endanger both the
existence of the Papal States and the continuation of the Council. And so the pope insisted more and more on finishing the
business in hand and proceeding to deal with papal infallibility.
By the end of April the time was ripe. The pope commanded
that the normal course of the Council be interrupted and the
constitution *Pastor Aeternus* be introduced for discussion—with

its two new dogmas of the pope's infallibility and his universal jurisdiction.

This decision reveals quite clearly how much the pope felt himself to be master of the Council and how he acted accordingly. For, up to this point many bishops had been willing to postpone the question of infallibility, out of fear of a schism, and to speak instead about the Church in general. Even the bishops of central Italy, under the leadership of their cardinals, Cosimo Corsi and Carlo Luigi Morichini, submitted a petition to this effect. In doing so, they knew that three of the Council presidents, Cardinals De Angelis, De Luca, and Bilio, were on their side.

Nothing infuriated the pope more than this defeatism in his own camp. "This petition is a shame for the bishops of Italy and an infamy for the bishops of the Papal States!" said Bishop Antonio Maria Valenziani, bishop of Fabriano-Matelica, according to Senestrey's diary.

The pope was now convinced that the Council presidents were weak-kneed and firmly set on taking the reins into his own hands so as to get the definition. "We have no men. At the Council of Trent there were more men, now we have more saints. One must be content with things as they are," the pope believed. In this case he also felt it necessary "to light a fire under the belly of the presidents," to use Emmanuel d'Alzon's drastic expression. Despite this zeal in his own cause, Pius IX was still enough of a diplomat to wait out the balloting for the constitution on faith and the fall of Daru as French Foreign Minister. Under the latter's successor the danger of intervention by France was staved off.

No Interest in
Real Discussion

Thus the Infallibilists got their wish: Papal infallibility finally came up on the floor for debate. But did they want a real exchange of views, an unbiased discussion weighing all the arguments brought forth? In its memorial to Cardinal Costantino Patrizi, president of the conciliar program commission, the majority declared the question of papal infallibility settled and requested the definition. All this occurred before the opponents of infallibility even had a chance to make their case. In this way the discussion was prejudiced from the outset. In fact, the very need to have a discussion was disavowed. Many Infallibilists considered their adversaries heretics. And the pope himself asserted that only Protestants and unbelievers would reject papal infallibility. So the most vital element in any dialogue was missing: the willingness to listen to counterarguments. "People talk, but they don't discuss," wrote Albert du Boÿs, a friend of Bishop Dupanloup, to the French Foreign Minister, Napoléon Daru, on January 29, 1870.

Not just the psychological but the material and formal prerequisites for a real debate were lacking as well. The great hall of the Council was acoustically defective. Most of the time the bishops could not understand one another. "I now sit right next to the Secretary's desk," wrote Bishop Hefele, "in the immediate vicinity of the cardinals and cardinal-legates or presidents, but often I can't hear what's being said from the speaker's platform." Many others fared no better. Before the Council several of them pointed out this inconvenience to the pope. "Thereupon the Holy Father asked them rather testily whether he would have to go to new expense to set up a council hall where the bishops could wrangle to their hearts' content," the Prussian ambassador, Friedrich Graf zu Limburg-Stirum, reported to Otto Fürst von Bismarck on October 5, 1869. Later attempts to improve the acoustics had no real effect.

Debate was greatly complicated by the stipulations of the agenda. Only members of commissions had the right of immediate reply to speeches. Everyone else had to make an appointment a day in advance of the session, and no one was allowed to speak until others of higher rank had finished. In addition, owing to the ban on printing speeches it was impossible to study the arguments carefully and give a response to them.

Because of all this, the conciliar minority repeatedly called for discussions in small groups. Pope Pius IX, however, would not hear of it. "The Holy Spirit," he replied, "is present at the Council, not at the national conventions." As the question of infallibility inevitably came closer and closer to the Council floor,

Cardinal Luigi Bilio, president of the
commission on faith and one of the
Council presidents

members of the minority's international committee asked the
Council presidents, in an official communiqué dated March 11,
1870, for the formation of a group comprising representatives of
the minority and the commission on faith. It was to discuss all
controversial points exhaustively, a proposal which found favor
with the majority of Council presidents Bilio, De Angelis, and
De Luca.

A conciliatory reply was already being drafted when Pius
IX objected and brought his presidents back to a sterner course.
Council Secretary Joseph Fessler, bishop of St. Pölten, had to
answer the leaders of the minority in the name of the Council
presidents: There were enough excellent prelates and theologians, he said, with whom the minority could discuss any
difficulties that might come up. The commission on faith was
overworked and had no time for such things.

It was now fully clear that the pope wanted no discussion.
"The pope thought people would only come to Rome to say
'Amen,'" wrote Bishop Félix Dupanloup in his diary on Jan-
uary 2, 1870. And Archbishop Darboy remarked what little

Cardinal Annibale Capalti, one of the Council presidents

confidence the majority must have in its own doctrine, since it rejected the proposed joint commission and failed to come up with five or six men to defend papal infallibility.

The partisan spirit was likewise continually evident in the conduct of debate in the Council hall. Important representatives of the minority, men like Bishops Joseph Georg Strossmayer, Augustin Vérot, Henri Maret, Ludwig Haynald, Giovanni Pietro Sola, and Giovanni Pietro Losana were interrupted in the middle of their addresses and prevented from continuing, often with the explanation that no one was allowed to speak so negatively about the Holy See. Cardinal Annibale Capalti, one of the five Council presidents, had a particularly authoritarian manner and not the slightest comprehension of the minority's motives.

People like Capalti created an atmosphere of hostility in the Council hall. Members of the majority often reacted to speeches with obstreperous signs of approval or condemnation: They applauded, grumbled, shouted, and sometimes let their indignation boil over in tumultuous scenes. The greatest storm broke out on March 22, 1870, when Bishop Joseph Georg Strossmayer affirmed in the great hall of the Council that even among Protestants there were many individuals who loved Jesus. When he went on to dispute the feasibility of deciding dogmatic questions by majority rule, the majority shouted him down. Many cried out, "Lucifer! Anathema, anathema!" Others screamed, "A second Luther! Throw him out!" All the Infallibilists loudly demanded, "Down with him, down with him!"

Complaints were heard everywhere about the lack of debate. According to Bishop Dupanloup, the bishops had the freedom to speak but not to discuss. He noted in his diary that the bishops' tongues had not been cut out, only caught in a vise—so the bishops couldn't use them to explain themselves. Bishop Maret considered the Council an acclamation disguised as a discussion.

Pius IX Agitates for Infallibility

The Roman pontiff personally bore no small share of the blame for this situation, as we have seen from the way he restricted and choked off debate. But he went much further than that. He personally intervened on behalf of the dogma of infallibility.

In his first encyclical letter of November 9, 1846, he had already laid implicit claim to infallibility. Three years later, in his encyclical *Nostis* (December 8, 1849), he spoke of his *"irreformabile magisterium,"* that is, his teaching office, which was not subject to any correction. Above all, however, he claimed infallibility de facto by declaring the dogma of Mary's Immaculate Conception on December 8, 1854, maintaining that, as the mother of Jesus, Mary had always been free of the stain of original sin.

Both before and during the Council Pius IX made no effort to conceal his belief that papal infallibility was a dogma of faith. Furthermore, he was so determined to push through the dogmatization that, as he revealed to the editor in chief of *La Civiltà Cattolica*, "My mind is so made up that if need be I shall take the definition upon myself and dismiss the Council if it wishes to keep silence."

In his "humorous" fashion the pope sometimes noted his

Pius IX's private train at Velletri, 1863

complete indifference to a definition. He remarked to the Belgian envoy in the summer of 1869: "People want to credit me with infallibility. I don't need it at all. Am I not infallible already? Didn't I establish the dogma of the Virgin's Immaculate Conception all by myself several years ago?" And speaking to the Austrian ambassador, Count Ferdinand Trauttmansdorff, around the end of 1869, he observed: "They're talking about the pope's infallibility. I believe in it. But in my recommendations to the Council there's not a word about it. I don't know whether we'll get it." That was diplomatic banter, and the Holy Father was not in earnest. "The pope wants it [the definition of infallibility]," Bishop MacQuaid wrote some time later, "and lets everyone see that he wants it." He believed he had received a special mission from God, an imperative to define the new dogma. Anyone who pleaded for infallibility would be showered with praise from the Vatican. That was the case, as already mentioned, for petitions from the clergy, books by theologians, and articles by journalists. It was also true for bishops who said the right things in the great hall of the Council. Pius IX often congratulated them personally, as he did for Bishops Charles Émile Freppel, Miguel Payá y Rico, Louis Pie, Pierre Henri Gérault de Langalerie, and Cardinal Henri Marie Gaston de Bonnechose. He publicly commended Bishop Ignatius von Senestrey when the latter forbade his theology students to attend Döllinger's lectures in Munich.

Towards the opponents of infallibility, however, the pope behaved quite differently. He did not hesitate to scold them repeatedly in official speeches, calling them leaders of the blind and friends of this world, ignorant and pusillanimous. In an address on the anniversary of his election as pope (June 1870), he rebuked them for "audacity, madness, foolishness, imprudence, haste, and violence." He took them to task for using methods ordinarily employed for getting votes at popular assemblies. On July 18, 1870, the pope once again reproached them, this time for impiety, rashness, and inconsistency.

And he treated them no better on an individual basis. Whenever Pius IX met with the bishops of the minority, he made them keenly aware that they were on the wrong side, even if they had done no more than sign the "false" petition. On such occasions he liked to insist on their kissing his foot—an old custom still in effect. No one who strayed from the party line could be sure of getting an audience with the pope. Despite his repeated requests, Bishop Henri Maret was not received once during the entire Council. "He is a viper," said Pius IX. At every opportunity he belabored the bishops over infallibility, pressuring men such as Wilhelm Emmanuel von Ketteler, Augustin David, François Victor Rivet, and Alessandro Ricciardi, along with Cardinals Henri de Bonnechose, Gustav Adolf von Hohenlohe, and Jacques Mathieu. He urged Archbishop Gregor Scherr of Munich to invoke sanctions against Döllinger.

Verbal Abuse

In his judgment of the minority bishops Pius IX showed no restraint. He looked down on them and on their resistance movement. The so-called opposition, as far as he was concerned, did not exist. "God breathed on them, and they were scattered," he

Giuseppe Garibaldi,
champion of Italian
unity

said, and burst out laughing. The bishops of the minority had
scarcely treated him any better than Giuseppe Garibaldi, the
Italian patriot and freedom fighter who had made several attempts to conquer the Papal States—and Rome in particular.
The only difference was that the bishops would spare him the
knife.

In the pope's eyes the French episcopate was not just in-
fected with false ideas, it was positively malicious. Bishop Félix
Dupanloup had given him the kiss of Judas. He considered
Georges Darboy dishonest: The archbishop of Paris was only
pretending to be a moderate, but the man was evil and his
thoughts were false. He couldn't fool the pope anymore—he
wouldn't get a cardinal's red hat. Speaking to a group of diocesan priests from Paris, Pius IX remarked of Darboy, "He's been
here a very long time." He characterized the theologian Alphonse
Gratry—the member of the French Academy who had defended
Dupanloup against Archbishop Victor Dechamps in some famous letters—as crazy and a rascal. In the presence of clerics
from the dioceses of Marseille and Perpignan, he declared that
their bishops had gone out of their heads. Bishop Charles

Philippe Place of Marseille complained of this incident in a letter to the pope—Pius IX denied the whole thing. He ordered Bishop Augustin David to devote further study to the infallibility question and recommended works by Ultramontane extremists for that purpose. He courted priests from the dioceses of Infallibilist bishops, while he often left the others standing there without saying a word to them.

The bishops from his immediate circle fared no better. On July 18, 1870, just before the solemn session defining the dogma, Archbishop Luigi Puecher-Passavalli (an opponent of infallibility) was reported sick. "Yes," the pope muttered, "he's sick in the head. That's a villainous trick." He viewed his almoner, Archbishop François Xavier de Mérode, as a cross laid upon him by God. When de Mérode broke his leg during the Council, Pius IX commented, "It would have been better if he had broken his tongue."

At an audience with clerics he accused Bishop William Clifford of working against him because he had passed Clifford over for the post of archbishop of Westminster. "But how could

Cardinal Gustav Adolf von
Hohenlohe-Schillingsfürst

I have made him archbishop," asked the pope, "since he can neither read nor write?" Alluding to Luke 22:31, which says that
Satan leads the apostles into temptation with God's permission,
sifting them like wheat, Pius IX chided Archbishop Johannes
Simor for beginning well but ending badly. He had first believed
that Simor loved him a little, but now he had to recognize the
fact that the Primate of Hungary had gone over to those who
waged war against him.

The opposition of the German-speaking bishops was likewise of little account to Pius IX. "Those German bishops make
me laugh." But the resistance to infallibility in Germany did not
seem quite so harmless to the pope. "The Germans are the worst
of all. The German spirit has spoiled everything."

He considered Cardinal Joseph Othmar Rauscher of Vienna
a nobody who greatly overrated his own education. Joseph
Georg Strossmayer was the chief of the sectarians who had come
to Rome to raise up altar against altar. Pius IX also spoke of
"that scoundrel Strossmayer," who was a political agent and had
connections with all the governments. The pope knew the names
of all the men who would shake Strossmayer's hand when he entered the Council hall. To his mind, Archbishop Paul Melchers
of Cologne was an ignoramus; Cardinal Friedrich Schwarzenberg of Prague "the subdeacon at the manger," that is, an ass;
Prince-bishop Heinrich Förster of Breslau nothing less than a
wild beast and soft in the head. Archbishop Friedrich Fürstenberg of Olmütz was useless except on the hunt.

His opinion of Cardinal Gustav Adolf von Hohenlohe was
scarcely higher. "He is a crazy fellow but an angel." And although he sometimes called him "our dear Gustav," there was a
grotesque scene when the cardinal threw himself at the Holy Father's feet after being rebuked for his attitude on infallibility.
Pius IX seized him by the ear and said, "Why are you so set
against your father, who has loved you so much and still loves
you?" A no less ridiculous moment occurred when the pope gave
free rein to his displeasure against Bishop Joseph Karl Hefele of
Rottenburg. On June 20, 1870, the Bavarian ambassador, Count
Karl von Tauffkirchen-Guttenburg, reported to King Ludwig II
of Bavaria: "The day before yesterday a German clergyman had
an audience with His Holiness. Upon being asked who he was,

the man said he was the secretary of the bishop of Rottenburg. Whereupon the pope turned away from him with a 'phew!' and left him standing there."

"I can't bear this skinny priest from Munich," remarked Pius IX of Professor Johann Friedrich, conciliar theologian of Cardinal Hohenlohe. "I even prefer Günther [Vienna-based philosopher and theologian Anton Günther, who had been condemned by Rome]. At least he doesn't speak out anymore." The influential English layman Lord Acton, who contributed greatly to the organization of the minority resistance, was favored by the pope with the epithet, "that blackguard Actonuccio [-uccio = ugly, nasty]."

It wasn't always just a war of words, especially when the bishops were very poor and therefore totally dependent financially upon the Holy See, as were most of the 285 Italians and approximately 70 prelates from mission countries. During the Council some three hundred bishops lived in Rome at the pope's

Lord John Emmerich Edward Acton, pupil of Döllinger

expense. There was opposition even among these council fathers, and Pius IX could not help quipping, "They're afraid to declare the pope infallible but not to have him go bankrupt [*fallire*]." But the pope often lost his sense of humor, and his level of annoyance rose, bringing on threats and intimidation.

Papal Chastisements

On January 26, 1870, a momentous scene took place at the Vatican. The Chaldean Patriarch Joseph Audu had been summoned by the pope because of a speech he had given at the Council the day before—and because of his opposition to the bull *Reversus,* which significantly expanded Rome's prerogatives in the filling of episcopal and patriarchal chairs.

As soon as Audu appeared in the papal chambers, a violent little drama occurred. According to Bishop Félix Dupanloup, the pope bolted the door behind him and warned the seventy-eight-

Joseph Audu, Chaldean
patriarch of Babylon

year-old patriarch that he would never get out of there till he had given his written consent to the bull in question. While the patriarch remained outwardly calm, the pope was trembling with rage. Audu had only two alternatives: to resign or submit. Out of fear he chose the second. Later on, however, further conflicts arose between pope and patriarch, and finally Pius IX removed him from office.[13]

This event stirred up extraordinary excitement—in the eyes of the council fathers it was yet another proof of the lack of freedom at the Council. Archbishop Georges Darboy spoke of a robber synod. Angriest of all was Audu's colleague, the Greek-Melkite patriarch Gregor Yussef. He told the French ambassador to Rome, Gaston de Banneville, that he would not give in: He was not yet eighty. He bravely withstood the first waves of pressure, and on June 14, 1870, gave a quite outspoken defense of the old rights of the patriarchs. In wild exasperation the pope ordered the patriarch to come see him. When Yussef kissed the foot of Pius IX in the traditional fashion, the pope placed his foot on the patriarch's head (some said his neck) after the manner of a pagan conqueror, and said, "Gregor, you hard head you." Then he rubbed his foot about on the patriarch's head a while longer. After Pius had died, the Holy Synod of the Greek-Melkite church (under the presidency of Patriarch Maximos IV Saigh) filed two separate reports of this event in Rome in order to block the pope's canonization. For a long time Yussef himself did not dare to speak of the incident, for fear of causing a schism in his church.[14]

Under such circumstances many bishops were afraid to speak their mind. Some of them, especially Eastern bishops, left the Council before it ended. Pius IX encouraged the departure of such "Gallican troublemakers." "Right-thinking" bishops, on the other hand, were detained in Rome.

Pope Pius IX and
Cardinal Guidi:
A Father-Son Conflict?

On June 18, 1870, emotions were running high in the great hall of the Council. A Dominican cardinal, Filippo Maria Guidi

Gregor II Sayour
Yussef, Greek-Melkite
patriarch of Antioch

Cardinal Filippo Maria
Guidi

had come forward to speak against the pope and the Infallibilists (the first Roman prelate to do so), emphatically stating
that the pope was not infallible in and of himself, independently
of the Church, but only insofar as he reflected the views of the
bishops and the tradition of the Church. Many believed that the
longed-for compromise had at long last been found; they embraced one another and wept for joy. But the happiness was
short-lived. That very evening Pius IX had Cardinal Guidi called
in and bitterly castigated him for his speech.

In reply to Guidi's protest that he had only spoken as a witness to tradition, the pope snapped back at him with the oft-
repeated phrase, "I am tradition." The incident greatly upset
Pius IX. More than one report claimed he became sick directly
afterwards.

Guidi's action struck the pope and the Infallibilists as likely
to encourage others to follow his example, and hence extremely
dangerous. Pius IX had the Dominican monastery of Santa
Maria sopra Minerva, where Guidi lived, kept under close surveillance. On the very day of Guidi's speech he also found out
the names of the people who had kissed the cardinal's hands
after he finished. And in the great hall of the Council the
reprimands were not long in coming. At the next session Bishop
Bartolomeo D'Avanzo upbraided Guidi in the name of the
commission on faith, saying he was worse than a Gallican. The
cardinal was not given an opportunity to reply. Instead, the
Infallibilists demanded that he recant his speech publicly in a
newspaper. Guidi held firm at first, but in the end he knuckled
under. On July 13, 1870, he gave his assent to the constitution,
though with reservations; five days later he finally went along
with it completely. Such were the obstacles to freedom of expression facing prelates who were dependent upon the Vatican,
materially and otherwise.

We know astonishingly little about this cardinal, the only
Roman prelate who dared to challenge Pius IX in public for any
length of time. In the historical literature his name is passed
over in silence. He has no biography, and a search of the
archives has brought only meager information to light.

Could the reason for this remarkable lacuna be that Cardinal Guidi was, in fact, the son of Pius IX? This was the claim

made by Polish Count Władisław Kulczycki in several dispatches to the Italian Foreign Minister, Emilio Visconti Venosta.
Kulczycki may well have had solid information about such
things. He had been in Rome since 1855 and since 1862 had
belonged to the papal family as a privy chamberlain. He was
connected to the group of Roman prelates who supported the
Italian cause and was an intimate friend of Augustin Theiner,
prefect of the papal archives. There are other indications as well
which make Count Kulczycki's allegation not altogether improbable.[15] No one denies, for instance, that Giovanni Maria Mastai-
Ferretti—Pius IX's civilian name—was a lady's man before he
began his theological studies at a relatively late age. The literature on the pope occasionally mentions children he is supposed
to have fathered. (This seems to be another reason why the
canonization of Pius IX is not making progress.) Oddly enough,
up till now scholars have passed over Kulczycki's letters in
silence, although all the other documents from the Italian
Foreign Ministry relating to the Vatican Council have been published.

Was Cardinal Guidi, then, both Pius IX's son and his opponent at the Council? This has not yet been proved, but neither is
it entirely unlikely. Of course, if it were true it would shed a still
more lurid light on the most oppressive scene from the Council:
the moment, so pregnant with symbolism, when the pope flings
at his son the line, "*I* am tradition, *I* am the Church," and then a
cardinal who takes a stand against his father, appealing to the
testimony of tradition, swearing that it runs completely counter
to his father's ambitions as pope—an unsurpassable confrontation with authority!

*Worldly Dominion in
the Service of
the Good Cause*

On April 6, 1870, the Prussian envoy to Rome, Count Harry
von Arnim-Suckow, wrote to Prince Otto von Bismarck: "The
king of Rome has put his mail service at the pope's disposal—as
he has, on other occasions, lent him his customs, his censors, and
even his police—for the purpose of disciplining the Council and

Pius IX blesses his kneeling troops at the Campi di Annibale (near Frascati) on July 2, 1868

bringing it around. This, of course, would never come about if the king and the pope were not on such good terms. This imposes a very serious restriction on the Council, since it prevents the Fathers from getting the information they need."

This report, which drew upon facts supplied by Bishop Heinrich Förster of Breslau, accurately described the situation. Bishops, theologians, journalists, and ambassadors of doubtful orthodoxy were closely watched. With all the discretion in the world this fact could not quite escape the attention of the anti-Infallibilists—and so the mutual mistrust grew deeper. The rump Papal States were, in any event, not the ideal place for free and open discussion. There was no political life, no freedom of assembly, no freedom of religion, no freedom of the press. Arrests for political reasons were the order of the day. The regime's paternalism went so far as to order doctors not to go on treating their patients unless the latter consulted their confessor (at the very latest) after the third house call.

The papal police force devoted special attention to the

press. Msgr. Lorenzo Randi, papal minister of police and later a cardinal, had all letters from newspaper correspondents intercepted at the post office and suppressed the most negative reports. Naturally, that in itself was not enough to stop the flow of information. Word soon got around how unreliable the papal postal service was, and reporters found other means of getting their stories out to the newspapers. The best proof of this is the "Roman Letters from the Council," which appeared in the *Augsburger Allgemeine Zeitung*. The police attempted to discover who the informants for these letters were in order to deport them. They suspected Dr. Albert Dressel, veteran correspondent for the *Allegemeine Zeitung;* Msgr. Nikolaus Vorsak, Bishop Strossmayer's conciliar theologian; Professor Johann Friedrich; Lord Acton; even the Bavarian ambassador, Count Karl von Tauffkirchen-Guttenburg. In the end, thanks to the intervention of the German embassy in Rome, none of them was forced to leave the Papal States.

The police had an easier time screening out all periodicals odious to the Vatican, as well as other undesirable printed matter. The *Allgemeine Zeitung* was subjected to this procedure

Cardinal Alessandro Barnabò, prefect of the Congregation for the Propagation of the Faith (the Missions)

Antonius Petrus IX Hassun, Armenian patriarch of Constantinople

with particular frequency. Bishop Ketteler commissioned a polemical piece entitled *"Quaestio"* by the Jesuit Fr. Francesco Quarella, but for four weeks it lay impounded at the post office until it was released after Ketteler protested and threatened to make trouble. Things didn't always work out so simply. Cardinal Pietro De Silvestri spoke of whole reams of brochures and other publications piling up at the post office—all held back with the noble intention of preventing the council fathers from becoming confused. Other occasional encroachments on the freedom and personal rights of Council participants, especially the denial of permission to leave Rome, strengthened the impression that they were not free.

This feeling was especially prevalent among the bishops subject to the jurisdiction of the Congregation for the Missions (the "Propaganda"), who were unwilling to accept the new dogma. The authoritarian regime of the prefect of the Propaganda, Cardinal Alessandro Barnabò, joined the pope in his ill will towards such bishops. Like the pope, Barnabò came down hard on subordinates who were opposed to the dogmatization of

infallibility. He violently reproved the Greek-Melkite patriarch
Yussef for speaking at the Council without showing him the text
beforehand. Yussef was told he was not allowed to speak without his permission. Barnabò threateningly advised him to act
differently in the future. The pope knew who his contacts were.
Barnabò likewise tried to browbeat Archbishop Connolly of
Halifax, warning him not to get into the bad books of the Propaganda. He also attempted to talk Archbishop Peter Richard
Kenrick of St. Louis and many other bishops into changing their
minds.

The bishops from the Orient were given a particularly
rough going over. Here Barnabò could rely on two loyal assistants, the Armenian patriarch Antonius Petrus Hassun of Constantinople and the Latin patriarch Giuseppe Valerga of Jerusalem. Special pressure was brought to bear on bishops who had
signed the postulate against the definition of infallibility. The
Propaganda succeeded in threatening them with suspension of

Giuseppe Valerga,
Latin patriarch of
Jerusalem

Placidus Casangian,
Armenian archbishop
of Antioch

its financial support, and most of the signatories withdrew.

The most serious incidents involved the Armenians. Not only did they prove to be recalcitrant on the issue of infallibility, they were also unwilling to accept Patriarch Hassun, who had been imposed on them by Rome. When Placidus Casangian, abbot-general of all Armenian Antonite monks, spoke out against infallibility, he was repeatedly threatened with dismissal unless he recanted. Casangian refused, nor would he permit an Apostolic visitation of the Antonite monastery in Rome. Pius IX was so infuriated by this that he commanded Casangian and Abbot Hanemian to perform compulsory spiritual exercises in a monastery.

The Armenians soon came to realize that such papal decrees were meant to be taken seriously. The papal police instituted thorough house searches and tried vigorously to enforce Pius IX's orders. As it happened, the Armenian archbishop of Diarbekir (Mesopotamia), Grégoire Bathiarian, was also an opponent of infallibility. The Propaganda concluded that this position was due primarily to the influence of John Stephanian, Bathiarian's vicar-general and secretary. At the instigation of Patriarch Hassun, it was decided to separate Stephanian from his archbishop and to order him to perform the same compulsory exercises. When Stephanian would not comply with this, the papal police attempted to arrest him in the street. Stephanian defended himself, and the ensuing scuffle led to a riot among the people. Only when Bathiarian intervened did the officers let him go. Both men wanted to return to Turkey immediately. The other Armenian bishops no longer felt secure either, and requested permission to leave Rome. When they were refused exit visas, two of the bishops fled, including Casangian. Once he was "on the other side of the Roman border," Casangian wrote separate letters to both pope and Council. In the face of the constant menace of imprisonment, he said, and owing to his serious illness, he had feared for his life and thought his only safety lay in flight. For Casangian, at least, there was no such thing as freedom of expression. Soon afterwards a schism broke out among Armenian

Grégoire Bathiarian,
archbishop of Diarbekir
(Mesopotamia)

Catholics and a large number of them returned to their non-Uniate fellow believers.

Nuncios as Informers

The nuncios, too, the advance guard of the Curia, were reliable assistants in the battle for infallibility. They were lavish with praise for those who shared their views. Bishops who said nothing either way were showered with petitions in favor of the dogma. And the nuncios cast suspicions of heresy on the opponents of papal infallibility, denouncing them to Rome. Nuncio Pier Francesco Meglia in Munich felt that pride was the leading characteristic of German theology professors and repeatedly complained during the Council that the bishops were taking no action against the University of Munich, that "school of pestilence," as he put it. He recommended the removal of the Franciscan Fr. Hötzl from his post for daring to defend Döllinger. Nuncios Meglia in Munich, Giovanni Battista Agnozzi in Lucerne, Giacomo Cattani in Brussels, and Flavio Chigi in Paris all advised Rome to put all books that departed from the Infallibilist line on the Index. Nuncio Chigi waged an especially fierce battle against the dean of the Sorbonne, Titular Bishop Henri Maret. He provided *La Civiltà Cattolica* with material for slanderous articles against Maret. With the help of the Spanish ambassador in Rome, Alejandro Mon, he even tried to bribe Maret's publisher, Henri Plon, to get hold of the galley proofs of Maret's book, *The General Council and Religious Peace*. At least that is how Maret tells the story, adding that the whole operation originated with the pope. When Maret's work appeared, the nuncio sent it posthaste to Rome, with the observation that it was nothing but unscholarly hackwork. He praised Bishop Louis Pie of Poitiers, who had published an attack on Maret, with the words, "You have done a good deed, something of lasting value."

Manipulation of the Press

Pius IX was quite aware of the increasing importance of the

Louis Pie,
bishop of Poitiers

press. He had shown this as early as 1869, when he gave his blessing to *La Civiltà Cattolica* to start up a discussion on infallibility. During the Council Fr. Carlo Piccirillo, S.J., the editor in chief of the journal, was one of the most frequent visitors to the Apostolic palace. Pius IX gave him exact directions as to what *La Civiltà Cattolica* should print and in what tone it should be written.

"Then Fr. Piccirillo came in," Giuseppe Franco, S.J., noted in his diary, "to talk about the *Civiltà Cattolica* business, and said he had come to ask the pope for guidance and direction. Gratry and Döllinger had now taken off their masks. Should we attack them? . . . The Holy Father ordered him to refute them, and refute them thoroughly. In *La Civiltà Cattolica* or elsewhere? In *La Civiltà Cattolica,* and above all in a clear, down-to-earth manner."

The pope's campaign had other targets, including the French politician and writer Charles de Montalembert; the anonymous article "Ce qui se passe au concile" (What's Going On at the Council), written by someone close to the French

Carlo Piccirillo,
editor in chief of
La Civiltà Cattolica

bishops; and the minority view that moral unanimity was imperative for Council decisions on dogma. Even bishops such as Maret, Hefele, and Rauscher were not spared.

Pius IX liked to play as direct a part as possible in such doings. He thrust aside intermediary authorities, such as his court theologian, Dominican Mariano Spada, who usually took care of censorship. He wanted to read the galleys himself and make the decisions on his own. He personally delivered the documents whose publication in *La Civiltà Cattolica* seemed useful to him. And he did not fail to provide financial support.

But *La Civiltà Cattolica* was by no means the only newspaper serving in the press campaign for papal infallibility. *L'Univers* and *L'Unità Cattolica* were just as important. They, too, along with *La Correspondence* [*sic*] *de Rome,* enjoyed subsidies from the Vatican. At times they carried out papal assignments as direct as those handled by *La Civiltà Cattolica.* Thus, Louis Veuillot wrote in his paper, "at the bidding of higher-ups," a series of articles on the freedom of the Council. Bishops complained continually of the hatred and discord such journalism spread among Catholics, but the complaints were of no avail.

To create a counterweight to the liberal press, the Infallibilists, particularly Emmanuel d'Alzon, proposed setting up
an international press bureau. They found a willing listener in
the pope. He assigned the suffragan bishop of Geneva, Gaspare
Mermillod, the job of forming such a bureau. For the practical
implementation of this plan, Mermillod contacted Fr. Carlo Pic-
cirrillo and ultimately succeeded in building up a large press
committee. Members included Bishops Manning, Dechamps,
and Pie, Paolo Mencacci, editor of *Il Divin Salvatore*, Fr. Emmanuel d'Alzon, Count Johann Anton von Pergen from Vienna,
Count Luca Gozze from Dalmatia, an adviser at the Austrian
embassy, Count Paul de Breda, Lord Dingsbey and Lord Bro-
denham from England, Giovanni Marchese Patrizi-Montoro,
Duke Scipione Salviati, and others. They met once a week, and
whenever else Mermillod thought it necessary, to pass out information or instructions to the Catholic press.

Gaspare Mermillod, suf-
fragan bishop of Geneva

As part of this program the pope released one bishop from each of the major language groups (Italian, Spanish, French, German, and English) from the oath of secrecy. In this way, for example, Archbishop Manning was allowed to tell all the news of the Council to the English chargé d'affaires, Odo Russell. Once Cardinal Henri de Bonnechose made it quite clear that he sided with the Infallibilists, he, too, was allowed to enjoy this privilege. It is not known that Pius IX ever granted this favor to any bishops of the minority.

3

Pius IX

Pius IX is the key figure in the First Vatican Council. Without him the dogma of papal infallibility would never have been declared. His personality, however, raises numerous difficulties.

The Pope's Epilepsy

Giovanni Maria Mastai-Ferretti, the future Pius IX, was born on May 13, 1792, amidst the chaos of the French Revolution in the little town of Senigallia near Ancona, the last of nine children. Since 1705 the Mastai-Ferretti family had borne the title of counts, but they did not belong to the lesser provincial nobility. In 1803, at the age of eleven, Giovanni Maria entered the secondary school of San Michele in Volterra. Four years later he had his first epileptic seizures. They lasted all through his youth and continued until his thirties. The young man reported having an epileptic disturbance as late as 1825. In the same year he wrote to Pope Leo XII that, owing to the effects of epilepsy, he had a very weak memory and could not concentrate on a subject for any length of time without having to worry about his ideas getting terribly confused.

Epilepsy was not the least factor in determining Mastai-Ferretti to enter upon a career in the Church. His admission into the pope's Noble Guard was denied the young count because of his disease. In 1816 he decided to become a priest. Three years later, after a rather summary study of theology, he applied for Holy Orders. On July 4, 1819, he received the indult (ecclesiastical dispensation) allowing him to be ordained a priest despite the epileptic fits. To be sure, there was a condition attached, namely, that he should never celebrate mass alone but always with another priest or deacon. Immediately after his ordination, Giovanni Maria Mastai-Ferretti worked in the "Tata Giovanni" orphanage. From 1823 to 1825 he accompanied the Apostolic delegate Giovanni Muzi as *uditore* (a diplomatic rank between secretary and counselor to the nuncio) on a trip to Chile.

After 1825 there are no reports of epileptic seizures for a long time. Mastai-Ferretti rose rapidly in the Church. The fact that he happened to have two uncles in high clerical positions may not have been irrelevant here. One was a bishop, the other

Pius IX, age eighteen

a canon of St. Peter's. In 1827, after a brief interlude as director of the Ospizio San Michele, Mastai-Ferretti was made bishop of Spoleto; in 1832 bishop of Imola; in 1840 cardinal. In 1846, at the relatively young age of fifty-four, he became pope.

In his years as a bishop, Giovanni Maria Mastai-Ferretti seems to have enjoyed good health. Only in 1849 do we hear of isolated instances of fainting spells. In 1870, the year of the Council, there was once again talk of epilepsy. The Austrian ambassador to the Holy See, Count Ferdinand Trauttmansdorff, reported to Vienna on June 4, 1870, that in the previous Lent the pope had once again been threatened with epileptic fits. Others, too, reported a momentary loss of consciousness and a recurrence of epilepsy. On the whole, it seems that the general public had no knowledge of all this—it would have been easy enough to keep it under wraps. Most of the historical sources are silent on the matter as well. On the other hand, nobody denies that the pope's epilepsy had lasting effects. Even writers favorably disposed to the pope have noted traces of it in Pius IX's physical makeup. The entire right side of his body, they point out, was slightly less developed than his left. This could be seen even in his face, which was asymmetric. His head leaned to the right, his lips were awry. The Roman prelate Francesco Liverani, Pius IX's confidant, felt that, owing to his earlier epileptic attacks, the pope was still very much a sick man.

The psychic effects of the pope's disease are more important than the physical ones—and they are also more freely conceded. Pius IX was considered highly impressionable, capricious, impulsive, and unpredictable. In the same vein, he was also characteristically given to mysticism and religious fanaticism.

Epilepsy probably offers one of the keys to understanding the pope's behavior during the Council, which was often puzzling. But other facts and phenomena deserve at least as much attention.

At the Pope's Mercy

The "sacred" disease of epilepsy, which he suffered from for decades, must have left deep traces in the pope's life. After all, had it not been for his illness he would most likely not have become a priest. But the experiences Pius IX had in the first years of his pontificate were of similarly critical importance. On July 16, 1846, Giovanni Maria Mastai-Ferretti became the successor of the archreactionary Gregory XVI. In their expectation of major policy changes, the people welcomed the new pope-king with jubilation. At first Pius IX let himself be swept along on this wave of enthusiasm and began to carry out a number of reforms (amnesty for political prisoners, relaxing of press censorship, installation of an advisory board, creation of a municipal guard). The legend arose of the liberal pope. But with these papal concessions the desire for reform grew stronger. The democrats managed to wrest a constitution from Pius IX, but that did not satisfy them. They demanded general, unrestricted elections, a parliament with broad powers, and the replacement of the army with a popular militia. Above all, however, they called upon Pius IX to place himself at the head of the movement for Italian emancipation and declare war on Austria. As head of the Catholic Church, Pius IX shrank from war with another Catholic

Popular rejoicing in Rome at the start of Pius IX's pontificate

country. Then he lost all his popularity. His Prime Minister, Pellegrino Rossi was assassinated, and the revolution broke out. Pius IX escaped the only way he could—by fleeing. Disguised as a simple priest, he slipped quietly out of the Quirinal Palace, got into the diplomatic coach of the Bavarian ambassador, Count Karl von Spaur, and headed for Gaeta, which belonged to the kingdom of the Two Sicilies.

The events of 1848 had a traumatic effect on the pope. Pius IX had never been a liberal, but he had felt some sympathy for liberalism. This feeling now turned to hatred. From 1848 on, Pius IX was haunted by fear of revolution. In 1850, shortly after his return to Rome, which French troops had retaken for him amidst bloody fighting, he revoked the constitution he had granted and branded freedom of the press and freedom of association as intrinsically evil. Liberalism was now the mortal enemy of the papacy and the Church. He laid all the more stress on his own authority. His rule became reactionary and dictatorial.

Despite this—or precisely because of it—Pius IX held an extraordinarily powerful fascination for a large number of Catholics. During his pontificate the papal cult reached a high point. Many people thought of Pius IX as saintly, selfless, deeply religious, full of charm and humor. The hostility of the liberals turned him into a martyr.

His followers' panegyrics, which often border on papolatry, are, however, only one side of the story. Many of his contemporaries, including some of the most eminent bishops of the period, viewed Pius IX as the greatest disaster for the Catholic Church—particularly on account of his role at the First Vatican Council. There they found themselves at the mercy of a man against whom they were powerless to do anything. The only way out would have been to break with him and pay the price of a schism. Their despair led them to attempt postponing any decision by the Council in hopes that the pope would die in the meantime.

Pius IX struck so many people as dangerous above all because he wished to dogmatize a teaching which, from the historical standpoint, was worse than dubious and which overturned the Church's basic organization. In their eyes the definition

Murdered Prime Minister Pellegrino Rossi appears to Pius IX in a dream. The pope fears a similar fate

would deprive the Catholic Church of the last shred of credibility.

The pope's epilepsy and the rest of his biography are important in understanding the mind of Pius IX. But they are not enough. They cannot explain why so many bishops at Vatican I found themselves in such a hopeless situation in trying to deal with him. The pope's words and actions and the impressions he made on a great variety of people shed new light on the figure of this pontiff, but they also create new problems. The picture becomes more dramatic.

"I Have the Mother of God on My Side"

Pius IX undoubtedly *was* a deeply religious man. Nevertheless there is no way of overlooking the fact that his piety often displayed abnormal traits. He was morbidly eager to believe his court prelates' stories about visions and prophecies.[16] He was always ready to take such things as apparitions of a cross in the sky or the stirrings of the corpse of St. Clare of Montefalco (ca. 1275–1308) as solemn signs from God. This was true both of the days when he was a bishop in Spoleto and Imola as well as later during his pontificate. "He often lapsed into mysticism," wrote Marco Minghetti, the Italian economist and statesman, of the period before 1848, "and it happened one evening during a session of the council of ministers, unless my memory deceives me, that he suddenly opened a window when a comet appeared in the sky, knelt down—and made all those present kneel down with him—and prayed to God to avert the scourge, of which the comet was the fateful portent. When he heard that the revolutionaries worshiped God and honored and respected priests, he rejoiced and thought he would surely find happiness even here below. But when the opposite occurred he broke into lamentations and saw the world hastening towards its ruin."[17]

Again in 1848 the pope was profoundly affected by the "illuminations" of a Neapolitan nun. In later years traumatic memories of the revolution helped to strengthen such mystical tendencies, and sound common sense increasingly gave way to a dangerously unhealthy mysticism.[18]

If we neglect his mystical side, the pope's behavior at the First Vatican Council becomes inexplicable. Pius IX obviously believed he had been given a divine mission to make papal infallibility a dogma of faith, and a number of visions played a part in this belief. The apparition of the Virgin may have had something to do with this. In 1846 Mary "appeared" to two shepherd children in the mountains of Savoy. In the secret message which one of the children, Melanie Mathieu-Calvet, had to write down for the pope, the word "infallible" occurs. More important than this, we have hints that Pius IX himself believed he had had a vision of the Mother of God, confirming his faith in the doctrine of infallibility. He looked upon Mary quite simply as his ally. When the Secretary of State, Cardinal Antonelli, and other cardinals pointed out the great difficulties that a definition would create with various governments, the pope answered, "I have the Mother of God on my side. I shall go forward."

On January 5, 1870, Giovanni Don Bosco (founder of the Salesians, canonized in 1934) also had a vision. In it he received the news that the time had come for Pius IX to elevate papal in-

Giovanni Don Bosco, founder of the
Congregation of the Salesians

fallibility to the status of dogma. The pope was to proceed to a
definition even if he had only two bishops on his side: At all
times he could count on God's protection and Mary's help.
Within a short space Pius IX received Don Bosco three times in
private audience. On February 12, 1870, the pope was given the
text of the revelation; on February 21 Don Bosco added some
material to complete his vision: Prussia would convert, the
Church would experience a great victory, and the papacy a bril-
liant triumph. Curial circles, too, prized the visions of Don
Bosco, and two years later even *La Civiltà Cattolica* reported on
them. The papal court seems to have consulted other visionaries
as well, both living and dead, such as Louise Beck (1822–79)
and Bartholomäus Holzhauser (1613–58).

Don Bosco only encouraged the pope along the way he had
already chosen. Even before this, numerous reports had arisen

The pope has a vision of the fall of
Bismarck's empire

that the pope considered himself inspired and believed in his
unique divine mission to define infallibility. Nothing could
deflect him from this path. Many people claimed that Pius IX
actually spoke of *feeling* infallible. He evidently thought of himself as enlightened by God in a special way. Bishops and diplomats talked about his extravagant mysticism and unhealthy
illuminism.

Pius IX wasn't the only one at the Council to have such extravagant experiences. Similar phenomena took place in the
heart of the Infallibilist camp. It took a peculiar psychic structure to begin with to make a vow to go to one's death, if necessary, for the sake of papal infallibility. It was no less eccentric to
view infallibility, as did Archbishop Henry Edward Manning, as
an absolute panacea, capable even of converting the Anglicans.
Add to this sort of thing a belief in miracles and a propensity for
esoterica. Cardinal Karl August Graf von Reisach—as the first

man named a president of the Council, he played a major role before the opening of Vatican I—belonged to the inner circle of the "visionary" Louise Beck in Altötting. This curial cardinal, who died at the beginning of the Council, was also evidently the Vatican representative who had consulted the prophetess of Lower Bavaria on the question of infallibility. After the Council, Bishop Ignatius von Senestrey likewise became a "child" of "Mother" Louise Beck, and thereby participated in the "mystery of the direction from on high." Despite the fact that Louise Beck was completely controlled by a pair of Redemptorist priests and that the whole thing led to mystical-erotic excesses (Louise slept with both of the priests in reparation for the sins of the world, a practice known as "the mystery in the mystery"), for years on end she exercised a crucial influence on the church politics of Bavaria, particularly through Reisach and his vicar-general, Friedrich Windischmann. Senestrey's behavior towards Louise Beck can only be explained as the result of religious delusions.[19]

Other Infallibilists were similarly susceptible. The Assumptionist Emmanuel d'Alzon credited Pius IX with miraculous powers and thought highly of all kinds of prophecies. For Archbishop Victor Dechamps, as we have already mentioned, a papal blessing had the effect of a stroke of Providence. Bishop Claude Plantier of Nimes wrote his speech on papal infallibility while lying ill in a state of divine illumination. Bishop Louis Pie of Poitiers was very much taken by the prophecies of the mystic Bartholomäus Holzhauser.

Despotic Traits:
Loss of a
Sense of Proportion

Along with his sense of possessing a divine mission, Pius IX had a strongly authoritarian character. "[The pope] is the object of the most intense flattery . . . and therefore his situation is the most distorted . . . no one dares to say a word . . . This secular and spiritual omnipotence destroys the mind and heart of a man . . . and everything around him," wrote Bishop Dupanloup in his diary on December 17, 1869.

Cardinal Karl August
Graf von Reisach

In Pius IX flattery found a fruitful soil. Reports about the pope constantly speak of his vanity. "The pope," wrote Count von Arnim to Bismarck on May 15, 1869, "insofar as he is merely human, is not free from the sort of personal overestimation which we usually call vanity. And he is not satisfied with the recognition he gets from himself. He places great value on the successes of his person and—I don't know how to say this in German—*il pose devant l'histoire.*" The court prelates bolstered such papal inclinations with their fawning obsequiousness. Pius IX had gone to the trouble of choosing certain types of people: mediocre, "fishy," unbalanced, sometimes even psychically disturbed. Their influence on the pope seemed so decisive to Bishop Dupanloup that he complained the pope was entirely in their clutches.

But this dependency did not at all lessen the pope's self-confidence. On the contrary, he acted in an altogether authoritarian fashion. This was especially evident in the issue of infallibility, which Pius IX saw as his own particular business. He worked so strenuously for a definition that many people got the impression that his own personal ambitions were at stake. "The popes had never shown so much zeal for the fundamental dogmas of Christianity," Bishop Maret believed. The Prussian envoy, Count von Arnim, talked about a papal caprice.

Pius IX wanted the new dogma at any cost. Not only did he make use of rather dubious methods, he was also blind to the dangers which might arise from a definition. But, above all, he displayed so much passion for his opinions that anyone who did not share them had to feel offended. A French bishop spoke of Pius' "feverish impatience," "willfulness," and "blind fanaticism." Bishop de Las Cases described the pope as an authority subject to no other control than his own whims and preferences. The new dogma, he felt, must lead to despotism. To others the pope was already acting the despot by applying massive pressures to dominate the Council. Every now and then Pius tried to pretend impartiality, but before long he would squelch any remaining doubts that everything depended upon him. Several bishops reported that the people closest to him were saying, "Don't count either the majority or the minority. The pope is everything."

The Council lasted longer than expected. The debate over infallibility dragged on into the Roman high summer. Many bishops fell ill because of the malaria still rampant in the city. But the pope would not hear of postponing the Council. "*Che crepino pure*" (let them croak) he is supposed to have snapped.

As mentioned before, the pope was toying with the idea of making the definition of infallibility all by himself, if need be, and without the Council. Had he done so, he would have only been following the advice given him by St. John Bosco's revelation. Such determination led Lord Acton to exclaim, "What wild passion!" "That isn't just passion," replied Bishop Dupanloup, "that's his personality." The Greek-Melkite patriarch Gregor Yussef went a step further and called the pope a tyrant.

"This is truly a difficult situation for the Church," wrote Fr. Henri Icard, a Sulpician priest from Paris, in his journal. "The most absolute power—in the hands of a man who will only listen to the people who think—or, rather, speak—the way he does." Pius IX felt that discussing his opponent's arguments was a waste of time. He knew that he would triumph thanks to the power of his office. Along these same lines, the Austrian ambassador, Count Ferdinand Trauttmansdorff, noted that the pope was extremely high-handed and given to bluster.

Pius IX with the prelates of the *Anticamera Segreta* (Secret Antichamber), ca. 1862. From left to right: Msgrs. Francesco Ricci Parraciani, Giuseppe Stella, François Xavier de Mérode, Antonio Cenni (kneeling), Edoardo Borromeo (majordomo), George Talbot de Malahide, Gustav Adolf von Hohenlohe-Schillingsfürst, Augusto Negrotto (kneeling), Secretary of State Cardinal Giacomo Antonelli, Bartolomeo Pacco (chamberlain), Marinelli (sacristan)

The pope believed that the bishops had come to Rome simply to say "yes" and "amen," Bishop Dupanloup wrote in his Council diary on January 2, 1870. When that turned out not to be the case, Pius treated all the reluctant ones as personal enemies. Only Protestants and unbelievers would deny papal infallibility. He reproached his episcopal opponents for their ignorance of both theology and history, as well as for violent impiety and inconsistency. Sometimes he called them Freemasons and tools of the Freemasons. The papal press did not lag behind here: The *Osservatore Romano* declared that the minority bishops were allied with the lodges.

More distressing than all this are the many abusive terms which Pius IX heaped on the bishops of the minority in private conversations and on public occasions. They covered the gamut from "crazy" to "ass," all the way down to "traitor" and "chief of the sectarians." The pope deeply injured the bishops with his biting remarks.

More clearly than any words, however, Pius IX's outbursts of rage revealed just how ungovernably passionate his temperament was. His anger had been feared even back in Spoleto and Imola, when Giovanni Maria Mastai-Ferretti was an archbishop. As pope he did not improve in this area. This matter comes up repeatedly in his canonization proceedings. His fury in private audiences could become so violent that older prelates might suffer heart attacks as a result and, on occasion, even die shortly afterwards. This was supposedly the case with Cardinals Vincenzo Santucci and Girolamo D'Andrea, who had advised the pope to make peace with the new state of Italy, as well as with the dean of the papal antichamber, Traversari, and a papal master of ceremonies.[20]

Such transports of rage were due not merely to Pius IX's impulsive nature but to his emotional poverty. Bishop Dupanloup spoke in his Council diary of a heart of stone, and others had the same impression. At times normal human feelings of affection, gratitude, and appreciation would be totally absent. After a massacre of Christians in Peking, the pope remarked with his usual callousness, "We shall canonize a few of these new martyrs."

In the pope's canonization proceedings there is also mention of his habit of mordant, wounding ridicule. Pius IX liked to be merry at others' expense. When, for example, he had to put the cardinal's hat on Bishop Frédéric de Falloux, he took care that the man's wig should fall off in the presence of all the spectators. Reports of Pius IX's heartless indifference do not necessarily contradict the previous picture of the pope's explosive temperament. Whatever did not touch him personally left him cold.

That was certainly not true for papal infallibility. Anyone who dared oppose this pet idea of his was made to feel his wrath. On June 22, 1870, the French ambassador to the Holy See, Gaston de Banneville, wrote to Paris that the pope greeted everything contrary to his *idée fixe* with childish outbursts of rage. Even his sense of humor deserted him: He ordered the confiscation of matches which were advertised as infallible (*fiammiferi infallibili*).

Mr. Talbot ecc.

Ricevetti a suo tempo la prima e lessi con piacere
la descrizione relativa al suo viaggio.
Notai l'ultima sua volontà di
consecrarsi al bene spirituale
dei suoi connazionali, fermandosi
in Oriente e principalmente nei
luoghi santi, per assistere quegl'Inglesi
che si conducano là a visitarli,
e amministrar loro specialmente
il sacramento della penitenza.
Benedica Dio questa sua buona
intenzione, e in quanto a me
l'approvo pienamente
Lo benedico di cuore
Dal Vaticano li 7. Luglio 1876.
Pio PP. IX.

In a letter dated July 7, 1876, Pius IX thanks his friend George
Talbot de Malahide for his account of a trip to Jerusalem. For decades Talbot had belonged, as court prelate, to the pope's inner circle,
but for the past few years he had been spending most of his time in a
psychiatric clinic in Paris

Pius IX in May 1876

This hyperemotionalism sometimes led to serious incidents —recall the scenes with the prefect of the Vatican archives, with Cardinals Gustav Hohenlohe and Filippo Maria Guidi, and Patriarchs Joseph Audu and Gregor Yussef. In all these episodes

Pius IX showed quite clearly how out of touch he was with reality. Papal diplomacy and the curial style in general, which grew out of centuries-long experience, had always aimed at avoiding needlessly painful confrontations.

The pope's tantrums were by no means affected: They upset him at least as much as they did his victims. In fact, during the decisive period, from the middle of June to the beginning of July 1870, Pius IX went through a crisis in his health.

Deceptive Maneuvers

In his Council diary Dupanloup repeatedly tried to make sense of Pius IX's character. He wondered whether much of the pope's behavior ought to be interpreted as professional hypocrisy or extreme stupidity. In the end he inclined to the view that both of these were present, coupled with violent willpower and a predilection for magnificence and display.

Dupanloup was not the only one to advance this opinion. Other bishops, too, had the impression that the pope was insincere, that he was striving to get infallibility defined by the use of trickery and cunning. In the presence of many witnesses Bishop Maret called Pius IX false and a liar.

Here are a few concrete instances of how the pope tried to conceal his real objective. In February 1869, as we have already seen, *La Civiltà Cattolica* began a campaign for the doctrine of infallibility. It was supposed to be made a dogma at the coming Council through acclamation by the bishops, that is, without discussion. Pius IX feigned ignorance of this before foreign ambassadors, although he himself had expressly approved the article in *La Civiltà Cattolica*. And when Bishops Clifford, Ramadié, and Place protested against the highly offensive language the pope had used in speaking of them at public audiences, he denied the whole thing. "I need no other argument," observed curial Cardinal Gustav von Hohenlohe to Professor Johann Friedrich in explaining his rejection of the proposed dogma, "than this single one, that in my entire life I never met a man who was less particular about the truth than Pius IX."

This two-faced demeanor was also evidenced by the fact that till the very end the pope spoke of his wish to leave the

Pius IX in 1871

Council completely free. Many people could no longer believe
that. "The facts proving the opposite are too numerous and too
obvious," wrote the usually restrained Count Ferdinand Trauttmansdorff to Vienna on June 22, 1870. This was the reason
Bishop Dupanloup spoke of professional hypocrisy and of a
long-lasting, far-reaching conspiracy. Even in the final days before definition the pope pretended to be utterly disinterested. On

July 12, 1870, he told Archbishop Georges Darboy that he had not read the new draft of the constitution *Pastor Aeternus.* In point of fact, he had already protested on July 8 to the commission on faith against its decision to strike out a passage in the revised constitution. The pope wanted to keep it exactly the way it was. Likewise, on July 15 he claimed ignorance before a delegation of the international committee of the minority.

With such facts in mind, it no longer seems quite so improbable when we read the allegation in diplomatic reports that the pope himself wrote articles attacking the minority bishops for various newspapers. The articles published in *L'Unità Cattolica,* for example, are supposed to have been personally dictated by the pope.

Pius IX's acts of duplicity concern us here less for their moral than for their psychological implications. They were an open secret and led to results the reverse of what the pope intended. Basically, they were as ill-adapted to the actual situation as his outbursts of temper.

*Faulty Theological
Training*

In his Council diary Bishop Félix Dupanloup explains that another reason for the pope's behaving the way he did was his simplemindedness. The pope, he thought, moved in the political as well as in the religious sphere without education or insight. He was at the mercy of his lackeys. He got his information from three newspapers and anonymous letters. Pius IX had, it is true, enough *esprit courant* and personal charm to create the impression that he had some notion of things. At bottom, however, he understood nothing. He could give a rational account of nothing, not even his own words. "We must pray . . . and trust ourselves to God alone," Dupanloup adds in concluding his analysis of circumstances which he viewed as terribly dangerous for the Church. Other bishops delivered similar judgments. The prefect of the archives, Augustin Theiner, spoke of Pius IX as "a pope who has scarcely any concept—or only very superficial knowledge—of history, secular or sacred, of theology and canon law. He only distinguishes himself—indeed, often makes himself ridiculous—by his blind, old wives' faith." On the issue of papal infallibility Pius IX had only the most flat-footed, categorical notions: He would not hear of limitations or conditions.

Effects of Advanced Age and Eccentricities

When Pius IX presided over the opening of the Vatican Council, he was already seventy-eight years old. His advanced age had taken its toll. The pope's intellectual capacities were deteriorating. "He no longer has any memory from one day to the next," remarked Bishop William Clifford. Many bishops spoke of him as an old man in his second childhood. Pius IX could no longer concentrate on a subject for any length of time and seemed to jump from one thing to the next. His speeches, even at official occasions, often caused embarrassment—the pope no longer paid attention to what he was saying. All too often Secretary of State Cardinal Antonelli had to undo the damage the pope had done at audiences by his thoughtless statements. There were occasional reports of the pope's speaking incoherently. This is difficult to prove from the speeches themselves, since they were usually not published in the form they were given.

The pope's physical and psychic condition was also important as far as infallibility was concerned. Many people, including not a few bishops, saw in Pius IX's determination to define the dogma not so much mature reflection as senile stubbornness: The pope was trapped by his own fixation.

Beyond this, there are instances of near megalomania which are still hard to evaluate. In 1866, some years before the beginning of the Council, Pius IX applied Christ's saying, "I am the way, the truth, and the life," to himself. On February 8, 1871, Count Harry von Arnim-Suckow reported to the imperial chancellor, Prince Otto von Bismarck, of Pius IX's attempt to work a miracle: "The story is making the rounds that sometime last year, as he was passing by the church of Trinità dei Monti, the pope bade a cripple who was lying out in front, 'Rise up and walk!' But the experiment failed." The historian Ferdinand

Pius IX as an old man, 1877

Gregorovius had previously noted in his diary on June 17, 1870: "The pope recently got the urge to try out his infallibility, like the French with their new *chassepots*. While out on a walk he called to a paralytic: 'Get up and walk.' The poor devil gave it a try and collapsed, which put God's vicegerent very much out of sorts. The anecdote has already been mentioned in the newspapers. I really believe that he's insane." Even if these accounts sound quite incredible, they nonetheless show what many people thought about the pope. Pius IX gave the impression that he was suffering from delusions of grandeur in other ways as well. Some, even bishops, thought he was mad or talked about pathological symptoms. The Catholic church historian Franz Xaver Kraus noted in his diary: "Apropos of Pius IX, Du Camp agrees with my view that ever since 1848 the pope has been both mentally ill and malicious."

Only Partially
Compos Mentis?

If the many negative reports about Pius IX had originated with notorious enemies of the Church, they could easily be ascribed to antireligious hatred. But this is not the case. In the first place, much of this material consists of undisputed facts.

Ferdinand Gregorovius, German historian resident in Rome

Beyond that, it was above all the more distinguished members of the episcopate, men who were deeply concerned for the welfare of the Church, who not only judged Pius IX harshly but viewed him as the greatest danger facing the Church. They themselves seemed to be caught in a trap. They felt powerless struggling with a pope who was possessed by his monomania and not accessible to rational arguments. They were literally at their wits end with this eighty-year-old man. "Oh, this unfortunate pope," wrote Félix Dupanloup in his diary. "How much evil he has done! . . . I mean, he has delivered the Church into the hands of these three or four Jesuit professors who now want to inflict their lessons on him! . . ." Dupanloup had noted earlier: "Back from [Bishop] Mérode's . . . The description he gives of this Holy Father makes one tremble . . . 'This is one of the greatest dangers the Church has ever known,' he said." According to a note jotted down by Dupanloup on April 15, 1870, several bishops said, "I'd rather die than see all that." Not a few bishops turned bitter from vexation and despair, or fell sick. Others left the Council in disgust before it ended. For many the Council looked like a degrading game, a tragic farce.

There can be no doubt that in their eyes the responsibility for all this lay primarily with Pius IX. They accused the pope of misusing his office. But if we assume that the pope were forced to answer for this crime before a modern West European court, wouldn't the prosecution have to concede many mitigating circumstances? Was the pope altogether *compos mentis* during the Council? Many of his personality traits suggest that this was no longer the case. The unhealthy mysticism, the childish tantrums, the shallow sensibility, the intermittent mental absences, the strangely inappropriate language even in strictly official speeches, and the senile obstinacy all indicate the loss of a solid grip on reality. These features suggest paranoia. They are, in any case, bound up with a strong ego-fixation. Pius IX seems also to have suffered from a narcissistic disorder, perhaps due chiefly to the attempt to compensate for his epilepsy and the failures at the outset of his pontificate.

Professor Paul Matussek, director of research in psychopathology and psychotherapy for the Max Planck Institute, to whom I submitted my research on Pius IX, responded as follows in a letter dated September 10, 1975: "The material presented permits one to conclude that we have here an abnormal personality, although without a more detailed case history it is impossible to say whether the abnormal traits are linked with the convulsions (epilepsy?) or other more purely psychic causes." And Professor Ludwig J. Pongratz, head of the Institute for Psychology at the University of Würzburg, wrote to me on October 16, 1975: "The points you make are all neatly documented, and your interpretation is very well prepared and cautious besides. The disease you describe has so many complex symptoms that it is hard to classify it in the usual scheme. In part, it is probably a case of epilepsy-related factors, both during and following the disease. Other symptoms might be put under the heading of the schizophrenic syndrome."

4

Vatican I:
A Free Council?

Even the vow of secrecy and repressive Vatican policies towards the press could not prevent the news from spreading of how much coercion and manipulation were being used to push through the definition of infallibility. In the eyes of the Infallibilists, this was not without its hazards. If, in the future, the freedom of the Council should come under serious question, then the dogma they had been fighting so hard for would be null and void. For an unfree Council could not claim to be ecumenical and hence could not insist that its decrees were binding. The Infallibilists tried to head off this danger by means of a revealing last-minute endeavor: They wanted the Council to attest to its own freedom. But here, too, the desired unanimity was unattainable.

The Council Shall
Declare Itself Free

At the last general session of the Council on July 16, 1870, all the bishops were handed a declaration signed by the five Council presidents. It was aimed at various pamphlets which "impugned the dignity and full freedom of the Council with the filthiest lies, violated the rights of the Apostolic See, and even heaped abuse on the person of the most holy lord [the pope]."

This protest, which had been prompted by Archbishops Edward Manning and Victor Dechamps, was, strictly speaking, directed against certain brochures written about the Council, but its real purpose was to pin the minority bishops down to a confession that the Council was indeed free. All the council fathers received two copies of the protest. Cardinal Filippo De Angelis, the first president, read out the text and then called upon all present to show their agreement by standing up and then handing in a signed copy for the archives, *ad perpetuam rei memoriam* (for an eternal remembrance). How did the bishops of the minority react? The official minutes of the Council state that all the bishops rose and gave their assent. But that is not, in fact, what happened, even if some of the bishops were surprised by this tactic and did stand up. "Quite a few men in the minority were caught napping," Bishop Joseph Hefele wrote on August 10, 1870, to Ignaz von Döllinger, "and gave way before the roaring fanaticism. It really took a little strength to fight off the importunate people from the majority, to remain seated, and not to sign." All the protests with the signatures of the bishops were bound together into two large quarto volumes which are kept today in the Vatican secret archives. Looking into them, one does not find a single minority bishop giving unconditional assent. There are actually very few signed copies from the minority on record. Many turned none in; others stayed away from the final session.

None of this, however, prevented the official papal newspaper, *Giornale di Roma,* from writing the next day: "In response to this invitation the Fathers unanimously endorsed the protest."

The whole operation, therefore, was a failure—the Infallibilists lost the insurance they had wanted so badly. Today, after decades when discussion of the freedom of the Council was simply not possible, what is more obvious than the need to take a fresh look at this painful issue? Nothing could highlight the weakness of the Infallibilist position more strikingly than the discord arising from their last maneuver.

Many bishops of the majority were probably not quite

aware of these manipulations as such. They were so completely convinced of the truth and justice of their own viewpoint—especially since they knew the pope was on their side—that they didn't even recognize the other side's right to exist.

In their opinion, moral unanimity in dogmatic decisions was of no importance. "Bishops allied with the pope are always in the right," wrote Archbishop Régnier of Cambrai. Bishop Ignatius von Senestrey did want to uphold the demand for moral unanimity, but in essence he fully agreed with Régnier: "Unanimity is achieved through the pope's adoption of a single position, whereupon his opponents either submit or leave the Church. Whether these opponents are many or few makes no difference at all."

At this point, interestingly, many Infallibilists shifted the focus in their concept of freedom from form to content: The free man was now the man who did what was right. The Ultramontane newspaper *L'Univers* extolled the sort of freedom the pope wished the Council to have as the loftiest embodiment of this ideal, since it meant only freedom for goodness and excluded freedom to do evil. Pius IX agreed. At an audience for the bishops he remarked: "You are free at the Council, but you must uphold sound principles so that the world, which has gone astray, may rediscover the true path."

"We Are Not Free at the Council"

As soon as the Council opened, complaints began to be heard from many bishops about the lack of freedom—owing to the way the agenda had been drawn up. As session followed session, these complaints grew continually louder. Bishop François Lecourtier spoke for many others when he wrote: "Our weakness at this moment comes neither from Scripture nor the tradition of the Fathers nor the witness of the General Councils nor the evidence of history. It comes from our lack of freedom, which is radical. An imposing minority, representing the faith of more than one hundred million Catholics, that is, almost half of the entire Church, is crushed beneath the yoke of a restrictive agenda, which contradicts conciliar traditions. It is crushed by commissions which have not been truly elected and which dare to insert undebated paragraphs in the texts after debate has closed. It is crushed by the commission for postulates, which has been imposed upon it from above. It is crushed by the absolute absence of discussion, response, objections, and the opportunity to demand explanations; by newspapers which have been encouraged to hunt the bishops down and to incite the clergy against them; by the nuncios who bring on reinforcements when the newspapers no longer suffice to throw everything into confusion, and who try to promote the priests ahead of the bishops as witnesses to the faith while reducing the true, divinely chosen witnesses to the level of delegates of the lower clergy, indeed, to rebuke them if they do not act accordingly. The minority is crushed, above all, by the full weight of the supreme authority which oppresses it with the praise and encouragements it lavishes on the priests in the form of papal briefs. It is crushed by the displays of favor to Dom Guéranger and of hostility to M. de Montalembert and others."

The French bishops in the minority began a petition to the Foreign Minister of their country on March 20, 1870, with the lapidary sentence, "We are not free at the Council." And to Prime Minister Émile Ollivier they complained, "The new dogma, which must lead to such grave consequences, is demanded of a Council which is both deeply divided and not free. Is there anyone in Europe who doesn't know the dismal facilities of the great hall of the Council, the restrictive rules governing debate, the refusal to do justice to the protest lodged on four separate occasions by duly authorized bishops, the adroit construction of the majority, the pressure applied by the Roman court and the Ultramontanes?" Bishop Charles Philippe Place of Marseille compared the Council to a cripple who may have the freedom to speak but not to move. Bishops Félix Dupanloup and Henri Maret were just as explicit. Archbishop Georges Darboy of Paris also addressed himself to the infringements on freedom in several letters to Napoleon III. The sort of discussion still possible at the Council had nothing to do with trying to find the truth. "There is a freedom of words," Dupanloup observed, "but no freedom of discussion." Archbishop Peter Richard Kenrick

Georges Darboy,
archbishop of Paris

considered the Council invalid and hence refused to speak at
any of the general sessions after June 4, 1870. Bishop Georg
Joseph Strossmayer of Diakovar shared this opinion. He confided
to Lord Acton: "There is no denying that the Council lacked
freedom from beginning to end." Speaking to Professor Joseph
Hubert Reinkens, who later became an Old Catholic bishop,
Strossmayer expressed his unshakable conviction, which he had
defended in Rome and would defend before the judgment seat
of God, "that the Vatican Council had not had the freedom necessary to make it a true Council and to justify its passing resolutions binding the conscience of the entire Catholic world. The
proof of this was perfectly self-evident."

Bishop Joseph Hefele also denied the freedom and validity
of the Council. In a letter to Ignaz von Döllinger dated August
10, 1870, he demanded that "(1) as many German, Austrian, and
Hungarian bishops as possible reject the submission to papal au-

thority; and (2) at the same time scholars reject the supposed binding force of conciliar decisions because of the lack of both freedom and unanimity." Archbishop Friedrich Schwarzenberg and Bishop Heinrich Förster seconded the motion. For Cardinal Gustav Hohenlohe the "conciliar status of this sad assembly" had been forfeited ever since the promulgation of the agenda. Such voices were heard everywhere, even among the English-speaking bishops. It would be tedious to enumerate them all here.

The bishops of the minority were not simply fighting for their own freedom: In their eyes the majority had as little freedom as they did. As a matter of fact, a good proportion of the episcopate was financially dependent on the Vatican and did not feel free to oppose the pope's wishes. One Eastern bishop declared that his bread was in one camp, his convictions in another.

The risk of having to act against one's own convictions was all the greater since there was no secret ballot. "The lack of privacy in voting is under the circumstances very dangerous since . . . those who . . . are dependent on the Roman Curia must willy-nilly vote in accordance with the pope's wishes," Strossmayer believed. Had there been a secret ballot, the results would undoubtedly have been different. In that case, according to the calculations of Bishop Luigi Riccio of Cajazzo, 150 Italian bishops would have voted "no." He was not the only one to make such estimates.

Bishop Henri Maret probed still more deeply into the problem of freedom at the Council. In his opinion the majority could not be free unless the minority was too. He argued that if the rights of such a large minority were curtailed, then the majority could not claim to have maturely weighed the question at hand and to have clarified it by every means available. Such a claim would become even less credible should the majority commit itself in advance of each discussion. The freedom of the minority seemed to Maret a condition for the freedom of the majority— and one can hardly challenge the justice of his conclusion.

The pope had said he wanted to give the Council so much freedom it would be surfeited with it. This could only sound like mockery: The bishops of the minority were driven to despair precisely because of the restrictions placed on their freedom by Pius IX.

"The Pope Is Devouring Us"

For many bishops the new dogmas of the primacy and infallibility of the pope meant a violation of the divine order of the Church and a destruction of episcopal power. They had the impression they were being forced to resign. "The pope is devouring us," said Archbishop Jacques Marie Achille Ginoulhiac of Lyon. This alteration of the Church's basic structure was being imposed on them with biblical, historical, and theological arguments which, in their eyes, were worthless. The Church, as a result, was losing its credibility. The new dogmas were the worst misfortune to strike the Church in a long time, for they were proving the unbelievers right. Bishop Wilhelm Emmanuel Freiherr von Ketteler spoke of a crime against the Church and humanity.

Beyond any doubt, the pope was forcing many bishops to go down a road they didn't want to take. "We have to eat what we have vomited up," commented Bishop Michael Domenec of Pittsburgh. The only possible way out would have been to break with Pius IX, but they lacked the courage for that. Thus the Council became for many of them the great trauma of their lives. A year after it ended, Bishop Félix Dupanloup was still talking about it as the greatest trial and most ghastly disappointment he had ever gone through.

For many the Council was no longer a Council at all. Dupanloup called it a comedy, Archbishop John Baptist Purcell of Cincinnati a comedy ending in a tragedy. Archbishop Georges Darboy felt the whole thing was frivolous and spoke of a Council of sacristans and a robber synod. Bishop Wilhelm Emmanuel Freiherr von Ketteler described it as a vile assembly and Bishop François Lecourtier of Montpellier coined the expression, "the Vatican farce." In the opinion of Joseph Georg Strassmayer, the Council had degenerated into "a sort of degrading game."

Michael Domenec, bishop of Pittsburgh

As time passed, irritation against the pope and the Infalli-bilists swelled. "I'm not going to the Council anymore," Dupan-loup noted in his diary on June 28, 1870. "The violence, the shamelessness, and even more the falsity, vanity, and continual lying force me to keep my distance."

Eventually the bishops of the opposition realized that they could not count on reaching a compromise. In their extremity they looked to what can only be construed as desperate meas-ures. Many bishops, especially from Germany and Austria-Hun-gary, threatened to resign if papal infallibility were defined. They were hardly thinking of schism, but Infallibilist groups did not exclude the possibility of schismatic movements led by bishops.

The minority repeatedly raised its voice in protest against

Reception at the French embassy in Rome. To the right of center, wearing civilian dress, French Ambassador Gaston Robert Marquis de Banneville

the agenda, the constraints on freedom, and majority rule on questions of dogma, but it was not heard and died away. Because of this, the minority entertained the idea—even in the early stages of the Council—of walking out en bloc. The plan never materialized because the minority was never resolute enough. Had it taken such an unequivocal stance against the pope, its unity would probably have shattered.

Thus the opposition came to an impasse. They knew they could hope for nothing, or almost nothing, from the pope and the Infallibilists. So they resorted to their governments and begged them to intervene in Rome to ward off the disaster. The French bishops were in the most convenient position to get results this way, since the Papal States survived only because of French military protection. In fact, the French bishops managed to persuade the government secretly to threaten the Vatican that it would withdraw its troops if papal infallibility were declared a dogma. But this move was as fruitless as the two protests sent to the pope by the French Foreign Minister, Napoléon Daru. In

April 1870 Daru was toppled with the help of the Curia and the Ultramontanes. Prime Minister Émile Ollivier temporarily took charge of the Foreign Ministry as well. Although this substantially lessened the chances of French intervention, the bishops made a further attempt at using the government to bring about a postponement of the Council, in the unvoiced hope that the pope might die before long. One mode of applying pressure they thought of was recalling the French ambassador to Rome. A bishop even suggested that in view of the way its protests had been scorned, the government ought to carry out a complete separation of Church and State in France.

The German, Austrian, and Hungarian bishops came to the support of their French colleagues. The Prussian ambassador to the Holy See, Count Harry von Arnim-Suckow, played a key role in efforts to bring about a joint intervention by the European powers. His hard line had the solid backing of the German bishops. In dealing with Arnim, Bishop Heinrich Förster showed sympathy for the idea of disestablishment if the pope were declared infallible. The Prussian Prime Minister and later Imperial Chancellor, Prince Otto von Bismarck, received a request from the majority of German, Austrian, Hungarian, and some French prelates to support and help to prepare a joint intervention. Bismarck felt quite flattered by this and expressed his amazement to the French ambassador in Berlin, Vincent Benedetti, that the bishops of Austria and Hungary had appealed to him only four years after their nation's army went down to defeat at Königgrätz.

That such requests were made of statesmen who could not be credited with much sympathy for the Catholic Church simply shows how desperate the bishops had become. Victor Conzemius, the church historian from Lucerne, is surely correct in writing that "most of the bishops felt guilty about suing for the support of diplomats and their governments. But they do not bear the final responsibility for this ill-assorted partnership. The onus for that falls on the leaders of the Council, who drove them first into isolation and then into that strange fellowship."

In their political overtures the bishops of the minority had made a fundamental miscalculation: The pope was only confirmed in the course he had embarked on. And the last-ditch efforts to change the pope's mind likewise came to naught. On

Heinrich Förster,
bishop of Breslau

July 15, 1870, Bishop Wilhelm Emmanuel Freiherr von Ketteler thrice fell to his knees before the pope and—as Bishop François Victor Rivet of Dijon reports—like a suppliant angel, with hands folded, joined the other delegates of the minority's international committee in begging the pope for an acceptable formula. But it was no use. On the eve of the solemn definition Bishop Félix Dupanloup implored the pope not to go through with the dogmatization. Again it was no use. Pius IX is supposed to have responded, "He's crazy, or he thinks I'm crazy."

The more hopeless the situation became, the higher the bishops' desperation rose. Sometimes it was expressed in violent agitation, sometimes in deep depression. Bishop Dupanloup speaks of his profound grief on almost every page of his Council diary. There were bishops who wept, others who wanted to die. In a fit of anger Bishop François Lecourtier threw his conciliar documents into the Tiber and left Rome prematurely. The papers were fished out of the water and brought to the Roman vicariat. Three years later Lecourtier had to pay the price for his gesture: He was dismissed as bishop of Montpellier.

The Primate of Hungary, Archbishop Johannes Simor, was

François Lecourtier, bishop of Montpellier

so upset by the pope's interference that for a long time he could neither eat nor sleep. After May 22, 1870, he stopped attending the meetings of the commision on faith. Some bishops, like Félix de Las Cases, Félix Dupanloup, and Joseph Georg Strossmayer, fell sick. Many others, such as Cardinal Friedrich Schwarzenberg and Bishop Giovanni Pietro Losana, found that the Council permanently embittered their lives.

A large part of the minority left Rome in an extremely agitated state before the solemn definition. Their resentment was directed, above all, at the pope, who not only treated them like schoolchildren but also forced them into a painful moral conflict. In compelling them to renounce their own rights, he outraged their humanity. The only way for the bishops to escape this powerlessness would have been to cause a schism.

The Council Wasn't Free!

The Infallibilists affirmed the Council's freedom; the minority denied it. Who was right?

The question is not so easy to answer, for when can any assembly be characterized as free? Certainly not just when no physical or material pressure is exerted. Moral pressure, too, can sharply limit freedom, indeed, it can altogether eliminate it. When a deliberative body has to clarify a theoretical issue, other criteria must also come into play: Were the necessary steps taken to shed sufficient light on the problem? Was there the opportunity for free, unlimited, unbiased discussion? serious examination of the arguments and counterarguments? consultation with experts? Any assembly is really free to resolve a question only when it is willing to look into the problems being debated. If the question has already been decided in advance, before discussion has begun, free choice is no longer possible, even in the absence of outside pressure.

But there is a further difficulty in judging the freedom of Vatican I. For the Roman Catholic Church the dogmas defined by this Council are strictly obligatory. Anyone who doesn't accept them is threatened with excommunication, that is, with exclusion from the Catholic community. The binding character of the dogma implies that the Council was a valid one (and therefore ecumenical and free). And so it was pointless for the opposition bishops to challenge the Council's freedom in the first place. Once the dogma had been proclaimed, the question was closed. In making their submission they were renouncing completely any possibility of calling the freedom of the Council into question. Modern Catholic historians, especially those who are dependent on the Church, are not much better off than the bishops.

Naturally, these historians no longer turn out such hasty apologies as did the Jesuit Theodor Granderath, who insisted that the freedom of the council fathers had been preserved as a sacred trust. That would be simply too unbelievable. Nowadays writers generally concede the existence of certain restraints on freedom at Vatican I. But, Catholic historians maintain, the lack of freedom was never so great as to endanger the ecumenicity— and hence the validity—of the Council. Evidently they overlook the intrinsic suspiciousness of the dictum, "The Council had enough freedom to ensure the legality of its decrees." This suspicion only grows when we read in the work of the Sulpician Henri Icard (the author of this formula) that one should never mention the lack of freedom at Vatican I for tendentious purposes—although Icard doesn't doubt it for a moment. He keeps returning to the idea of how dangerous it would be to deny that the Council was free. "To affirm that the Council lacked the freedom necessary to validate its ordinances is impossible . . . Under no circumstances would God abandon his Church in such a way that we should one day be justified in going back and questioning what the great majority of the bishops, together with the pope, decided on matters of faith! . . . Can we run the risk of such a scandal? And what would then become of the Holy Church?" This passage, with its obvious apologetic intent, is cited by the respected church historian Roger Aubert, who bases his case for infallibility on Icard. Immediately after the above section, Icard asks what would become of the Church's authority if Catholics were permitted to discuss the legality of the conciliar decrees. Aubert does not quote this passage . . .

Such intellectual contortions only strengthen one's conviction that there is no way to uphold the freedom of the First Vatican Council without silencing, softening, or embellishing the facts. A typical example of this procedure may be found in the writings of Remigius Bäumer, a church historian from Freiburg. He admits that the freedom of the Council was curtailed by the agenda, the moral pressure applied by the pope, and the intermittent restrictions on free speech, but he still fails completely to take a serious look at the facts. Like Aubert, he quotes Icard's remark about the validity of the decrees without realizing its context. He dismisses Bishop Lecourtier's complaint about papal coercion as a mere trifle. He is obviously unaware of Lecourtier's many other statements and activities. In order to reach the verdict he has in mind, Bäumer prefers to lean on the scholarly authority of his colleague, August Franzen, who finds that the debates were thoroughly open and the Council itself was free, as proved by the fact that many bishops voted *non placet*. After a very brief and superficial coverage of the manipulation by the pope and the Curia, Bäumer turns to the issue of intervention by foreign governments. On the basis of a handful of examples he concludes that "the freedom of the Council was impaired to a much greater extent by the political powers of Europe than by the Curia." But, in fact, it was the minority bishops themselves, for the most part, who in their desperation went out and sought help from the governments and encouraged intervention. We find nothing of this in Bäumer.

On the whole, pressure from foreign governments had barely any impact at all compared to pressure from the Infallibilists, the Curia, and the pope. Judging from the testimony of both bishops and diplomats, there can be no doubt about this. With only a few exceptions, reports from ambassadors in Rome return again and again to the heavy moral coercion and the lack of freedom. Even in the Curia and groups close to it people were very conscious, right from the start, of the danger that the validity of the Council's resolutions might one day be questioned on account of this.

Practically all independent church historians of the post-conciliar period dispute the freedom of Vatican I. In his four-volume *History of the Vatican Council,* Professor Johann Friedrich makes it especially clear just how much the Council was manipulated. True, the opponents of infallibility were allowed to speak, up to a point, but every method, fair or foul, was used to make sure that such critical voices had no effect. Professor Joseph Hubert Reinkens and Johann Friedrich Ritter von Schulte in Prague, both of whom, like Friedrich in Munich, later became Old Catholics, argued the same point in their writings. And their books were put on the Index along with Friedrich's. But Old Catholics were not the only ones to take this stand. "There could likewise be no sense in talking about *actual freedom* at the Council, where absolutely everything was subject in advance to the almighty influence of the papal will"—was the judgment of the Protestant theologian Theodor Frommann, writing a few years after the Council. And several decades later the Orthodox theologian Sergei Bulgakov suggested, "The Vatican Council has as much right to call itself a Council as today's meetings of delegates from the Soviet republics can claim to be a free expression of the will of the people."

Such conclusions find their place in a still older tradition. As

Johann Friedrich Ritter von Schulte, professor of canon law in Prague and Bonn; one of the leaders of the Old Catholics

early as August 26, 1870, fourteen German theologians assembled in Nuremberg declared apropos of the First Vatican Council: "Freedom from every sort of moral coercion and from influence through superior force is a sine qua non for all ecumenical councils. Such freedom was missing from this gathering because, among other reasons: (a) in contradiction to the practice of previous councils and despite the protests of a great number of bishops, the pope imposed an agenda on the members which cramped their freedom. This agenda was later modified without their consent and upheld over their continual objections; and (b) the pope used the manifold tools at his disposal to exert moral pressure on the members over an issue which was still very much undecided and which personally concerned the pope."

Was Vatican I a free council? This study deals with the definition of infallibility—the high point of this great church assembly. And so the question can be reworded: Were the bishops free from material and moral coercion in presenting their opinions on papal infallibility?

After the foregoing presentation, there can be no doubt: Any talk of such freedom is meaningless. Material pressure (e.g., the threatened withdrawal of financial support) and, even more, moral duress were applied in every conceivable way. Only bishops who were sure of their position (and financially secure as well) could avoid this coercion, and then only to a degree.

The others could neither speak nor vote freely. The limited opportunity to speak which the pope granted the bishops should not obscure this fact. That was all part of Pius IX's strategy: The pope only pronounced his judgment when he felt his goal was endangered.

Thus, from the very beginning the external preconditions for a discussion were simply not there. Also missing—and this seems to me still more important—was the inner freedom to discuss and examine the doctrine of papal infallibility. The measures taken by pope, Infallibilists, and Curia show they had no interest in it. Such an attitude led to a discussion which neither had nor could have any real substance. And so the further we press the analysis of the debate on infallibility, the more clearly we shall see how little freedom there was.

5

The Arguments
For and Against
Papal Infallibility

The Controversy

Despite the complex nuances and the variegated interplay of views, there were two easily distinguishable positions at the First Vatican Council. One side (the minority) had fundamental misgivings about a definition of papal infallibility. The other (the majority) considered a dogmatic definition possible. Opposition to infallibility on exclusively pragmatic grounds— people who held that the moment wasn't ripe for a definition— was rare in its pure form. During the Council bishops used this argument for tactical reasons, as a sort of escape hatch. They wanted to leave themselves a way out, should the definition eventually take place.

The so-called third party, which tried to mediate between the two opposing standpoints, never succeeded in carving out a clear position all its own, and in the course of the Council it was absorbed into the majority. It had belonged there de facto from the very first.

Of course, even within the majority there were some considerable differences of opinion. The gamut ran from the extremely intransigent, aggressive campaigners of the stripe of an Ignatius von Senestrey or a Henry Edward Manning through relatively

John Martin Spalding, archbishop of Baltimore;
leader of the third party at the Council

moderate bishops like Konrad Martin of Paderborn to council
fathers who joined the majority shortly before the definition out
of resignation rather than conviction, such as, for example, the
archbishop of Salzburg, Maximilian Joseph Tarnóczy. The most
sharply contested point among the Infallibilists—this was seen
particularly in the sessions of the commission on faith—was the
extent of papal infallibility. The intransigent bishops, under the
leadership of Ignatius von Senestrey, wanted to extend infallibility far beyond the realm of revealed truth. The pope was to
be infallible in his encyclicals (they were thinking especially of
the *Syllabus,* the list of modern errors, of 1864), in canonizations, and in passing judgment on theological errors. In the end,
in wise Roman fashion the question was left open: The pope

was entitled to infallibility in all the areas in which the entire Church could claim it. Unfortunately, this formulation was as problematic as any other: There had never been agreement on what those areas were.

For the opponents of the new dogma Vatican I was a battle for conscience' sake. Is the pope infallible all by himself or only in conjunction with the bishops? That, in a word, was the whole point at issue. And that was how Bishop Vinzenz Gasser framed the question in his final summation at the Council. While the minority representatives insisted on the absolute necessity of the advice and consent of the bishops for papal decisions to be infallible, majority representatives saw it as only a relative necessity. In their view the pope was infallible in and of himself in *ex cathedra* decisions on faith and morals, independently of the bishops and the Church. This principle was not at all affected by saying that in his decisions the pope relies on the testimony of Scripture and church tradition. Apart from the fact that *Pastor Aeternus* says nothing about this reliance being mandatory, there is simply no authority capable of examining and confirming or denying the congruence of papal decisions with Scripture and tradition.

Thus far we can observe a major difference between the two positions. On one side we have a perfectly clear-cut, unambiguous criterion, namely, the decision of a man who in his own right, and without the concurrence of the Church, is infallible. The minority, on the other hand, rejects such an unequivocal standard. A papal decision, for the minority, would only be infallible with the consent of an ecumenical council and hence, in the final analysis, of the Church. It is just this condition which reveals how much more open the latter view was to the truth, how much more leeway it allowed for freedom.

Obviously, all the power gained by an independently infallible pope meant power lost to the bishops. The final decision on infallibility had crucial practical consequences. In addition, one must always keep in mind the link between infallibility and the second dogma proclaimed at Vatican I, namely, the primacy of papal jurisdiction, which effectively reduced the bishops to satraps. "It follows from this doctrine," wrote Secretary of State Cardinal Ludovico Jacobini to the nuncio in Madrid on April 13,

1885, "that the pope can intervene authoritatively at any time in any situation in any diocese, and in every instance where the pope intervenes the bishops are obliged to obey and submit to his decisions."[21]

But there was more at stake than this. The Council minority was not struggling primarily for their own rights as bishops. For them the credibility of the Church was on the line. They could see no solid foundation for the new dogma, neither in the Bible nor the tradition of the Church. Nothing ought to be defined, in their opinion, without absolute certainty that it was a revealed truth. Most of the arguments by the minority dispute this certainty. On the other side, the majority used hundreds of arguments in trying to prove that papal infallibility was part of Revelation.

The Evangelists
as Evidence of
Infallibility

The Infallibilists were convinced that the doctrine of infallibility could be found in Holy Scripture, which would qualify it as revealed. Many of them believed it was even more explicitly present than such other articles of faith as, say, Mary's perpetual virginity or her Immaculate Conception. Cardinal Henri Marie Gaston de Bonnechose found traces of papal infallibility back in the Old Testament, and Bishop Nicholas Joseph Dabert of Périgueux believed that Christ conferred a sort of infallibility upon the teachers of Israel.

Otherwise, however, the Infallibilists restricted themselves to the New Testament. Their *loci classici* were Matt. 16:18–19, Luke 22:32, and John 21:15–17.

The conciliar minority was not to be persuaded by such arguments. These passages, to their mind, could not be construed as teaching any sort of personal papal infallibility.

"You Are Peter, and on This Rock . . ."

The most important proof text cited by the Infallibilists

comes from the Gospel of Matthew: "You are Peter, and on this rock I will build my church, and the powers of death shall not prevail against it. I will give you the keys of the kingdom of heaven, and whatever you bind on earth shall be bound in heaven, and whatever you loose on earth shall be loosed in heaven" (Matt. 16:18–19). The minority rejected the idea of deducing infallibility from this passage on several grounds: Not just Peter but the other apostles, too, had been called the foundation of the Church. The power to bind and loose had been awarded to them as well. The Fathers of the Church, for the most part, had interpreted the "rock" to mean Christ and faith in him. But even if it were applied to Peter, it was not at all clear how one could infer from it the pope's personal infallibility.

Modern exegetical scholarship holds that the passage about the "rock" only makes sense when applied to Peter. Nevertheless, it fully confirms the minority's final judgment. Most scholars today read the passage not as a statement by Jesus but as a creative interpolation by the Christian community in Palestine or Syria, or by Matthew himself. Besides, Peter's symbolic function as rock was not a Church office, but served Matthew as an illustration of the bond between the tradition conveyed by his gospel and the earthly Jesus. For contemporary Catholic exegetes the notion of deducing the infallibility of Peter and his successors from the passage in Matthew seems so inept that they no longer bother discussing it.

Jesus Prays that
Peter's Faith
May Not Fail

The Infallibilists' second proof text was, from the standpoint of the minority, even more problematic. This one came from Luke, who hands down the words of Jesus to Peter: "I have prayed for you that your faith may not fail; and when you have turned again, strengthen your brethren" (Luke 22:32). The opponents of papal infallibility presented a series of objections to this passage, the most important being: (1) The context shows that Jesus was interceding for Peter in person. There could be no question here of a transferable endowment. (2) In addition, the word "faith" meant confidence and loyalty to Christ. In no sense did it refer to an infallible theological faith. (3) The passage speaks only of Jesus' prayer. One cannot conclude from this that the prayer was answered.

Modern exegesis backs up the minority on all these counts. The kind of interpretation proposed by the Council majority is no longer even discussed: Catholic biblical scholars are simply unwilling to defend it.

"Feed My Lambs, Feed My Sheep"

The third proof text was John 21:15–17. Jesus charges Peter three times to feed his lambs and sheep. The Infallibilists claimed that Peter could not have carried out this mission unless he were infallible. Once again the minority threw up its hands: This passage, like the others, implied nothing about infallibility and had never been interpreted by antiquity in that sense. Modern exegetes once more find for the minority. No one ever brings up the episode of Peter's appointment as shepherd in connection with infallibility anymore.

When the minority raised its objections, the Council majority argued over and over again that the passages from Scripture previously mentioned had to be construed in accordance with the decrees of the Church's magisterium. This was an obvious begging of the question, one which kept reappearing in the Infallibilists' case: They presuppose what has to be proved. A teaching is true because the Church says so. Scripture is expounded strictly in accordance with the Church's magisterium and is therefore stripped of any independent critical capacity. But this retreat to the magisterium's testimony in its own behalf cannot conceal the fact that the Infallibilists' attempt to prove their dogma from the Bible failed right down the line.

Church Tradition: The Second Mainstay of Infallibility

The proof which the Infallibilists tried to establish from tradition was a much broader and more comprehensive affair. The tradition of the entire Church, they argued, bore clear witness to the pope's infallibility. But the minority bishops could find no such doctrinal tradition. There was no evidence of it in the first eight hundred years of church history. The doctrine did not appear until the Middle Ages, and the popes themselves had not taught it distinctly until the sixteenth century.

Bishop Joseph Hefele of Rottenburg, a former professor of church history at Tübingen and author of what is, to date, the most exhaustive history of the Council, addressed the assembled fathers on an emotional note: "Forgive me if I speak simply: I am very familiar with the old documentary sources of the history and teaching of the Church, with the writings of the Fathers, and the acts of the Councils, so that I can say with Horace that I have had them in my hands night and day. But in all those documents I have never seen that doctrine [of papal infallibility]."

Thomas Connolly, Capuchin archbishop of Halifax, Nova Scotia, had come to Rome as a convinced adherent of infallibility. After thorough study he became one of its declared opponents. At bottom, though, he would have liked to go on believing it, and so he repeatedly challenged the Infallibilists in the Council hall to come up with clear texts from the first three centuries—always in vain. He made a private offer of one thousand pounds (perhaps thirty thousand dollars today) to anyone who could provide the text he wanted. All he got was a forgery.

The minority based its resistance on the rule of St. Vincent of Lerin (d. 450), which states that a teaching can only be defined if it has been held to be revealed at all times, everywhere, and by all believers. The majority declined to accept these conditions for a possible dogmatization. If this rule always had to be observed, there would be practically no dogma at all. Universality and unanimity were not necessary: The doctrine's antiquity was the only requirement.

The minority gave yet another reason for excluding a dogmatization: Many facts of church history belied papal infallibility. The Infallibilists replied that the doctrine was clearly contained in both sources of divine revelation, Scripture and tradition. It would, therefore, be quite impossible for it to be

Thomas Connolly, O.F.M.
Cap., archbishop of Halifax

contradicted by anything in church history.

Such apodictic formulas awaken mistrust—which the more detailed analysis that follows will do nothing to allay.

Controversy over the
Fathers of the Church

The Infallibilists asserted that the unanimous testimony of all the Church Fathers favored papal infallibility. The minority countered that there was no clear and unambiguous evidence for this teaching in the Fathers, who knew nothing about it.

To prop up their thesis, the majority gathered a total of some forty Church Fathers. For some of these the minority had contrary interpretations; in other cases it felt that a reply was obviously not worth the trouble. The discussion centered around three names in particular: Irenaeus of Lyon, Ambrose of Milan, and Augustine of Hippo.

St. Irenaeus, bishop of Lyon (d. ca. 202), had written that all churches must concur with the Church of Rome because of its greater preeminence (*potentior principalitas*). The Infallibilists viewed this as evidence for papal infallibility: Rome was the rule of faith for all the other churches. But the minority could not go along. Irenaeus, they noted, also spoke of the other Apostolic churches as the rule of faith. For him the criterion of true faith lay in the consensus of all these churches.

Subsequent research has reinforced the minority's objections, and the passage from Irenaeus is no longer seriously considered as evidence of papal infallibility. In fact, the question has been raised whether Irenaeus can even be claimed as a witness to the primacy of Rome. The current tendency is to deny that he accorded the Church of Rome any fundamental superiority, to say that he thought all the Apostolic churches enjoyed equal rights. In theory each Apostolic church could be the model of the true faith. In fact, however, Rome had certain privileges: the doubly Apostolic origin, its position as a world capital, and its busy traffic with the other Christian communities. These things made Rome the proper measure of orthodoxy, but it did not for that reason possess any unique authority.

The Infallibilists also appealed rather frequently to Bishop Ambrose of Milan (ca. 339–97) and liked to cite his dictum, "Where Peter is, there is the Church." The minority rejected the reading of this passage as an Infallibilist proof, and here, too, it has been fully supported by modern scholarship. Besides, the large amount of autonomy which Ambrose claimed for his episcopal see (in his day he overshadowed the bishop of Rome) makes the majority's version of his position seem utterly irrelevant.

More important than Ambrose for the Infallibilists was the great Latin Father of the Church, St. Augustine of Hippo (354–403). They particularly liked to quote the saying attributed to him, "Rome has spoken, the matter is settled." But the minority proved that Augustine had never made the statement. For him the consensus of the churches had been the rule of faith. In backing up the minority, scholars nowadays point out that Augustine did, in fact, concede an important role to Rome's decisions, but he never accepted it as definitive. He believed the authority of a plenary council was more important than Rome's. The question as to whether Augustine recognized papal infallibility has become irrelevant.

Ecumenical Councils
as Evidence
of Infallibility

The Infallibilists also considered the ecumenical councils one of the underpinnings of their whole argument. But they fashioned a completely unhistorical picture of them. In it the pope appears from the very first as the lord of the councils. Such a view was made possible by the bishops' projecting much later circumstances back into the past. They maintained that the councils never recognized any decrees without the prior endorsement of the pope. It was his approval alone which rendered the decrees irreversible and infallible.

To this the minority objected that the early councils had subjected papal writings to a thoroughgoing scrutiny. The commission on faith at Vatican I responded with a distinction: The councils were indeed in a position to approve papal decrees, but not to deny them their consent. Understandably, the minority had little sympathy for such quibbling. Whoever has the right to approve must also have the right to contradict. Otherwise the right of approbation becomes a pure fiction, indeed an absurdity. The facts clearly showed that the majority's interpretation just didn't add up. For councils had sometimes not only denied their approval to papal documents but had actually condemned them. The anti-Infallibilists recalled the condemnation of the letters of Pope Honorius I (625–38) to Patriarch Sergios I of Constantinople (610–38) by the sixth, seventh, and eighth ecumenical councils.

More or less, all the ecumenical councils figured in the Infallibilist chain of proofs. The list began with the Apostolic Council of Jerusalem. "Not Jacob, bishop of Jerusalem," wrote Archbishop Giuseppe Cardoni, "but Peter was the head of this Council, and everyone submitted to him. Through the presence of Peter this Council received authority from God to impose obedience on all believers and silence on all those who thought otherwise." For the minority, however, the Apostolic Council stood as a counterproof: The events that took place during it would make no sense at all if Peter had been held to be infallible.

The Infallibilist reckoning went on, stretching from the First Ecumenical Council of Nicaea (325) to the Council of Trent (1545–63). The Infallibilists said nothing about the Councils of Constance (1414–18) and Basel (1431–37 or 1438). Only Bishop Vinzenz Stephan Jekelfalusy of Stuhlweissenberg admitted that during them papal infallibility had been denied—for the first time in history. The bishops opposed to a definition, on the other hand, were glad to appeal to the Council of Constance to show how it had rejected papal infallibility. According to Constance, the Council derived its power directly from Christ and was above the pope. Even in the case of Trent, the Infallibilists found themselves clearly on the defensive. The minority stressed that the silence of this Council indicated the absence of any general belief in papal infallibility in the sixteenth century.

The majority felt it had its strongest arguments in the Fourth Council of Constantinople, the Second Council of Lyon, and the Council of Florence.

"The Catholic Religion
Preserved Intact . . ."

Because the Eighth Ecumenical Council (the Fourth Council of Constantinople, from 869 to 870) approved the formula of Pope Hormisdas (514–23), the Infallibilists took this Council as a proof of their position. The Hormisdas formula, which was later appropriated by Pope Hadrian II (867–72), states that in the Apostolic See the Catholic religion had been continuously preserved intact.

For the minority this text was inconclusive chiefly because of the dubious circumstances under which the bishops' consent to it had been obtained. "All Greek bishops," wrote bishop and conciliar historian Joseph Hefele, "who had previously belonged to the party of Photius had to sign this formula before they were admitted to the Council. Afterwards, however, many regretted signing it. They stole the document bearing their signatures. Whether such signatures prove very much about papal infallibility I don't know."

But even the formula itself, as the minority read it, said nothing about papal infallibility. It didn't mention the bishop of Rome, only the Apostolic See. The pope could well err for a time; in fact, he had erred in individual cases (Honorius!) without destroying the faith of Catholics in Rome, in the Apostolic See.

These arguments are convincing. Of course, the minority could have made its case even stronger had it pointed out the doubtful ecumenical character of this Council. For on January 26, 880, the papal legates, in the name of Pope John VIII (872–82) had annulled the Fourth Council of Constantinople and had it stricken from the list of ecumenical councils. John VIII wrote to Patriarch Photius of Constantinople (ca. 820–901) to the same effect. Only at the end of the eleventh century did the Fourth Council of Constantinople gradually find its way back (through an "error" of the canonists) into the list of ecumenical councils: Gregory VII's (1073–85) new concept of papal primacy had reawakened interest in it. In addition, the pope found in canon 22 of this Council (dealing with lay investiture) a most powerful weapon against the Western emperor. Still, it was only at the end of the sixteenth century that the Fourth Council of Constantinople was again called the Eighth Ecumenical Council.

The majority was cutting into its own flesh with its arguments. It appealed to a council which had been annulled by the pope for centuries, and which by its own standard could therefore not rate as ecumenical. The minority, too, revealed its weaknesses. It accepted all too uncritically the Roman list of ecumenical councils which had been put together under the influence of the Jesuit cardinal Robert Bellarmine.

Judge in Disputes
over Faith

As their second important proof from conciliar history, the

Infallibilists adduce the Second Ecumenical Council of Lyon (1274). For the so-called Greek confession of faith from this Council ascribes the primacy on matters of belief to the Roman Church over all the others. Disputes about the faith had to be decided by the judgment of Rome.

The minority was not convinced by this argument and created some difficulties over it. The confession of faith had not been signed by the Greek bishops, but only by the Byzantine Emperor Michael VIII Palaiologos (1224/25–82). To that extent, therefore, it wasn't a conciliar decision at all. In addition, the text of the confession said nothing about an independent, personal infallibility of the pope apart from the bishops and the councils. It spoke not of the pope but of the Church of Rome. Its call for resolving disputes by Rome's decision did not imply the infallibility and irrevocability of such a judgment.

The majority replied to this objection, but it could not refute it. In point of fact, the Council neither discussed the Byzantine emperor's confession of faith nor proclaimed it in a legally binding manner. Michael Palaiologos had accepted all the pope's dogmatic demands out of fear of losing his empire because of attacks by Western princes. The Greek Church did not stand behind him, and the involuntary union of emperor and pope seems more farcical than anything else. The Greek confession of faith from Lyon is merely the pope's testimony in his own behalf. It was neither accepted by the Greeks nor passed by the Council.

"The Supreme Teacher"

The Infallibilists maintained that the Council of Florence had implicitly defined papal infallibility when it declared that the pope was the supreme teacher of all Christians.

The bishops of the minority were not impressed. Florence never implied that the pope held the supreme teaching authority in the absence of participation by bishops and councils. The majority defended itself by arguing that Peter's primacy was also a primacy of faith. Infallibility was bound up with the primacy of the pope on the basis of his divine right.

We can easily see that this argument presupposes what it's trying to prove. Beyond this, modern scholarship views the Florentine compact on the primacy of Rome as so ambiguous that each side could legitimately read its own interpretation into it. In any case, the Greeks were by no means under the impression that they had defined the doctrinal primacy of the pope.

The minority did not contest the ecumenicity of the Council of Florence. In reality, however, the decree of union only came about under the heaviest political pressure. The Byzantine emperor at that time, John VIII Palaiologos (1392–1448), was in desperate need of papal assistance against the Turks, who were now threatening to capture Byzantium itself. This imperial pressure on the Eastern participants was the reason why Florence was later denied ecumenical status in the East. In the West, too, it did not go unchallenged, but Pope Eugene IV (1431–47) used it as a political tool against the reform-minded Council of Basel. In addition, with the exception of the Greeks, practically all the bishops at Florence were Italian. In France the Council of Florence was not considered an ecumenical council for centuries. Before the opening of Vatican I, Döllinger announced his doubts about Florence—they have yet to be resolved. The fact that the minority avoided bringing up all this at the Council shows once more, apart from any possible tactical considerations, how timid it was in the face of Roman traditions.

*Conflicting Images of
the Church in History*

The foregoing exchanges make it clear that the Infallibilists, unlike the minority, believed that papal infallibility had been taught and practiced down through all the centuries of the Church's history. This basic divergence was possible only because the majority and the minority had altogether different notions of that history. The Infallibilists saw it something like this: From the earliest times local churches brought their disputes before the Apostolic See and accepted its decisions as final. The pope was the one who overcame and annihilated the heresies of the first three centuries, for the ecumenical councils did not yet exist. In the following centuries the Roman pontiff maintained his leading role. The ecumenical councils accepted the pope's decisions without question. They had no binding power to begin with, except by the authority of the bishop of Rome.

Papal infallibility, the argument continues, was taught throughout the Church in all ages, was confirmed by the blood of the martyrs, and attested to both in the Latin and Greek liturgy. This state of affairs went unchanged for more than eighteen hundred years. The popes acted in cognizance of their supreme, infallible magisterium and as teachers never committed an error in questions of faith and morals. The doctrine of papal infallibility, therefore, was no longer a mere opinion but had to be believed.

Luigi Natoli, archbishop of Messina, was only reflecting such thinking in a particularly crass form when, on May 14, 1870, in the great hall of the Council he went so far as to claim that there had never been a time when the people of his city had not championed papal infallibility with might and main. He proceeded to speak of a delegation of nobles from Messina who had confessed this belief in the presence of the Virgin Mary—shortly after their conversion by the Apostle Paul. The Irish bishop, William Keane of Cloyne, was no less simpleminded: "When Peter came to Rome, so that he could rule the whole Church more easily from the center of the Roman Empire, he brought with him, either written down or in the form of oral tradition, the entire body of the faith (*depositum fidei*)."

The bishops of the minority drew a sharply different picture: In the first centuries the Christian churches took pains to preserve the unity of the faith by means of synods and councils. No one had any idea of papal infallibility. Religious controversies were settled by councils and not by the pope's authority. Even the bishops of Rome appealed to the consensus of the Church and awaited confirmation of their decrees from the councils. For their part the councils did not hesitate to reject papal decisions. Sometimes the popes themselves revoked their own judgments or those of their predecessors. The possibility of error could not be excluded, not even from their solemn definitions.

There is no mistaking the fact that the majority's image of the Church was determined by the forgeries of Pseudo-Isidore and others. The Infallibilists present church history as if the life of the early Christians were already being regulated by papal decretals. The minority rightfully resisted such a falsification.

The Popes as Evidence for Their Own Case

In every century the Infallibilists found popes who taught that they were infallible or acted as if they were. The list begins with Peter, the Prince of the Apostles, and ends with Pius IX. Every now and then the examples chosen have a certain comical flavor. Thus, for instance, someone adduced as proof of infallibility the fact that the Corinthians, racked by religious controversies in the first century, had not turned to the still surviving apostles (John, to name one, lived in the neighborhood), but to the Roman Pope Clement. Even then he supposedly passed judgment as the supreme arbiter in matters of faith.

The Infallibilist claims were very often roundly denied by the minority. The bishops in the opposition could not find a single pope before the sixteenth century who had clearly and unequivocally pleaded for the doctrine of infallibility. Not only that, in their opinion many facts from church history could not be explained unless one assumed that papal infallibility had been unknown at the time. Thus, for example, the controversy over baptism between Pope Stephen I (254–57) and Bishop Cyprian of Carthage (ca. 200/10–58) made no sense at all without that assumption.

The majority thought of Pope Leo I (440–61) as a particularly crucial witness. His letter to Patriarch Flavian of Constantinople (446–69) was, they said, accepted by the Council of Chalcedon (451) without examination. The minority dissented here, claiming that Chalcedon had closely scrutinized Leo's letter, tested it for orthodoxy, and finally approved it. Pope Leo himself was fully aware of this.

But the minority had a still weightier objection: Some of the popes had themselves become teachers of error. The most famous case was Pope Honorius I (625–38), who will be dealt with separately. Alongside him Pope Liberius (352–66) was also mentioned as a heretic. He made common cause with the Arians, who maintained that Jesus Christ was not essentially equal to God the Father. Pope Virgilius (537–55) had also been accounted less than orthodox. Under pressure from the emperor of Byzantium, Virgilius in his weakness condemned the *Three Chapters* (works by three theologians from the time between the Councils of Ephesus in 431 and Chalcedon in 451). He disavowed de facto the doctrinal resolutions of the Council of Chalcedon, whereupon the bishops of North Africa excommunicated him.

The minority bishops then counted up a whole series of popes who, in the following centuries, committed errors on questions of marital ethics, the sacrament of Holy Orders, and issues regarding natural and international law. The minority regarded as especially compromising the case of Pope Boniface VIII

"Am I infallible? . . . fallible? . . . infallible? . . . fallible? (contemporary caricature)

(1294–1303). If the pope was infallible, then his bull *Unam sanctam* must also be considered infallible. But in it Boniface maintained he had secular authority over all Christians and declared that faithful obedience to the papacy was required for salvation. Boniface VIII and his successors, who confirmed the bull, had arrived at such conclusions on the strength of historically false accounts of the first centuries. Today no one bothers to defend this bull anymore.

The minority did not object when pre-Reformation bishops of Rome were treated as proponents of infallibility. On the other hand, it repeatedly underscored the fact that all the way up until Vatican I the popes had no choice but to tolerate anti-Infallibilist opinions. Rome condemned the Declaration of Gallican Articles but not its teaching. As late as 1820 and 1831, the Apostolic Poenitentiaria explained that Rome had not censored the teachings of Gallicanism. Pope Innocent XI (1676–89) twice praised Bishop Bossuet's (1627–1704) exposition of the Catholic faith, although Bossuet said nothing about papal infallibility.

The minority's arguments show just how far the Infallibilists had wandered away from the realities of history. And the findings of modern scholarship make this even more evident. Specialists in early church history, for example, have discovered that not only did the African Bishop Cyprian (who carried on the controversy with Pope Stephen I) *not* teach papal infallibility, in their opinion Cyprian hadn't even heard about Rome's supreme jurisdiction. Cyprian thought that the Church should be led by a loving fraternity of bishops, all of them equal, and that in case of conflict decisions should be made by synods. The African Church remained true to this notion for centuries. In 424 the Council of Carthage would not admit Roman legates, and it forbade appeals to Rome.

In subsequent centuries the popes tried to extend the range of their leadership—with mixed success—but none of them, not even Pope Gregory VII (1075–85), spoke of their own infallibility. Indeed, Pope John XXII (1316–34), as we have seen, rejected infallibility as a limitation of his rights as a sovereign, and in the bull *Qui quorundam* (1324) condemned the Franciscan doctrine of infallibility and irreformability as the work of the devil. Only later on, in the struggle against Protestantism and Gallicanism, did the popes once more consider infallibility a practical weapon. At all events, until the eve of the First Vatican Council the popes had willy-nilly tolerated anti-Infallibilist views.

Pope Honorius I
Condemned as a Heretic

In the centuries-long effort to explain the connection between the divine and human nature in Jesus Christ, some theologians tried to solve the problem by arguing that Christ had only a single will. The idea was to put a heavy emphasis on the unity of two natures in one person. Pope Honorius I (625–38), among others, got involved in this, and in an official letter to Patriarch Sergios of Constantinople (610–38) declared that he believed in the existence of only one will in Jesus Christ. A few decades afterwards this doctrine, known as Monothelitism, was condemned as heresy by the Sixth Ecumenical Council (the Third Council of Constantinople, 668–81). The anathema was expressly leveled at, among others, Pope Honorius. The Seventh Ecumenical Council (the Second Council of Nicaea, 787) and the Eighth (the Fourth Council of Constantinople, 869–70) repeated the condemnation.

These indisputable facts gave the Infallibilists all sorts of trouble even during the preparatory stages of Vatican I, and cast long shadows over the whole infallibility debate. The majority could not dare to deny the conciliar decrees per se, as Cardinals Robert Bellarmine (1542–1621) and Caesar Baronius (1528–1607) had done. Only Archbishop Georgios Ebedjesu of Diarbekir did not shrink from calling them later interpolations. But the Infallibilists nevertheless tried to cleanse Pope Honorius of the stain of heresy. Honorius, they insisted, was not a teacher of error. He had merely shown negligence in the struggle against heresy, and for that reason had been censured by the Council. The word "heretic" had a broader meaning then. But the Infallibilists did not feel so sure of themselves in this affair. They had a second argument ready just in case: Even if Honorius I *had* been a heretic, that did not disprove papal infallibility. The pope's letter to Sergios could in no way be considered an *ex cathedra* decision.

The Infallibilists' defensive attitude reveals the precariousness of their situation. The minority would not budge from their claim that Honorius I had erred on a question of faith. For Bishop Joseph Hefele the letter to Sergios containing the heretical expression "one will" was an *ex cathedra* decision. Still more crucial for the anti-Infallibilists, however, was the fact that three ecumenical councils and several popes had called Honorius a heretic. Even the slickest interpretation could not make these facts disappear. "In the face of all the efforts to smooth over the sentence passed on Honorius," wrote Georg Kreuzer in 1975, "we must emphatically repeat the historically attested fact that Honorius I was condemned in due form by the Third Council of Constantinople because, according to their lights, he was a heretic."

Constantinople's decision had long been a thorn in the side of Rome. For more than two hundred years, since the middle of the seventeenth century, the Roman Curia had obstructed publication of the *Liber Diurnus Pontificum Romanorum*. Decree 84 of this book pronounces the anathema on Honorius I. To this day it is hard to see how this condemnation can be reconciled with the supposition that Honorius' contemporaries believed in papal infallibility.

A Cloud of Witnesses: The Theologians

The Infallibilist proof from tradition also drew upon the theologians and doctors of the Church. The spokesmen for the new dogma took pains to show that there was a moral consensus among these interpreters of the faith on the question of infallibility. They claimed for their side whole schools of theology, such as the Augustinians, Thomists, Scotists, and the Franciscans, following the line of the latter's great leader Bonaventure (1217/18–74). They did the same for the most important Catholic universities, the Sorbonne in Paris, the University of Louvain, and those in Spain. Many Infallibilists did not hesitate to claim that *all* schools of theology and all the better theologians taught papal infallibility. The minority was unimpressed. They could match the many witnesses for infallibility with an equal number of equally significant opponents of the doctrine. Besides, the value of their evidence was doubtful. The witnesses called by the Infallibilists would often garble, falsify, interpolate, or totally misinterpret their supposedly clinching proof texts. But in any case, the minority asked, what did all these arguments mean? Even if practically all theologians had taught papal infallibility, that would have no significance. "Ten thousand sixteenth-century theologians speaking without unambiguous evidence from divine tradition," Archbishop Thomas Connolly of Halifax argued in the great hall of the Council, "do indeed tell us something about Scholastic opinions during that period, but when we're dealing with the certainty of divine faith, they might be completely immaterial."

These fundamental objections explain why interest in the "cloud of witnesses" for infallibility began to wane. From the early Middle Ages to the nineteenth century the Infallibilists adduced about one thundred theologians, and for most of these their case went unchallenged. Only with the more important theologians did the Infallibilists get any argument from the opposition. Thus, both parties claimed St. Thomas Aquinas (ca. 1225–74), the great Latin Doctor of the Church. But although Thomas warmly supported the pope's jurisdictional primacy (on the strength of the forgeries by Pseudo-Isidore and Pseudo-Cyril) and thought that the pope alone had the right to call ecumenical councils, he cannot be treated as an advocate of papal infallibility. His statements on the subject are too sporadic and vague. The whole thing was only of peripheral concern to him. He does admit the pope's supreme teaching authority, but he never mentions the infallibility of doctrinal decisions by the pope. The Councils of Constance, Basel, and Trent demonstrate how few theologians, in the time after Thomas Aquinas, shared a belief in papal infallibility.

Every now and then the Infallibilists even appealed to Jacques Bénigne Bossuet (1627–1704), the leading theologian of seventeenth-century France. But the minority rightfully stressed that Bossuet was living proof for the other side. Bossuet was the chief author of the *Declaration of the French Clergy* (1682).

The second of these Gallican articles establishes the superiority of the Council over the pope. The fourth makes the conclusiveness of papal decisions on faith contingent upon the consent of the Church. In a separate book Bossuet bolstered these concepts with arguments from history.

The Gallican theses set the tone in France till the mid-nineteenth century and also had a broadly influencing effect on English- and German-speaking countries—even northern Italy. Episcopalism, Febronianism, Josephism (all movements strongly promoting the rights of bishops against the pope), and the theological trends of the Enlightenment went out of their way to thwart the doctrine of papal infallibility. The Infallibilist assertion that they had the unanimous backing of the theologians proved to be utterly misleading.

The Church's Sense of Christian Faith

When the overwhelming majority of Catholics hold a teaching to be revealed truth, then it can be declared a dogma. The Infallibilists appealed to this principle, which is based on the presupposition that the Church as a whole could never err on matters of faith. They argued that both now and in the past Catholics have always believed unanimously in the pope's infallibility. It was only in the most recent days that some Catholics had begun to deny this truth. For this reason it had to be elevated to dogma.

The Council minority flatly challenged this supposed consensus of the faithful. Up until Vatican I the doctrine of papal infallibility could be considered an opinion of the schools but not official church teaching. In the sixteenth, seventeenth, and eighteenth centuries the contrary point of view had predominated. In many regions the faithful had still not heard of the idea. Up till now it had been possible, when discussing infallibility with non-Catholics, to reject it as a malicious Protestant calumny. In addition, the doctrine could not be found either in the Church's *kerygma*, its confessions of faith, liturgical documents, or in the most widely used catechisms. The most impor-

tant theological faculties in the world—the Sorbonne, Alcalá,
Kilmacduagh, Louvain, Salamanca—had always taught some
form of anti-Infallibilism.

In the course of the debate both parties tried to claim individual countries for themselves. The majority, in particular,
came up with a superabundance of arguments to back up its
case on this point. The Infallibilists had a clear title to the Catholic East, Yugoslavia, Holland, and Luxembourg. In the case of
Italy, Spain, Hungary, England, the United States, and Canada,
the minority strongly demurred. Portugal was considered largely
opposed to infallibility. The greatest controversies raged over
Ireland, France, and Germany.

The Infallibilists maintained that Ireland, too, had nurtured
a strong faith in infallibility over the past few centuries. Archbishop Paul Cullen of Dublin could actually report that even St.
Patrick (385–461), the apostle of Ireland, had proclaimed the
doctrine in the course of building up the Irish Church. Alluding
to the weakness of Cullen's sources, Archbishop John Baptist
Purcell of Cincinnati ironically countered that Patrick had
busied himself with the slightest details of his people's lives. He
had gone so far, for example, as enjoining priests to wear under-

Cardinal Paul Cullen,
archbishop of Dublin

John Baptist Purcell,
archbishop of Cincinnati

clothes when they celebrated mass—but he had not insisted on papal infallibility. He must have been quite unfamiliar with this doctrine, otherwise he would surely have brought it to the attention of his flock. There was no other way of explaining it. "The Irish believe in the infallibility of the pope," Bishop Augustin Vérot of Savannah conceded, adding, "but then they also believe in the infallibility of their pastors."

In France the Infallibilists could discern a unanimous belief in infallibility that stretched from the ninth to the nineteenth century. The Gallican articles, they thought, were only an apparent obstacle to this continuity. They had not been drawn up in freedom, and real Catholics had never accepted them. The minority took a totally opposite stance: The doctrine of infallibility had never been generally accepted in France. On the contrary, it had often been unanimously disapproved.

The dispute over Germany broke down along the same lines. The Infallibilists heaped argument upon argument to illustrate their unbroken tradition—and the conciliar minority would have none of it. Bishop Johannes Beckmann of Osnabrück couldn't find a trace of papal infallibility in his diocese. Likewise, Bishop Philipp Krementz of Ermland could not conceal the fact that in his diocese there was no Infallibilist tradition in either preaching or catechesis. It had also vanished from the schools of theology.

Bishop Ignatius von Senestrey had busied himself as the Infallibilist representative for Bavaria. His episcopal colleague Pancraz Dinkel of Augsburg rejected his arguments as inconclusive. Senestrey had adduced six authors to cover as many centuries. But one would have had to make inquiries among the bishops and priests who lived during that period. Besides, the catechism of Peter Canisius, whose use had long been obligatory in Bavaria, said not a word about papal infallibility. "How, then, can Senestrey still talk about a continuous tradition?" Dinkel wondered.

For further corroboration of their theses the Infallibilists appealed to the ten provincial councils held in the decades immediately before Vatican I. This was not enough to change the mind of the minority. They knew only too well what to make of the decisions by the provincial councils, for they had—or some of them had—themselves taken part in those meetings. Thus, Cardinal Friedrich Schwarzenberg of Prague and Bishop Johann Valerian Jirsik of Budweis (České Budějovice) contested the claim that the Prague Synod of 1860 had confirmed anything relating to infallibility. Furthermore, as far as the minority was concerned, the First Vatican Council itself was proof enough that the allegedly unanimous consent of the faithful on infallibility did not exist. Over one hundred bishops would reject the new dogma. In this connection, they once again broached their demand for moral unanimity on dogmatic decisions. Otherwise, thought Bishop Ketteler of Mainz, the Council would be committing a crime against the Church.

*The Need for
an Infallible
Supreme Head*

The arguments based on Scripture and tradition stand at the center of the infallibility debate. Occasionally, however, speculative theological proofs were also brought up.

According to the Infallibilist view, the Church, as a community incapable of erring in matters of faith, had to have an infallible leader and judge. Otherwise it would not be safe from error, it would lack both unity and order, and it would be vulnerable to fragmentation, as could be seen so clearly in Protestantism.

For their part the bishops of the minority accused the Infallibilists of using the proposed dogma to introduce a double infallibility. Along with the infallibility of the Church, which no one denied, there was now papal infallibility. The question might be asked whether the pope's infallibility did not make the Church's superfluous. On a more profound level, the minority argued that the definition of infallibility destroyed the divinely willed structures of the Church by abolishing the rights of councils and bishops and making the pope separate and independent.

Infallibilist reasoning was often hopelessly speculative. For example, in his opening address in the infallibility debate Bishop Louis Pie of Poitiers tried to prove that just as history tells us Paul, not Peter, was beheaded, therefore Peter (and with him the popes) as the head of the Church would never be separated from the body of the faithful. And along with Pope Leo IX (1049–54) Pie interpreted the fact that Peter was crucified head downward to mean that he was the cornerstone which supported the whole structure of the Church.

In other conciliar debates the arguments were often even more curious. Bishop Pierre Simon Dreux-Brézé of Moulins pleaded for the appointment of a single vicar-general in his diocese by referring to the Letter to the Ephesians, 4:4–6: "One God, one Christ, one faith, one baptism, one pope, one bishop in each diocese, one vicar-general, so that Christ's prayer may prove efficacious." And with the same ideological unity in mind, on February 21, 1870, the bishop of Havana, Jacinto Maria Martínez, called for a single catechism for the entire world. Though mothers were of different races and colors, their milk was always white, and so the catechism, the milk of the Church, must likewise be the same for all. On January 31, 1870, Bishop Gennaro Acciardi of Anglona and Tursi entered the lists to champion the priestly cassock. His reason: Jesus himself always' wore such a robe. Even on the island of Patmos he appeared to the Apostle John wearing this garment.

But to return to infallibility. The Infallibilists brought in a second, related line of proof similarly based on papal primacy. Since the pope had a universal jurisdiction and therefore the supreme teaching authority, he had to be infallible. Otherwise he might lead all the faithful into error, carrying the entire Church with him into the abyss, since all Catholics were obliged to obey him on questions of faith.

The minority rejected this inference from supreme magisterium to infallibility as an impossible leap. Primacy and infallibility were altogether different things. As the minority saw it, the Infallibilists had not only not come up with any new proofs, they had only conjured up new difficulties with the dogma they were pressing for. If the pope were infallible, independent of the college of bishops, then one had to question who would be capable of passing judgment on him in the event he fell into heresy— a possibility even popes and curial theologians had reckoned with. What of the no less thorny cases of a pope whose election had been questionable, a pope robbed of his freedom and forced to make dogmatic declarations and, above all, a pope suffering from mental illness?

*Logic and
the Definition
of Infallibility*

On June 3, 1870, the dean of the Sorbonne, Bishop Henri Maret, aroused the wrath of the Council presidents and the Infallibilists. He was interrupted by Cardinal Luigi Bilio and reprimanded for maintaining that if the Vatican Council declared the pope infallible by a dogmatic resolution, it would *ipso facto* prove itself to be superior to the pope. In the very act of making the definition the Council would be limiting the pope's rights, would be, strictly speaking, *giving* him rights.

Cardinal Bilio publicly reproved Maret. This was intolerable, a great injustice to the Holy See. The Council was not giving the pope any rights, it was merely recognizing the rights the

Henri Maret,
dean of the Sorbonne
and titular bishop

pope already had. In attacking Maret, Bilio was pretending to more assurance than he really had: During the period of preparation for the Council, the Infallibilists had been occupied with the same questions as those raised by Maret. At that stage they had likewise calmed themselves with the thought that the pope already possessed infallibility, and hence the Council could not truly award it to him. To make that as clear as possible, the consultants proposed to define infallibility on the basis of the Council's advice, not its consent.

Subsequently, however, the Infallibilists accepted the idea of a conciliar resolution. But since the Council could only be considered infallible when it was acting in unison with the pope, they had not avoided the danger of having to confess the new dogma on the grounds of the pope's testimony in his own behalf. But how can I know if the pope is telling the truth? No matter, the certainty afforded by saying, "The pope is infallible because the First Vatican Council says so," would be no greater. The truth of such statements can never be recognized with any certainty except by an act of faith. It is much more feasible to to prove their falsehood.

6

The Infallibility Debate and the Science of History

Forgeries and Misinterpretations

For some time now we have been following the various disputes among the bishops. Perhaps the most surprising feature of all this is the enormous number of arguments and counterarguments. On both sides they ran to upwards of two hundred. The Infallibilists tried to be persuasive, but the sheer bulk of their evidence had the opposite effect: People became skeptical. Every conceivable text (including passages from the Old Testament), fact, and person was dragged in to prove papal infallibility. The whole operation showed how little intellectual seriousness there was on the Infallibilist side—it all looks like a childish romp. The utter worthlessness of most of the arguments often makes it hard to believe that the people who proposed them were completely candid.

What were the Infallibilists trying to establish? Officially, they wanted to prove the revealed truth of papal infallibility from Scripture and tradition, that is, from history. For Scripture and tradition are historical sources even if they qualify as revelation for believers. But the Infallibilists were on uneasy terms with history. As their opponents kept pointing out, the arguments used by the majority were out of touch with historical reality. Indeed, the proposed dogma directly clashed with many known historical facts. Hence the suspicion arises that history weighed rather lightly in the Infallibilist scales. A report from the commission on faith (which was totally controlled by the Infallibilists) sheds some revealing light on the situation. In response to the historical difficulties raised by the minority, the report asserted that the pope's infallibility was an incontrovertible, divinely revealed truth. Historical facts, therefore, could never disprove it: Insofar as historical data contradict revelation, they are to be looked upon as false. And so history was dethroned by ideology.

History proved to be a sore point all through the infallibility debate. Both majority and minority appealed to it—with diametrically opposite results. The explanation for this discrepancy cannot be historical reality itself. It lies with the council fathers and their different methods of interrogating the past.

The Infallibilists are vulnerable to the charge of appealing to texts which were either forged, spurious, mutilated, or interpolated. Take the instance of Archbishop Giuseppe Cardoni, the leading Infallibilist consultant. The evidence he produced included unquestionably fabricated material by Pseudo-Isidore purported to be written by Popes Lucius (253–54), Felix I (268/9–73/4), and Mark (336), as well by Patriarch Athanasius of Alexandria. True, the Infallibilist council fathers did not quote Pseudo-Isidore directly, but they were nonetheless dependent on forged documents by him and others. They believed that from the very beginning the Church had been regulated by papal decrees. Still worse, they confidently based their arguments for infallibility on theologians who were deeply indebted to Pseudo-Isidore and Pseudo-Cyril. One of these theologians was St. Thomas Aquinas. Relying on texts concocted by Pseudo-Cyril, he raised papal authority to the brink of infallibility. Later curial theologians, such as Juan de Torquemada (1388–1468), Thomas Cajetan (1469–1534), Robert Bellarmine, and Caesar Baronius made still more extensive use of forged works in building their case for the papacy. The fact that such forgeries had long since been unmasked did not stop the Infallibilists from calling in these theologians as their star witnesses. The majority forgot about that fact or, rather, wanted to forget about it. Their whole approach to their sources was grossly uncritical.

This rather dim picture is not brightened by the hermeneutical methods of the Infallibilists. They wrench proof passages out of context and overinterpret them. They find explicit evidence of papal infallibility even where the document does not so much as mention the pope's supreme authority. The cause of these often grotesque misinterpretations was their habit of reading contemporary theories back into earlier times instead of looking at texts against the background of their own time and place. Preoccupied as they were with the present, the Infallibilist bishops constructed an image of the past that had very little to do with historical reality. Hardly a single one of them suspected what was going on. In general, their knowledge of history was extremely shallow.

Perhaps the reason why the Infallibilists did things this way was that tradition to them meant no more than the prevailing opinions of the Church's magisterium. Perhaps they advanced this version of church tradition because that was how the dominant curial party wanted it. These conjectures are confirmed by a glance at the Infallibilist approach to Scripture. They demand that the Bible be expounded along lines acceptable to the teaching authority of the Church, that is, of the pope. In its constitution on faith the First Vatican Council explicitly sanctioned this ecclesiastical monopoly on interpretation.

"Dogma Has Conquered History"

The Infallibilists' strained relationship with history was no accident. For some time, most notably since the middle of the nineteenth century, Roman theologians had been extending the concept of tradition to the point where it embraced the entirety of Catholic faith—as authoritatively proclaimed by the Church's magisterium. According to this view, whatever the Church teaches and preaches must qualify as divine tradition. The content of tradition is no longer decided by critical scrutiny of the old texts but by ecclesiastical authority.

This active, creative role of the magisterium was spelled out with all the clarity one could wish when the Immaculate Conception of Mary was made a dogma in 1854. A proof from tradition was called for here as always, but the point of departure in presenting it was not the documents and records from the past but the Church's current teaching and religious practices. Because the Church now believed in and preached about Mary's Immaculate Conception, this truth must likewise have been believed and preached in earlier days. But such strategies of internal immunization were not enough for Pius IX. He also considered it necessary to set up an external shield against historical criticism. He did want the bishops to be on hand in Rome for December 8, 1854, but not to discuss anything—simply to consent to the new dogma. When the bishops had last been canvassed, there had been 56 negative votes along with 546 positive ones. And university professors, especially in Germany, had voiced objections on historical grounds. Pius IX didn't want to be bothered with all that. So, despite the dubious value of his arguments from Scripture and tradition, the pope succeeded in proclaiming the new dogma as an unbroken church tradition.

Roman Jesuit theologians like Giovanni Perrone, Carlo Passaglia, Clemens Schrader, and Johann Baptist Franzelin viewed the critical methods of modern history with animosity—a feeling which they passed on to their students. Archbishops Henry Edward Manning, Victor Dechamps, and Bishop Ignatius von Senestrey, who were probably the most important Infallibilist leaders, had all studied under the Jesuits.

Archbishop (later Cardinal) Manning made no secret of his deep aversion to historians. There was nothing ambiguous or jesuitically subtle about his notion that historical criticism undermined the faith. "It is time," he demanded, "for 'historical science' and the 'scientific historians,' with all their arrogance, to be thrust back into their proper sphere, to be kept within their proper limits. And this Council will do just that, not with controversies and condemnations but with the words, 'it has pleased the Holy Spirit and us.'" Manning's remarks were aimed principally at Ignaz von Döllinger and the historical school.

In his notes on the Council, Manning wrote that a tremendous gap divided tradition and history. Tradition was divine, history human. Tradition could never be either proved or refuted with historical evidence. The divine magisterium, guarantor of the Church's tradition, towered over all of human history and was in no way dependent on it. Only the Church's teaching office, not historical science or any other authority, could decide what tradition was. "No one," Manning affirmed, "who wishes to keep the name of Catholic may descend from the unshaken Rock of Truth, the Church's magisterium, into the swamp of human history when the truths of the faith are at stake." When Bishop Hefele brought up several historical difficulties in the great hall of the Council, the archbishop of Westminster heatedly replied, "We are not at school but at an ecumenical council. We are not to bring our questions to historians and critics but to the living oracle of the Church."

For Manning, once the Church had spoken, all historical problems were liquidated. The Holy Spirit, he believed, was so closely allied with the Church that errors or false steps were impossible; and this faith gave him utter certainty. The story goes —and it seems quite believable—that Manning and his circle had a motto, "Dogma must triumph over history," or "Dogma has conquered history." Bishop Félix Dupanloup reports a similar remark from the no less intransigent suffragan bishop of Geneva, Gaspare Mermillod: "Infallibility sets the nations free from history."

With Bishop Ignatius von Senestrey we find the same sort of organic thinking as with Manning. He, too, believed that the help afforded the Church by the Holy Spirit excluded the possibility of false developments. Of course, Senestrey's theory puts the Church's doctrinal statements beyond the reach of any kind of historical criticism.

Archbishop Victor Dechamps of Mechlin displayed an ignorance of the critical historical method scarcely inferior to that of the other Infallibilists. To back up the abstruse thesis that the Latin Church had always upheld the law of clerical celibacy, and that the Greek Church had done so in its early years, Dechamps thought it enough to cite two contemporary Ultramontane theologians. He had no patience with bishops who raised historical objections against infallibility. He nervously scribbled the following on his copy of the conciliar document dealing with this question: "One more German who doesn't seem to realize that this job is finished, done with, *usque ad nauseam*" (to the point of nausea).

It is obvious that the anti-Infallibilists felt differently about historical criticism. As advocates of a serious confrontation with the past, they not only called for a clarification of the historical problems regarding the dogma but they demanded clear texts, especially from the first centuries of Christianity. They succeeded, to a far greater extent than the Infallibilists, in placing the sources in context and letting them speak for themselves. In the course of conciliar debates, some of the representatives of the minority, such as Archbishops and Bishops Joseph Hefele, Joseph Othmar Rauscher, Henri Maret, and Jean Baptiste Landriot, proved that they were excellent students of church history.

The clearest instance of this different attitude towards history is probably found in the person of Ignaz von Döllinger, the church historian from Munich and one of the most influential minority theologians. Döllinger insisted that the Church could not make a dogma of any teaching found in neither the Bible nor tradition. But the task of determining this—and here is the critical difference separating him from the Roman theologians— does not belong to an infallible ecclesiastical magisterium but to critical historians employing scientific methods.

It was the question of infallibility in the first place that drew Döllinger into the broader problem of religious authority: "We are standing here," he wrote, "on the solid ground of history, of evidence, of facts." Wherever solid results of critical research were available, Döllinger refused to accept contrary pronouncements of the Church's magisterium. As he wrote to Bishop Johann Baptist Greith before the Council: "Before I could ever inscribe this modern invention [the doctrine of infallibility] on the tablet of my mind, I would first have to plunge my fifty years of theological, historical, and patristic studies into Lethe [river of forgetfulness] and then draw them forth like a blank sheet of paper."

Taking the same ground, Bishop Joseph Hefele of Rottenburg offered bitter resistance at the Council to the definition of infallibility. But Hefele is also an example of how long apologetic biases, some of which never lost their power over the minority, could blunt the thrust of their criticism. Thus, Hefele's famous history of the Councils was marred at several points by an uncritical acceptance of dogmatic and canonical norms. Following the lead of Cardinal Robert Bellarmine, he ascribed to the popes a role in the ecumenical councils which they had never had. He also adopted Bellarmine's list of the councils without question. True, Hefele's eyes were opened by his experiences at Vatican I, but by then it was too late to revise his great work.

Another famous theologian, John Henry Newman (who was later made a cardinal), could never work himself free from old prejudices. He, too, had once described as scandalous the way infallibility became a dogma.[22] Nevertheless, in 1875 he dissociated himself from Döllinger and defended the use of authority in intepreting history. In an open letter to the Duke of Norfolk, Edward George Fitzalan Howard, written the same year, he declared, "It is the Church's dogmatic application of history that the Catholic believes in."

History Misused

In contrast to other dogmas, papal infallibility is linked to history in two ways. First, it makes statements about a series of concrete personalities by affirming that when past, present, and future popes speak *ex cathedra* on faith and morals, they invariably teach only revealed truth. It follows logically from this that St. Peter's successors have never contradicted one another, and that they never will. And since the Church as a whole is also infallible, it can never have rejected any *ex cathedra* papal decisions. Second, the definition itself binds the dogma to history in that it appeals to the continual faith of the Church.

Let us take the second point first. We have already seen how convinced the Infallibilists were that the Church had believed in papal infallibility from the very beginning. Hence they had no need to meddle with Newman's efforts to reconcile history and dogma. The First Vatican Council paid no attention to the development of dogma. The most the Infallibilists would admit was that Christians hadn't always spoken expressly of papal infallibility in the past. But they had used different words —which merely needed to be explained—to say the same thing.

Johann Joseph Ignaz von Döllinger, professor of church history in Munich

There was no need to infer anything from the text; a simple explication would suffice. Various other terms found in ancient documents implied the doctrine of infallibility.

As harmless as all that might sound in theory, in practice it was often strange and fantastic. The Infallibilist commission on faith, for example, saw a proof of infallibility in Pope Hormisdas' dictum that the faith had always been preserved intact in the Apostolic See at Rome. They found another in the Greek confession of faith from the Second Council of Lyon: The formula that the pope's judgment must put an end to doctrinal controversy was tantamount to papal infallibility. And when the Council of Florence called the pope the supreme teacher, that carried along with it the notion of his infallibility, because otherwise the pope might lead the faithful into error.

On the second point binding infallibility to history (viz., in their official doctrinal decisions the popes must never have either contradicted themselves or been repudiated by the Church), the Infallibilist efforts at immunization against intellectual difficulties are still more obvious. The magic word that sweeps away all the problems here is *ex cathedra*. Only *ex cathedra* pronouncements are to be infallible. Since this concept did not even exist before the sixteenth century, it cannot be said with certainty of any papal declaration from the first fifteen hundred years that it was made *ex cathedra*. This did away with all sorts of unpleasantness, such as the condemnation of Pope Honorius I as a heretic by three ecumenical councils. Furthermore, papal proclamations endorsing murder and manslaughter could not tarnish the luster of infallibility: By classifying them as not *ex cathedra* the situation was saved.

In the process, the dogma of infallibility had become so vague that it could never run afoul of history. As Brian Tierney remarks with biting irony, "All infallible statements are certainly true, but no statement is certainly infallible."

At this point it is clear, at least, that the Infallibilists did not ground their proofs in history and the findings of historical research. Their arguments were essentially based on what the Church, and still more the pope, taught and preached at that point in the nineteenth century. Since prevailing opinion within

the Church supported the thesis of papal infallibility, it had to
be true. Most of the time the crude logic underlying the Infallibilist position remained hidden. Only every now and then was it
abruptly illuminated by such things as Pius IX's outburst at Cardinal Filippo Maria Guidi, "*I* am tradition (i.e., the Church)," or
Cardinal Manning's remark that dogma must conquer history.

The Infallibilists went to great lengths to obscure the real
foundation of their proofs. They trotted out hundreds of historical arguments, leaving the crucial elements in their thinking out
of sight. Hence, they cannot escape the charge of having
misused history to push through the definition of infallibility.
They erected a facade of serious historical reasoning and arranged to have an inconsequential "ritual discussion," with the
(mostly unconscious) intention of glossing over their own dogmatism.

A very large number of majority bishops had barely an ink-
ling of these contrivances. Still, one cannot overlook the care-
lessness, frivolousness, and ignorance they displayed in presenting their historical arguments. Many of them may have been
acting in good faith, aided and abetted by intellectual laziness
and lack of critical sense. Others were probably urged on by
fear of sanctions or calculating opportunism. But even then it
was possible to know better—the minority bishops are proof of
that.

Cardinal Camillo Di Pietro may be taken as a particularly
eloquent example of the cautious attitude adopted by some of
the fathers. He complained to Lord Acton that he couldn't commit himself to the anti-Infallibilists as strongly as he wanted to.
He could not afford the luxury of opposition, "because he would
be subject to terrible attacks, and since everyone has some weak
point in his life, he could not expose himself to such ruthless assaults on his character and honor."[23] This murky allusion is
clarified by the fact that when Cardinal Di Pietro had been a
nuncio in Portugal in 1845 he had had an affair with a dancer
(who, in turn, was deceiving him with a Russian general). The
cardinal had managed to avoid a duel but not a scandal.[24]

Cardinal Camillo Di Pietro

The small group of convinced Infallibilists clustered around the pope—consisting of Manning, Senestrey, and the Jesuits of *La Civiltà Cattolica*—succeeded in arguing that for many of the council fathers the question had long since been settled and that discussion was pointless. The majority bishops accepted and came to believe the Infallibilist version of things. On the other hand, it often took years to bring the bishops of the opposition around, and in some cases the operation never quite succeeded.

7

How the New Dogma Was Passed

As the day of the vote on infallibility approached, resistance began to crumble. Many bishops dodged the decision and left Rome, others became conveniently sick, while still others again forced themselves to come up with a "yes."

Nonetheless, on July 13, 1870, a surprisingly large number—88 bishops—voted against the constitution *Pastor Aeternus*. And 62 council fathers only assented with reservations—many of them were de facto opponents of the definition. Only 451 bishops voted "yes," representing less than half of the 1,084 members entitled to take part in the Council, and less than two thirds of the seven hundred bishops present at the opening of the Council.

In response to a petition by a number of Infallibilists on July 14, 1870—in which they called for an explicit declaration that there was no need of episcopal consent to render the pope's declarations infallible—Pope Pius IX wrote in his own hand that same day: "Let Cardinal Bilio read the enclosed comments and try to make use of them. Let the cardinal also be assured that the admonition, 'Don't waste your words where there is no one to heed them,' was never truer than in our case." This order was the reason why the formula of definition stipulated that the pope was infallible "without the consent of the Church."

Dal Vaticano

14 Luglio 1890

Il Card. Bello legge,
le unite osservazioni
e procuri di farne uso.
Si assicuri pure il Cardinale
che nel caso nostro è
più che mai vera
quella sentenza

= Ubi non es auditor
= non effundas
= sermonem =

Just before the solemn vote on July 18, 1870, the minority made a desperate attempt to change the pope's mind. But all their efforts, including the visit by a delegation of six archbishops and bishops, got nowhere. On the contrary, their request to incorporate the Church's consent in the definition only antagonized the pope. He directed Cardinal Luigi Bilio to sharpen the terms of the formula and to strike out any mention of the need for the Church's endorsement.

On July 17, 1870, 55 bishops of the minority renewed their *Non placet* and let it be known, moreover, that out of reverence for the Holy Father they did not wish to take part in the solemn session of the following day. They then left Rome in protest. (Other bishops had already departed before this.)

At the last meeting of the Council on July 18, 1870, the number of "yes" votes rose to 535. Only 2 bishops voted "no," Luigi Riccio of Cajazzo and Edward Fitzgerald of Little Rock. (They had not been entirely clear about the strategy agreed on by the minority.) But both men submitted immediately after the definition passed. In terms of the original number of participants, 20 percent boycotted the solemn final session of the Council. Their doubts had not been cleared up.

As the new dogma was being proclaimed, a violent electrical storm burst over St. Peter's. The thunder rolled and growled, the lightning flashes threw a ghostly light into the darkness which had filled the cathedral—for some a sign of God's approval, for others of his wrath.

The Opposition
Plans to Resist

The definition of the new religious truth sealed the fate of the conciliar minority. Its unity broke into pieces. Before leaving Rome on July 17, the anti-Infallibilists did hold one more meeting where they resolved to keep in touch, to act in concert, and to advise one another before making any decisions. But that very day Bishop Wilhelm Emmanuel Freiherr von Ketteler and

A moment during the proclamation of the dogma of infallibility. Bishop Antonio Maria Valenziani of Fabriano and Matelica reads the constitution *Pastor Aeternus*. At the extreme right Pius IX on

Archbishop Paul Melchers of Cologne broke rank; they wrote to the pope and indicated their readiness to accept the conciliar decrees.

Most of the minority bishops weren't capable of such an abrupt about-face. When they left Rome in such agitation, they were in no mood to submit to the definition. "Persons of trust

the throne between Cardinal Deacons Mertel and Grassellini. The photomontage is by G. Altobelli, "painter to the Council."

and authority tell me," wrote the nuncio in Vienna, Mariano Falcinelli, to the Secretary of State, Cardinal Giacomo Antonelli, on July 22, 1870, "that almost all the bishops of Austria-Hungary now returned from Rome are *furious* over the definition of infallibility. The few who have visited me did not dare to talk about the Council." And on July 25 the nuncio reported to Antonelli,

Edward Fitzgerald, bishop of Little Rock, Ark.

"The bishops who have come back from the Council have once more left Vienna after scandalizing clerics and lay people with their speeches attacking Rome. In the case of two bishops in particular, the vexation and exasperation reached such a fever pitch that they had the temerity to say that the discussion of infallibility must be reopened and the definition corrected. The persons who spoke with the bishops got the impression that *many* people do not wish to return to Rome for the Council. In their opinion the bishops will stand firm on this intention." In a manifesto Professor Friedrich Michelis of Braunsberg described Pius IX as a "heretic and devastator of the Church." Neither Cardinal Friedrich Schwarzenberg nor Bishop Joseph Hefele contradicted him. In speaking of the pope, the bishop of Rottenburg himself used the term *perturbator ecclesiae* (disturber of the Church).

Since the bishops could hardly profess belief in something they had rejected as untrue only a few days before, they found themselves in a hopeless situation. Some thought of resigning, as they had threatened during the Council. In letters to theologian friends and episcopal colleagues the bishops vented their feelings over this profound crisis of conscience. They spoke of their historical and theological objections, which had yet to be answered, and challenged the freedom and ecumenicity of the Council's decrees.

In this kind of atmosphere, it is not surprising that individual bishops tried to organize the resistance. These efforts centered around Bishop Félix Dupanloup and Cardinal Friedrich Schwarzenberg. Schwarzenberg commissioned two reports on what steps the minority would have to take when the Council reopened. Both experts he conferred with suggested a solemn challenge to the ecumenicity of the resolutions on papal primacy and infallibility. This suggestion could count on the support of the bishops.

Should it fail, however, there remained only the "pathetic expedient" of interpretation. The minority bishops should call

Cardinal Friedrich von Schwarzenberg, archbishop of Prague

for an explanation of the dogma that suited their theological and ecclesiastical interests, and which required the collaboration of the bishops in infallible dogmatic decisions. They should further demand a guarantee of the restoration of freedom at the Council and of the inclusion of theological experts from all over the world in the work of the Council.

Both consultants also advised the minority to make concrete preparations before the Council reconvened. A small group of bishops (one report named Bishops Joseph Hefele, Pancraz Dinkel, and Matthias Eberhard; another Friedrich Fürstenberg and Heinrich Förster) should begin by working out a definite plan of action, drawing upon suggestions from a wide circle of sympathizers, and eventually presenting it to the international committee of the minority.

However well thought out the minority's resistance may have been in its details, within a few months it had fallen apart. This was not simply owing to the lack of cohesion in the opposition. Outside events had something to do with it too. Hardly had the Council proclaimed the infallibility of the pope, when the Franco-Prussian War broke out and paralyzed communications between the two most important centers of resistance. The war also diverted public attention from the Church's problems. This gave the Curia a better opportunity to work undisturbed at building up esteem for the new dogmatic provisions. Rome set all sorts of machinery in motion to bring the vacillating bishops to submission. It was especially clever at denying its opponents any chance to get together; this was accomplished by suspending the Council. The Italian siege of Rome immediately suggested itself as a welcome excuse for this action.

A few bishops continued to resist for quite a while, but the opposition's back was broken. The bishops were now slaughtered one by one, as Hefele put it. There was only one exception: the Hungarian episcopate. It kept up its determination and managed to put off submitting for almost a year. But by the end of 1871 the job was practically finished. Save for a few bishops, all the members of the minority had handed in their depositions of consent to Rome. "You have all submitted," Pius IX remarked to Bishop Augustin David of St. Brieuc in a voice full of satisfaction. "That is good."

Rome Forces Compliance

Months before papal infallibility was declared a dogma, the Infallibilists were treating the contrary point of view as heresy. They longed to put an end, at long last, to the "wicked speeches." The bishops in the opposition would later have to make satisfaction for their scandalous statements; Pius IX, in particular, stressed this point. During the Council he had been unable to do anything to them, but the time would come to demand a reckoning for the scandal they had caused. Whoever opposed the faith of the Church, he told Louis Veuillot on July 18, 1870, would be struck down. To the undersecretary of the

Friedrich Fürstenberg,
archbishop of Olmütz

Council, Monsignore Ludovico Jacobini, he wrote in his own hand, "Even the bishop of Cincinnati, Purcell, has submitted. But he still owes reparation for the scandal of having spoken from the pulpit against the decree . . ."

The first bishops of the minority to feel Pius IX's irritation and anger were those prelates living at his court in Rome who had ventured to object to papal infallibility. Pope Mastai-Ferretti declared that he wanted no heretics in his own house. He was referring, among others, to the papal almoner, Archbishop François Xavier de Mérode. He had stayed away from the solemn session of July 18, 1870. When, at the next official papal audience, de Mérode shrank from giving his consent to the conciliar decrees, Pius IX lashed out at him, saying he had had enough of his childishness. He expected an act of faith from him. By August 2, 1870, the official papal newspaper *Giornale di Roma* could write that de Mérode had given his full, clear, and explicit consent to the new dogmas. De Mérode and his friends were indignant at this sort of collusion.

François Xavier de Mérode, archbishop and papal almoner

Pius IX felt even greater animosity towards his court preacher, the Capuchin Archbishop Luigi Puecher-Passavalli. He, too, was no friend of the new dogma and had been absent when it was solemnly proclaimed. In retaliation the pope fired him on the spot as vicar of the chapter of St. Peter's. The fact that the Capuchin made a full submission failed to mollify the pope. The First Vatican Council was the prelude to a lifelong alienation between Pius IX and his court preacher. Guglielmo Audisio, canon of St. Peter's, likewise paid the price for his opposition; he lost his post as professor of law at the Roman university "Sapienza."

Putting his own house in order posed no serious problems for Pius IX. It was harder to take in hand the more independent cardinals and bishops outside of Rome. One means of accomplishing this was the papal press. In order to conceal the real strength of the opposition, on the day the dogma was proclaimed the *Giornale di Roma* spread the story that the great majority of the two hundred absent bishops advocated papal infallibility. Some of them, it claimed, had already given their assent in writing. This consciously distorted reportage—the Prussian ambassador, Count Harry von Arnim-Suckow, spoke of an out-and-out lie—soon took on still crasser forms.

From June 22 to August 22, 1870, various Ultramontane newspapers, such as *Unità Cattolica,* the *Osservatore cattolico di Milano,* and the *Giornale di Roma,* published reports that along with several bishops all the cardinals of the minority—to wit, Friedrich Schwarzenberg, Jacques Mathieu, Joseph Othmar Rauscher, and Gustav von Hohenlohe—had submitted. In the case of Schwarzenberg and Hohenlohe, that was a barefaced lie; with regard to Mathieu and Rauscher, it was misleading.

The newspaper campaign was a clever ploy against the opposition cardinals. The only way they could have protected themselves would have been to issue an official denial, to insist that they had not accepted the new dogmas. Rome was not mistaken in assuming that none of the cardinals would have the courage to do that. This device also succeeded in creating uncertainty among the opposition bishops who still held out, and in putting salutary pressure on them. When Archbishop Johannes Simor of Gran found a copy of the *Giornale di Roma* in his mail,

Cardinal Joseph Othmar
Rauscher, archbishop of Vienna

sent by an anonymous Roman source, with an article on recanting council fathers, he got the hint. The nuncio in Vienna,
Mariano Falcinelli, made it his duty to apply this tried and true
method. In order to bring the stubborn Hungarians to heel, he is
believed to have leaked to the press a list of bishops who had already submitted.

Rome did not always limit itself to that kind of indirect
summons. Sometimes it was the nuncios, sometimes Cardinal
Alessandro Barnabò of the "Propaganda," and sometimes the
pope himself who reminded the dilatory bishops of their duty.
For especially stiff-necked individuals Rome liked to operate
through a third party instead of on its own. Cardinal Jacques
Mathieu was brought to submission in this way. And he, in turn,
was supposed to work on Bishop Félix Dupanloup. The Munich
nuncio, Pier Francesco Meglia, assigned the archbishop of Cologne, Paul Melchers, to Bishop Joseph Hefele. When this failed
to get results, he passed the job on to the suffragan bishop of
Freiburg, Lothar Kübel.

The declarations of consent were important to Rome: They
were to bind the bishops permanently. By 1872 the Vatican had
its people busily and carefully collecting these letters: The Curia

very much wanted every one of them. But in 1883, while involved in this effort, the nuncio in Vienna, Serafino Vannutelli, suffered a setback. As he reluctantly admitted, three bishops, Stephan Pankoviés of Munkács, Georg Smiciklas of Kreutz, and Alexander Bonnaz of Csanád and Temesvár, had continually managed to avoid making a written submission. Mansi's great edition of conciliar documents hushed up this painful state of affairs by not printing any of the submissions.

Split in the German Opposition at Fulda

The Roman Curia maneuvered with striking success against the Fulda Bishops' Conference at the end of August 1870. It drove a wedge into the German resistance and broke its back.

Soon after the promulgation of papal infallibility, the archbishop of Munich, Gregor Scherr, approached Archbishop Paul Melchers of Cologne and Bishop Wilhelm Emmanuel Freiherr von Ketteler with a proposal to convoke a conference of bishops at Fulda in order to make a joint declaration on the dogma. This plan must have been long in the works, for Ketteler had two printed drafts of the declaration with him when he arrived at Fulda. In all probability the chief movers behind the scene here were the Secretary of State and the Nuncio Pier Francesco Meglia of Munich. In any event, the nuncio from Vienna, Mariano Falcinelli, was given the assignment of starting up a similar conference of bishops in Austria. Fulda was also cited to Nuncios Flavio Chigi of Paris and Giovanni Battista Agnozzi as a model to be imitated. Falcinelli believed that because of logistical problems the bishops could only meet at the provincial level in Austria. But even these gatherings broke down when individual bishops balked at passing joint declarations on infallibility. Likewise, nothing came of the plan in France. In Switzerland Nuncio Agnozzi got better results: In 1871 the Swiss bishops issued a joint pastoral letter on the definition.

In Fulda a whole group of bishops previously opposed to papal infallibility came out in favor of it. They also recognized

Wilhelm Emmanuel
Freiherr von Ketteler,
bishop of Mainz

the freedom and ecumenicity of the Council. For the bishops still intent on resisting the dogma, Fulda came as a great shock. This split in their ranks seemed the greatest misfortune that could have struck the minority. They couldn't figure out this sudden change of heart. "The Fulda group," Joseph Georg Strossmayer wrote to Joseph Hubert Reinkens, a professor of church history in Breslau, on November 27, 1870, "wise as they were before the Council, are now acting every bit as foolishly and unwisely after it. No power in the world will ever convince the world that the Council was really free." There was a widespread impression that the bishops at Fulda had sacrificed the integrity of their convictions.

*Denial of
Marriage
Dispensations*

When, in spite of everything, the bishops of the opposition still failed to show a proper docility, the Roman Curia had other means available to coerce them: It denied them important authorizations and privileges.

Bishop Joseph Hefele characterized the refusal to grant marriage dispensations as one of the main forms of pressure brought to bear on him. Before long, sixteen couples in his diocese were unable to get married. In Germany, Johannes Beckmann of Osnabrück was hit with the same penalty. In the Hapsburg Empire, Bishop Joseph Georg Strossmayer had especially harsh treatment meted out to him. Rome ignored his urgent requests for help. After repeated inquiries he was informed by his Roman confidant, Canon Nikolaus Vorsak, that he would have to go on waiting for an answer until he had obediently accepted the conciliar decrees. This procedure is reported to have been used against other bishops in Austria-Hungary as well. The driving force behind such harsh measures was Pius IX himself. The number two man in the Dataria Apostolica, Monsignor Carmine Gori-Merosi, confided to the counselor at the Austrian embassy, Joseph Palomba, that he needed three audiences to talk the pope out of his position on marriage dispensations. This method, however, did not always work. Archbishop Friedrich Fürstenberg was denied permission to dispense individuals from marriage impediments. The Curia often made use of this tactic in France, where, despite their isolation and lack of information, the bishops still persisted in resisting pressure from Rome.

The minority bishops came to feel the brunt of Rome's ill will in other ways as well. Until they made a clear and unequivocal submission, they were given no suffragan bishops, no dispensations from the local rules for fasting, and no memorial medallions of the Council, as other bishops were. Sometimes they lost their jurisdiction over religious congregations in their diocese, as did Bishop François Lecourtier in Montpellier and Bishop Étienne Émile Ramadié in Perpignan. Above all, Rome made a point of barring them from advancement for a number of years even after they submitted. In addition to this, it appears likely that Félix Dupanloup, one of the leading French members of the minority, was forbidden to exercise important episcopal functions. Along with others, Dupanloup was under a cloud as long as Pius IX lived: The pope believed Dupanloup was conspiring against him and the Church.

Retraction
of Writings
on the Council

The moment of reckoning was particularly inevitable for the bishops who had attacked the new dogma in print—a true scandal in the eyes of the Infallibilists. First in line for censure was the dean of the theological faculty of the Sorbonne, Bishop Henri Maret. After Vatican I the congregation of the Index opened proceedings against his book, *The Council and Religious Peace*. Maret was threatened with condemnation unless he formally recanted. All his protests and excuses went for nought. Rome was not satisfied until Maret officially disavowed his work and withdrew it from sale. And so the titular bishop from Paris publicly trimmed his sails and followed the course prescribed by Rome. At the reopening of the Sorbonne in 1871, Maret's first job, as he informed the new archbishop of Paris, Joseph Hippolyte Guibert, was to register the declarations of assent to infallibility on the part of faculty members in the minutes of the conference.

Archbishop Peter Richard Kenrick also wrote a piece on infallibility which was belatedly condemned by the Congregation of the Index. For personal reasons, however, the Vatican took its time in pronouncing sentence. In contrast to Maret, Kenrick managed to appease the Roman Curia without having to make a formal retraction.

Forced Resignation
of Bishops

In France the punishments for recalcitrance sometimes proved to be still harsher—even after the bishops submitted. Some of them lost their dioceses. Bishop Félix de Las Cases of Constantine had his nerves so unhinged by the war, by the debts burdening his diocese and, above all, by his experiences at the Council that he had to enter a sanatorium. While recuperating there from a state of temporary nervous exhaustion, he was talked into resigning from his diocese. He, too, later recanted, but to no avail.

Félix de Las Cases,
bishop of Constantine

Pius IX wanted a special sort of reparation from Bishop
François Lecourtier of Montpellier. Back in 1865 Lecourtier had
complained about the Ultramontanes to the Minister of Religion,
Pierre Jules Baroche. Later he had written anonymous newspaper articles about the lack of freedom at the Council, and
when he left Rome prematurely, as already mentioned, he threw
his conciliar documents into the Tiber. Despite his quite explicit
act of submission, the Curia's anger went on smouldering. In
1873 Lecourtier was slanderously accused of writing antireligious letters to a priest friend of his, now deceased. The
nuncio in Paris, Flavio Chigi, with the connivance of the secretariat of state, made use of this calumny to prepare the final
blow. At the nuncio's behest, Cardinal Charles Lavigérie assigned Lecourtier's former vicar-general, Auguste Lamothe-
Tenet, the mission of employing false information, threats, intimidation, and appeals to Pius IX's express wish in order to force
the bishop into retirement. Lecourtier was caught unawares;
once he had signed his resignation, all his later recantations
were in vain.

Bishop Frédéric Marguerye of Autun also resigned after the

Council. The circumstances surrounding his move are quite obscure, but he was certainly under pressure from his own clergy and still more from Nuncio Chigi in Paris. It appears that Bishops Nicolas Gueulette, Giovanni Pietro Sola, Jean Pierre Bravard, and Jean Jules Dours were also forced to step down in a similar fashion.

"The Jesuits, Too, Are Satisfied"

Long before papal infallibility was solemnly proclaimed as a new dogma, the bishops of the minority began to worry about returning to their dioceses. Even during the course of the Council, many of them switched over to the dominant trend in their dioceses, while others, out of fear of their own lay people, ducked a decision and left Rome before the final vote.

In the beginning, at least, the German and Austrian bishops had no reason for such fear. Indeed, after the Council Cardinal Friedrich Schwarzenberg of Prague could write his colleague, Joseph Othmar Rauscher, in Vienna, "I believe I can say that the majority of the faithful entrusted to me would not accept the dogmatic decrees with the devotion of true belief." And Bishop Philipp Krementz of Ermland told Nuncio Pier Francesco Meglia that he doubted whether even a dozen of his three hundred priests believed in the newly defined doctrine. Joseph Georg Strossmayer's homecoming turned into a genuine triumphal procession.

Of course, things in France were another story altogether. Bishop Flavien Hugonin of Bayeux had to go into hiding for months to escape the wrath of the Infallibilists in his diocese. And Bishop Frédéric Marguerye of Autun was greeted by a deafening uproar at a retreat for parish priests when he tried to explain the position he had taken at the Council.

But even in Germany, as a victory for the Roman party began to look more and more likely, the Ultramontanes were increasingly buoyed up. These groups of intransigents could always count on the support of the nuncio in Munich. When, for

Flavien Abel Antoine
Hugonin, bishop of Bayeux

example, Bishop Pancraz Dinkel of Augsburg forbade the editor of his diocesan newspaper, Professor Matthias Merkle, to publish the Vatican decrees, Nuncio Pier Francesco Meglia, acting on orders from the Secretary of State, Cardinal Antonelli, had copies of the decrees distributed to all the important parishes of Augsburg. It was hoped that this would offset the bishop's disparaging comments about the Council.

"I'm sitting on a volcano," Bishop Joseph Hefele of Rottenburg wrote a few months after the end of the Council. At first he had felt quite sure of his diocese. Now many of his clergy, with the encouragement of the nuncio in Munich, were putting pressure on him to accept the doctrine of infallibility.

In the United States it was, above all, the Jesuits who incited clerics and lay people against refractory bishops and forced them into submission. Before long, one of the key figures in the resistance movement, Archbishop Peter Richard Kenrick of St. Louis, succumbed to the pressure. The authorities of the Roman Inquisition accepted his declaration of submission, not-

Peter Richard Kenrick,
archbishop of St. Louis

ing that he had not only satisfied the faithful but the Jesuits as
well.

*We Have Always
Believed in
Papal Infallibility!*

Despite the conciliar oath of secrecy and the restrictions of
Vatican press policy, the fact that many bishops had fought
against the dogma of infallibility in the name of history did not
escape the attention of the laity. Now, just after the end of the
Council, these same bishops were calling for devout acceptance
of the Vatican decrees. Many Catholics would understandably
have liked to hear an explanation for this sudden change of
mind.

Once the definition had passed, the easiest thing by far for a
bishop to say was that he had always believed in papal infalli-

bility and had merely thought its dogmatization would be inopportune. Only a few bishops resisted the temptation to take this easy way out. In the interests of the new dogma, the Infallibilists also did their utmost to popularize this legend. Cardinal Henry Edward Manning, writing several years after the end of the Council, claimed that not even five bishops could rightly be considered opponents of infallibility; fundamental objections to the dogma had only been voiced in two or three speeches. Catholic historians repeated this groundless assertion so frequently that it soon qualified as incontrovertible truth. Only in recent times have they once again begun to question it seriously.

As the entire foregoing presentation of the Council has shown, Manning's assessment could hardly be further from the facts. Apart from extremely rare cases, the bishops did not limit themselves to attacking the opportuneness of the definition; they also advanced historical and theological reasons against the dogma. Of course, not all of them did this with equal vehemence. Among the many bishops who later metamorphosed into mere "Inopportunists" were a good number who had stayed out of the conciliar limelight. This rapid ostensible conversion made a much more painful impression in the case of bishops who had loudly voiced their weighty historical and theological misgivings. For some of them—such as Archbishops Thomas Connolly of Halifax and John MacHale of Tuam, or Bishops Michael Domenec of Pittsburgh and Matthias Eberhard of Trier—one might almost think someone had blotted out of their memory all convictions they had held only a few months before.

With others the changeover took place gradually. The best example of this is the bishop of St. Gall, Johann Baptist Karl Greith. He had raised a whole series of factual objections against the dogma, and on May 17, 1870, had spoken in the great hall of the Council in a paroxysm of exasperation. "The bishop of St. Gall was so violent in his speech against infallibility," wrote Bishop Jacob Chadwick of Hexham and Newcastle in a letter to England on May 22, 1870, "that through the very force of his enunciation he lost a false tooth. He had to pick it up from the ground and put it back into place before he could go on."[25] And the conciliar theologian Victorin Galabert noted in his diary for May 17, "Msgr. Greith of St. Gall . . . shouts

Matthias Eberhard,
bishop of Trier

Johann Baptist Karl Greith,
bishop of St. Gallen

like someone hard of hearing." Nonetheless, not long after this the bishop was saying he had been careful not to speak against the doctrine itself. His objections, he declared, were not of a "thetic" nature. What Greith meant by this is hard to figure out. In any event, he wanted to soft-pedal his difficulties with infallibility. Shortly thereafter he took a further step and reported to Bishop Félix Dupanloup that he had merely presented other people's difficulties in order to draw out the discussion. And soon after that he informed the laity that, like the rest of his colleagues in the conciliar minority, he had at bottom only been concerned about the inexpedience of the definition. He dismissed all criticism of his position during the Council, claiming once again that he had never challenged the doctrine itself, only its opportuneness. A few years later the last reservation fell away. He now praised Pius IX as the prophet sent by God into the chaos of the world to separate light from darkness, day from night.

The temptation to "whitewash" the minority bishops after the fact and to stamp them as mere Inopportunists was widespread, since it was believed that this would enhance the credibility of the new dogma and the honor of the Church. The temptation was so great that Bishop Félix de Las Cases thought it necessary to put a codicil in his will expressly forbidding anyone to baptize him an Inopportunist in his grave, as had already happened to some of his colleagues.

No More Serious Misgivings?

The minority bishops at the Council had not been won over by the majority's arguments. After the definition passed, however, many of them began to send out pastoral letters crammed with evidence for the dogma from Scripture and tradition—evidence which the Infallibilists had presented a short time before. How to explain this *volte-face?*

At the Council in Rome Bishop Philipp Krementz had stated that history posed enormous problems for the new dogma, that the condemnation of Pope Honorius I by the Sixth Ecumen-

Philipp Krementz,
bishop of Ermland

ical Council made papal infallibility look extremely dubious. As late as August 7, 1870, he could write to Archbishop Johannes Simor, Primate of Hungary, "It is hard for me to reconcile what has been decided in Rome with my old theology and the facts of history." But that did not stop him, on December 11, 1870, from offering the proof from tradition in his pastoral letter. When he came to speak of the traditions of his own diocese of Ermland, he contradicted himself with particular crudity. At the Council he had insisted that, as the testimony of many bishops proved, in various dioceses in Germany, France, Bohemia, Hungary, Transylvania, and other countries the very term "papal infallibility" was completely unheard of. He could not conceal the fact that in his own diocese this doctrine had not been handed down either in catechesis or in preaching. It had long since disappeared from the schools of theology. But then, in a complete reversal, Krementz went to great pains in his pastoral letter to point up Ermland's unbroken Infallibilist tradition. He began his list of witnesses with Anselm, the first bishop of Ermland (1250), mentions Cardinal Stanislaus Hosius (1504–79), and came at last to the Jesuits, who had taught papal infallibility to the clergy of Ermland for two hundred years. Only at the beginning of the nineteenth century had this doctrine been eclipsed, but fundamentally the people of Ermland had always had a deep attachment to it.

Krementz was not the only one to go through this evolution. Others who did likewise included Archbishops and Bishops Gregor Scherr of Munich, Paul Melchers of Cologne, Michael Deinlein of Bamberg, Matthias Eberhard of Trier, Johann Baptist Karl Greith of St. Gall, Pancraz Dinkel of Augsburg, and Aimé Victor François Guilbert of Gap.

But it was the archbishop of Gran and Primate of Hungary, Johannes Simor, who made the most heroic belated endeavor to furnish a proof from tradition. In a pastoral letter issued in September 1871 he maintained that everyone in Hungary had always believed in papal infallibility. This was clearer than noonday light from the evidence he had produced. Obviously Simor

Johannes Simor, archbishop of Gran and Primate of Hungary

had quite forgotten what he had declared more than a year before in the great hall of the Council—that the Hungarian people knew nothing of papal infallibility, an assertion strongly supported by several of his fellow bishops from Hungary. In subsequent pastoral letters of December 18, 1871, and August 15, 1872, Simor likewise forgot all the other objections on principle he had previously voiced against the definition. At times he stood his old arguments right on their head. On May 20, 1870, when the Infallibilists cited the Second Council of Lyon as a point in their favor, Simor replied that only the Greek emperor, Michael Palaiologos, had made the so-called Greek confession of faith. The Greek bishops—even the ones still in union with Rome—had refused to accept it despite the insistent pleas of Pope Innocent IV. A year and a half later, however, in his pastoral letter of December 18, 1871, Simor could now report that the Greek bishops *had* accepted the confession of faith, had, in fact, signed it, and thereby recognized the infallibility of the pope. Rome knew how to appreciate such services: Simor was the first minority bishop to become a cardinal.

Perhaps such abrupt shifts in opinion were due simply to repression, as the case of Archbishop Michael Deinlein of Bamberg suggests. On September 8, 1870, he wrote to Archbishop Paul Melchers in Cologne that his studies in history still forbade him to endorse the dogma of infallibility. But only a few months later he was giving people the impression that his complete conviction "of the Vatican doctrine's solid foundation in Scripture and tradition" dated from as far back as July 1870.

Or was it the decision by the magisterium that led the council fathers to this brand-new evaluation of Scripture and tradition? Many bishops, including former members of the opposition, lead us to believe that this was so. They repeatedly affirm that when papal infallibility was defined, the highest authority simultaneously determined that this doctrine was contained in Scripture and tradition. "Since the Church has reached this solemn decision," Bishop Philipp Krementz wrote in his pastoral letter of November 8, 1870, "it is therefore certain and self-evident that her resolution is grounded in Holy Scripture and tradition, the two sources of Christ's teaching, which she interprets unerringly." Archbishop Gregor Scherr was even more ex-

Michael Deinlein,
archbishop of Bamberg

Gregor Scherr, archbishop
of Munich-Freising

plicit in his struggle with Döllinger, who had offered to let the controversy "be decided by the verdict of all the scientifically trained historians in Germany." Scherr replied that there was no longer any need for historical science to examine the question of whether the doctrine of infallibility was contained in tradition. This had been decided once and for all by the ecumenical council in the Vatican. The definition had also completely eliminated all historical objections, as Cardinal Joseph Othmar Rauscher and Bishops Johann Baptist Greith and Matthias Eberhard logically stressed.

From now on, anyone who refused to submit to the authority of the Church's magisterium would be slapped with the bishops' verdict: guilty of intellectual arrogance and scholarly conceit.

But even among the bishops there were a few who could not forget their former theological and historical difficulties, men like Peter Richard Kenrick, Ludwig Haynald, and Joseph Hefele. Archbishop Kenrick of St. Louis did, in fact, submit out of obedience, but in later years he would never teach the doctrine of papal infallibility nor justify it in terms of Scripture and tradition. He left it to others to demonstrate the compatibility of the doctrine with the facts of church history. As for Bishop Hefele, on April 20, 1871, he wrote to the former Minister of State, Baron Joseph von Linden, "I am still convinced that the proofs adduced for this dogma are not valid." He had confided to his friend Ignaz von Döllinger on September 14, 1870, "I cannot say 'no' to 'yes,' and vice versa . . . Let him who can acknowledge something as divinely revealed which is not true in itself, *non possum* [I cannot]."

*For the Sake
of the Church's
Authority and Unity*

By far the largest number of minority bishops submitted on the grounds than an ecumenical council had spoken—and so the controversy had been settled. Some French bishops explained their new position by noting that at the Council they had exercised their roles as judges of the faith. But now they were only simple members of the Catholic people, for whom the proper attitude was unquestioning belief. Obedience, humility, piety, and willingness to learn are other words mentioned as motives for submission.

But had not the bishops of the minority just recently questioned the freedom and ecumenicity of the Council? Yet once the definition passed, many of them wanted to let all that drop. In dealing with the laity, they made a great deal of the ecumenicity and binding force of the Vatican decrees. Some of them now explicitly disclaimed the need for unanimity in dogmatic decisions. The whole thing depended on which side the pope was on. Besides, the minority had waived its right to vote by boycotting the solemn final session. Those who were unwilling to accept such a distorted picture of the situation appealed to the fact that almost all the bishops of the minority eventually consented to the dogma. Although these erstwhile members of the opposition had otherwise shown a sharp eye for manipulation, in this case they were blind to all the pressure and coercion used to effect this tardy consensus.

The fear of having to carry on the resistance alone helped prod Cardinal Friedrich Schwarzenberg and Bishop Joseph Hefele into submission. "The position of a suspended and excommunicated bishop strikes me as something terrible," Hefele remarked to Ignaz von Döllinger on March 8, 1871. "I could hardly bear it."

But in Hefele's case it was another motive that turned the scale: fear of a schism, concern for the unity of the Church. He considered a schism a still worse misfortune than infallibility, as he wrote in a confidential letter to Bishop Joseph Fessler of St. Pölten on April 2, 1871. Caught between Scylla and Charybdis, he had preferred to sacrifice his intellect rather than encourage a schism. Hefele's opinion was shared by Bishop Charles Philippe Place of Marseille, who thought the supreme value of church unity warranted many sacrifices.

The authority of the Church and a concern for unity were thus the reasons motivating many bishops to submit. The issue of the truth of papal infallibility, which had played so large a role at the Council, faded out completely. But this gave rise to

Charles Philippe Place,
bishop of Marseille

the suspicion that the bishops' assent to the doctrine remained
purely external.

*Interpretation
as a Loophole*

In September 1870, when Cardinal Schwarzenberg's two
consultants wondered how the minority bishops might contest
the new dogma, they thought—as we have already seen—of the
"pathetic" loophole afforded by interpretation. Of course, what
they had in mind was an authentic declaration by the Council itself. But on September 20, 1870, Italian troops captured the
Eternal City and the pope postponed the Council indefinitely.
The bishops would now have to find the loophole by themselves.

As a matter of fact, many of them did just that. The process
began during the Council. The more inevitable the definition became, the more the bishops began to take thought for what
would come afterwards. Some of them explored the possibility

of giving the texts the sort of meaning they could live with. Thus, during the last phase of the Council, for example, Wilhelm Emmanuel Freiherr von Ketteler began to behave more amicably towards the decree. For on July 7 the definition of infallibility had been prefaced by a historical note which enumerated the various means employed by the popes in finding the truth. Ketteler saw in this the other side of the reciprocal obligation between the pope and the entire Church for which he had been pleading so vehemently. Others took comfort in the thought that the extreme Ultramontane demands had all fallen short.

After the definition had passed, the recourse to interpretation became a more pressing necessity. To begin with, many bishops tried to limit as much as possible the cases where papal infallibility applied, which would prevent conflicts with history from arising. Still more important, they felt, was the linking of papal infallibility to the Church as a whole. Although the Council had clearly defined that the pope was infallible in himself, without the concurrence of the Church, the anti-Infallibilists tried once more to bind the pope to the consensus of the Church by way of exegesis.

Joseph Hefele took to the way of interpretation with more vigor than anyone. Hefele made a critical norm out of the brief historical note that the popes had ascertained the faith of the Church through councils, synods, and so forth, before proceeding to *ex cathedra* decisions.

But Henri Maret is by far the clearest example of how tortuous the path of interpretation could be. After the definition, Maret found himself in a desperate situation. Should he accept the new dogma and sacrifice his former convictions? While Maret worried over this quandary, his friend Augustin David, bishop of St. Brieuc, advised him to accept the dogma out of obedience without believing in it. Maret himself preferred the idea of a mental reservation—to believe in the dogma, but only as *he* understood it. Yet in the final analysis he found that both approaches divided him against himself. "A sincere declaration would doubtlessly be better. But is it possible?" Obviously Maret thought not. In the end he found a sort of Columbus' egg solution to his dilemma. He decided that the Vatican definition

Augustin David, bishop
of St. Brieuc

of infallibility in no way ran counter to his own views. As he put
it, to his great satisfaction he found in the decrees exactly what
had to be found there.

What had Maret found after all? Taking Hefele's use of interpretation one step further, he believed he was justified in saying that the Council had not excluded the Church's concurrence,
both before and during a papal decision. On the contrary, each
of these modes of consent were necessary. If they were lacking,
the Church would have to supply a subsequent ratification. But
if this were the case, then the Vatican decree did not teach that
the pope was personally and absolutely infallible. In this manner, Maret saw his way clear to give the dogma his unconditional
assent. His friends repeatedly criticized his interpretation for
misconstruing the natural and explicit sense of the Vatican
decrees, but Maret would not waver.

Bishop Maret has had imitators down to this day. Along
with many others, theologians Heinrich Fries and Klaus Schatz
have argued that the First Vatican Council only rejected the necessity for ratification after the fact by the Church. Nowadays
such interpretive finesse seems perfectly suitable, but in his day

Maret and his secretaries did not dare publish any of their conclusions in any form for fear of sanctions from Rome. Maret should have been able to notice from other indications that all was not well with his compromise solution. Rome insisted, for example, that the dean of the Sorbonne disown his book on the Council and withdraw it from circulation.

We can see why the defeated opposition later opted for the strategy of explaining the dogma away. Bishop Pancraz Dinkel went so far as to claim that "the decree should really be considered a victory for the minority rather than for the majority." There was no trace of such a sentiment among the Infallibilists. Ignatius von Senestrey and his group viewed the formula passed by the Council as a triumph. According to Emmanuel d'Alzon, they were generally delighted with the (fourth) chapter on infallibility even before the final addition of language increasing the pope's power. Even the Ultramontane extremist William George Ward had no complaints. Few were as candid as Cardinal Friedrich Schwarzenberg, who wrote to his Viennese

Pankraz Dinkel, bishop
of Augsburg

colleague Joseph Othmar Rauscher on August 16, 1870, that the Council had simply condemned the minority viewpoint.

Rome Makes Concessions

How did the Roman Curia react to efforts by the opposition to soften the dogma and by the Infallibilists to harden it? Declarations of submission from the bishops were handled principally by the Congregation of the Inquisition and the Congregation for Extraordinary Church Affairs. In October 1870 Pius IX created a special commision within the Congregation of the Inquisition "for all matters concerning the Vatican ecumenical council and the current situation in Rome." All these Roman institutions showed a great deal of elasticity. Authors of both broad and narrow interpretations of infallibility got letters of recognition. Even Joseph Hefele received a vaguely worded testimonial. True, Hefele's exposition of the dogma was handed over to the authorities of the Inquisition, but they looked the other way. Secretary of State Cardinal Giacomo Antonelli repeatedly told the Bavarian ambassador, Count Karl von Tauffkirchen-Guttenburg that "the Curia agreed completely with the bishop of Rottenburg's explanation." But that was a mere diplomatic flourish. Nobody in Rome thought seriously of adopting Hefele's opinion.

What interested the Curia more than anything else was the actual submission. For this reason it generously overlooked reservations on the part of the Eastern bishops, and in troublesome but less important cases did not demand the publication of the Vatican decrees.

Even when six theologians from the University of Munich and, after them, Archbishop Ludwig Haynald argued that the binding power of the Vatican decrees was contingent upon the approval of the bishops, the Curia made some concessions to this position, although it judged it to be utterly untenable theologically. The main thing was that bishops and professors submitted and kept silent. This held true likewise for the theology professors of the University of Tübingen. Although everyone knew that they didn't believe in the new dogma, they were left in peace provided they kept quiet. This led Ignaz von Döllinger to

Ludwig Haynald, arch-
bishop of Kalocsa and
Bacs (Hungary)

remark to the Protestant theologian Adolf von Harnack that the
Tübingen people were only allowed to discuss tomfoolery in
their official journal.

Other professors, such as Eduard Herzog of Lucerne, the
man who later became an Old Catholic bishop, had rejected as
dishonorable the same offer of immunity in exchange for silence.

Submission Pro Forma?

In July 1870 two diplomatic observers at the Holy See, the
Spanish chargé d'affaires, José Fernández Ximenes, and the Italian agent, Imbro I. Tkalac, agreed that the bishops' approval of
infallibility would not be sincere, a mere political formality to
hold on to their episcopal chairs. The two men thought there was
no reason to expect a schism on account of the prevailing
religious indifference. Were they right? The earnest tone of
many of the declarations of submission belies the diplomats'

Cardinal Jacques Mathieu,
archbishop of Besançon

assessment. On the other hand, our analysis has shown how extraneous the motives for submission largely were. The bishops did not accept the Vatican decrees because they suddenly realized their truth but rather because of the Church's authority which validated them. Another extraneous motive was the less frequently voiced one of concern for church unity. Similarly, the attempts by various bishops to interpret their way around the dogma hardly suggest a deep inner commitment to it. Statements by the bishops themselves and reports from their intimates add to the suspicion that many of them never abandoned their reservations.

One of the first to submit was Cardinal Jacques Mathieu of Besançon. "I confess," he wrote to the pope on August 11, 1870, "that I consent, totally and completely, with my whole heart and soul to the dogmatic definitions made by His Holiness at the session of the Vatican Council on July 18." Pius IX was overjoyed. Any unprejudiced reader, in fact, would have assumed that the cardinal was indicating his unconditional consent to the decrees of the Council. But that was not the case. In various letters to his episcopal colleagues Mathieu confided that he had not given up the old minority position—both his honor and his conscience forbade his doing that. His understanding of the definition implied restrictions and proper limits, and only under those conditions had he made his submission.

Bishop Henri Maret also submitted on the same terms and with the same qualifications as Cardinal Mathieu. (He expressly mentioned this in a letter to Bishop Félix Dupanloup.) After pondering the matter for three months, he believed he had found a justification for interpreting the Vatican decrees to suit his own beliefs. Many of his colleagues could not go along with Maret in this. In making their submission, most of them were merely rendering an act of obedience to the pope, as Maret himself and his associates must have known.

The terms Mathieu employed for his submission reoccur in those of Bishops Georges Darboy, Augustin David, and Charles Theodore Colet. On September 21, 1870, Mathieu wrote to Cardinal Friedrich Schwarzenberg that the minority bishops from France were generally inclined to accept the decrees "simply as is" and not to meddle with the question of the obligations imposed by the fourth session. Evidently, a number of French bishops, probably including Charles Philippe Place and Félix Dupanloup, had reached an agreement on this point. There is also a good deal of evidence suggesting that, along with Mathieu and Maret, David, Darboy, Dupanloup, and Place did not, in their heart of hearts, concur with the dogma despite the fact that all of them submitted.

Mathieu's formula of submission even turned up in America. Archbishop Peter Richard Kenrick of St. Louis made use of it, although, according to several witnesses, he, too, did not really believe in infallibility. Lord Acton claimed that two English bishops, William Clifford of Clifton and Thomas Brown of Newport, gave only outward consent to the definition.

It is especially hard to believe that Bishop Joseph Hefele truly subscribed to the dogma. All his motives remained foreign to the matter in hand: concern over church unity; fear of a schism; the likelihood of excommunication if he resisted any further; the increasing restiveness among his clergy as well as the government of Württemberg. Hefele made the "sacrifice of the intellect," as he called it, and submitted. He informed his friends, however, that this didn't mean he directly accepted the Vatican decrees. And at no subsequent time did he clearly say that he was ever convinced of the truth of infallibility or of the arguments supporting it. Hefele made it very difficult for posterity to come any closer to knowing what he really thought. He burned his papers and tried to get his friends to return his confidential letters for the same purpose.

No less puzzling is the attitude of Bishop Joseph Georg Strossmayer. For years neither friend nor foe could move him to a declaration of submission. When Fr. Augustin Theiner and Strossmayer's Roman contact, Croatian Canon Nikolaus Vorsak, advised him to make a perfunctory profession of faith since Rome was dead set on it, Strossmayer rejected this request. "I'd rather die," he protested to Fr. Theiner on March 1, 1871, "than go against my conscience and my convictions. Better to be ex-

Joseph Georg Strossmayer, bishop of Diakovar (Croatia)

posed to every humiliation than to bend my knee to Baal, to arrogance incarnate."

But Strossmayer's resistance was visibly crumbling. "Rome will never see me again," he had written to his friend, Canon Franjo Rački, on June 6, 1870. But in 1871 Strossmayer was back in Rome again. In 1872 he condescended to publish the Vatican decrees in his diocesan newspaper *Glasnik*, though without commentary. In 1875 he was reconciled with Pius IX. "I am making peace with the pope out of love for my friends," he reported on January 16, 1875, to Rački. Canon Vorsak added, "The bishop owes it to the position he has in our nation—and my position, too, would become still more precarious." Strossmayer, however, did not formally consent to the definition until 1881, when he made a profession of sorts under the pontificate of Leo XIII. At the end of his life he swore he had only opposed the dogma as inopportune.

Neither Cardinal Friedrich Schwarzenberg of Prague nor Cardinal Joseph Othmar Rauscher of Vienna ever expressly declared their approval of infallibility. Their personal convictions remain a mystery. "Schwarzenberg did not believe in the new dogmas and never forced anyone else to. He complied in silence because he didn't have the strength to carry on open resistance after the other bishops had succumbed," noted Friedrich von Schulte, professor of canon law and a friend of the cardinal. There were others as well, such as Prince-bishop Heinrich Förster, whose verbal declarations of faith may not have jibed with their inner beliefs.

This "emigration inward" occurred everywhere, even within the Roman Curia. Although Cardinal Gustav Adolf von Hohenlohe repeatedly insisted that he had always believed in papal infallibility, he did not recognize the validity of the resolutions by the Vatican Council. But he avoided making public statements on the subject. Still more contradictory, despite his official submission, was the attitude of the Capuchin archbishop and preacher to the papal court, Luigi Puecher-Passavalli. In 1871 he sponsored various reformist theses calling for the rejection of infallibility and a solemn protest against the despotism of Rome. Such notions are not surprising, coming as they did from an archbishop who viewed the fetishist adoration of the Church's hierarchy (and especially of the pope) as the chief error of Ca-

Luigi Puecher-Passavalli,
Capuchin archbishop and
papal court preacher

tholicism, and who, as late as 1891, held the definition of infallibility to be a sacrilegious offense against the Holy Trinity. It had, he said, transformed the office of the supreme shepherd into a despotic sultanate of Mohammed and Christ's sheepfold into a herd of slaves.

But despite all this, not a single bishop held out to the end. All of them gave in—at least externally. To many this seemed an unforgivable weakness, a surrender of honor, a form of moral decay, indeed, an apostasy. On the Catholic side the bishops were praised as impressive witnesses of solid fidelity to the faith and the Church.

*Resistance from
the Professors,
or It Might Have
Turned Out Differently*

After the new dogma was proclaimed, and especially after the bishops' protests proved to be milder than expected, opposition from the professors slowly disintegrated. The declaration of the Fulda Bishops' Conference, so favorable to the Council, did more than its share of damage. Anti-Infallibilist theologians convening in Nuremberg on August 25, 1870, could only muster fourteen participants. All of them sharply rejected the Vatican decrees on the grounds that the Council was neither free nor ecumenical and had defined a doctrine which was not contained in tradition and which destroyed the God-given rights of the episcopacy.

Opposition from the bishops progressively weakened, and with it resistance from the professors collapsed. All the reasons invoked by the bishops for accepting the definition came into play once more. Many professors (e.g., from the Catholic theological faculty of the University of Tübingen) joined the inward emigration. Like a good number of others, they did not believe in infallibility, but neither did they speak out against it.

In contrast to the bishops, however, there were many professors who could not, and would not, be silent. In German-speaking countries alone, twenty professors of theology and clerical teachers of philosophy were excommunicated within a short time after the Council. Two thirds of all Catholic historians teaching at German universities left the Church. Five historians from Munich took this step. Other countries, too, saw theologians leaving the Church in protest against the dogma.

In presenting their objections, the professors shifted the emphasis from form to content. They focused not on the lack of freedom and ecumenicity but on the contradictions between the decrees and the facts of history, between dogma and historical science. The leading figures in this struggle were Professors Ignaz von Döllinger in Munich, Johann Friedrich Ritter von Schulte in Prague, and Joseph Langen and Franz Heinrich Reusch in Bonn. Archbishop Paul Melchers took Reusch to task for "thinking too much of science and too little of authority . . . You talk altogether too much about conviction." The bishops were not interested in conviction; they wanted obedience.

Not surprisingly, those who accepted infallibility tried to impute other motives to the professors' rebellion. They were accused of national conceit, scientific vanity, alienation from the Church, scholarly bias, individualism, and aristocratic hauteur. Above all, however, they were guilty of fighting a bugbear in-

Paul Melchers,
archbishop of Cologne

stead of coming to grips with the true doctrine of infallibility—
as though the bishops themselves had not struggled against the
dogma month after month at the Council.

The Pope's Official Historian

Even before the Council came to an end, the Infallibilists
were thinking of having someone write a history of the event to
meet their specifications. With this purpose in mind, Pius IX
summoned Canon Eugenio Cecconi from Florence to Rome in
June 1870. "Fr. Cecconi has arrived here from Florence," wrote
Archbishop Vincenzo Tizzani—one of the few men in the Curia
who were committed to the opposition—to Cardinal Friedrich
Schwarzenberg on February 1, 1871. "He has been given the
task of writing the history of the Vatican Council. So an official
history will be available. Many people suspect that Cecconi will
merely supply his name, while the Jesuits will do the writing. I
don't care what it's all about. I shall do my duty and write what
I heard when I took part in the Council. Readers will see

whether they should believe me or Cecconi or both of us."

Cecconi soon published four thick volumes on the Council, whereas Tizzani published nothing. During the Council Tizzani had gathered a good deal of material and had begun using it to sketch out a history of the Council, but it was never printed in his lifetime. The total victory of the other side made it look inadvisable. When Tizzani died in 1892, the Vatican bought all his manuscripts from his niece, the Countess Lucrezia Accursi Gazzoli. But though it promised her one hundred thousand lire, it only paid a fifth of that, which led to litigation. To this day Tizzani's papers have been kept under lock and key in the Vatican secret archives.

Tizzani was not the only minority bishop who planned to do a history of Vatican I. Bishop Étienne Émile Ramadié of Perpignan had similar ideas. "The bishop of Perpignan carefully records everything said and done at the Council," the French Sul-

Vincenzo Tizzani, titular archbishop and professor of church history at the papal university of Rome

pician, Fr. Henri Icard, noted in his diary on April 23, 1870. "He writes all the time and edits it when he gets back home." In June 1871 Ramadié, like Tizzani, thought the time was not ripe to publish a history of the conciliar minority based on his material. Events had not gone in their favor. In 1872 Ramadié betook himself once more to his notes. He remarked to Bishop Félix Dupanloup that they would be useful to the Church and that he would put them into final shape as soon as he had the time. But nothing ever came of it. Ramadié waited in vain for more favorable circumstances. Today even his notes have disappeared.

With Rome's encouragement, Cecconi, the official conciliar historian, was much more successful. Cecconi did have to agree to let Cardinal Luigi Bilio revise his four volumes, but, on the other hand, the office of the Secretary of State saw to it that they had a wide circulation. Not only did all the bishops receive copies of Cecconi's work, but the nuncios in Paris and Munich had to arrange for French and German translations.

As early as 1875 the process of compiling the official conciliar history had come to a standstill. Cecconi had been made archbishop of Florence. In 1893, after a hiatus of almost twenty years, Pope Leo XIII commissioned the Jesuit Theodor Granderath to do a full-scale presentation of the First Vatican Council. He granted him free access to all existing material in the Vatican archives. "All the documents are at your disposal," said the pope. "Not one has been withheld from you. Now set forth the course of events at the Council just as they actually happened." The records Granderath was allowed to inspect have remained shut to all other researchers for over seventy years. The Jesuit knew how to show his gratitude for this privilege: His picture of the Council followed the Infallibilist party line with complete fidelity. It set the standard in the Catholic world for treatments of the subject.

The plans of Bishops Maret, Ramadié, and Tizzani to present the Council from the standpoint of the defeated minority were never carried out for fear of sanctions from Rome. As a matter of fact, the Congregation of the Index put all the significant writings by the anti-Infallibilists—for example, the works of men like Johann Friedrich von Schulte, Lord Acton, Johann Friedrich, Joseph Hubert Reinkens, and Joseph Langen

—on the list of forbidden books. But Rome was still not satisfied. In a systematic campaign it called upon the Infallibilist bishops to combat "enemy" publications. On commission from Cardinal Bilio (and ultimately from the pope), Bishop Joseph Fessler polemicized against von Schulte, professor of canon law in Prague. To help him refute von Schulte's book more effectively, Fessler was released from the conciliar vow of silence. Bishop Ignatius von Senestrey of Regensburg and others were to take the field against Schulte's and Aemil Ruckgaber's writings on Honorius.

While on the one hand the Roman Curia cut off the flow of information to the outside, on the other it was interested in staying as *au courant* as possible. It had the nuncios send to Rome all pastoral letters and other episcopal statements concerning the Vatican decrees. Later it called in all other writings on the Council.

The curial suppression of unpleasant facts and opinions quickly made itself felt. Books on both the majority and minority

Joseph Fessler, bishop of
St. Pölten and secretary
of the Council

bishops often glossed over the facts. Documents dealing with the anti-Infallibilists left out "awkward" material. This occurred even in the Mansi collection of documents from Vatican I, as re-edited by Louis Petit and Jean Baptiste Martin. Distasteful items, such as a key letter of protest by Strossmayer or the dossier on Lecourtier's submission, were hushed up.

To this day no one has published a history of the First Vatican Council based upon the sources.

"All That Has to Be Burned . . . Has to Disappear . . ."

This repression also had telling effects on potential archival material. Thus, as previously mentioned, Bishop Joseph Hefele not only burned all his papers but asked his friends to return his letters so he could burn them too. All the papers of Cardinal Charles Philippe Place were also incinerated on order from Richard, his secretary. Archbishop Georges Darboy directed some of his documents to be burned during the siege of Paris. After he was arrested by the Commune, Darboy's sister carried on the job; a few pieces, however, were spared.[25a] In Hungary, Gustáv Jánosi, an episcopal secretary and Roman correspondent for the newspaper *Fövarosi Lapok,* consigned his two volumes of personal notes on the Council to the flames. Benedictine Archabbot Krizosztom Kruesz from Pannonhalma/St. Martinsberg likewise destroyed important private documents relating to the Council.

Bishop Joseph Alfred Foulon had a bout with fear when he read over his conciliar correspondence. "All that has to be burned," he wrote his friend Abbé Tapie on December 29, 1873, "with the exception of the first and perhaps the second letter. For my part, I shall see whether the same goes for the copy which you were kind enough to make. All that has to disappear. I am counting on the courage of your friendship to give you the strength which you, perhaps, will need. But I implore you, do it." Abbé Tapie calmed Foulon, promising to burn anything with the faintest resemblance to conciliar polemics. All compromising letters would disappear. Tapie did not burn much, but some

Joseph Alfred Foulon,
bishop of Nancy and Toul

things he must have destroyed. For example, the reply to Tapie's question as to whether it was true that the pope had had a vision of the Mother of God declaring him infallible is no longer to be found among Foulon's letters. The papers left by other minority bishops have either vanished or were heavily expurgated.

There was also some burning on the Infallibilist side. In the archives of the Jesuit Curia, for instance, all the letters from Germany for the period 1860–70 are missing. They were probably destroyed on purpose before the Italian troops entered Rome. In the same archive, it is impossible to get hold of the correspondence of Jesuit General Pierre Jean Beckx with *La Civiltà Cattolica* for precisely the years 1865–75. Again, in the archives of this Jesuit journal, which played a central role in the pope's conciliar policies, all documents concerning the activities of the Jesuits during the Council are missing. Most notably, the diary of *La Civiltà Cattolica* from 1860 to 1890 has vanished. It would have told us a great deal about the part played by the Jesuits at the Council. Before the Italian occupation of Rome on

September 16 and 17, 1870, officials of the papal police burned large portions of their secret archives. Such destruction of documentary material was already a tradition in papal Rome. In the years 1815–17 Vatican agents in Paris, with the approval of the Secretary of State, Cardinal Ercole Gonsalvi, had taken 4,158 volumes of trial documents belonging to the Roman Congregation of the Index—they had been carried off to the French capital by Napoleon I—made them illegible, and sold them off to dealers in old paper.

Ever since July 18, 1870, a stigma had been attached to the bishops of the minority, which greatly lessened any incentive to publish their papers. This attitude of negligent indifference almost brought about the total destruction of Bishop Maret's extremely important and well-organized documentation. Some sections had already been burned in Chartres, when the French historian Xavier de Montclos saved the rest. To date, the most important documents of the French minority have not been published. The papers of von Senestrey and Manning, the chief exponents of infallibility, remain inaccessible.

Worst of all, however, the Vatican still continues to practice its old restrictive archival policy. In December 1966 the Vatican secret archives opened up all materials touching on the pontificate of Pius IX to researchers. This included the archives of Vatican I. But before this wealth of manuscripts and records could really be looked into, the doors were shut once more. In a tedious effort that had consumed years, three employees of the Vatican secret archives had sorted through all the material down to the last box, completing all the necessary preparations for an exhaustive index. Then, at the end of 1969, Pope Paul VI announced plans for a critical edition of the conciliar documents. Publication would take a long while, but in the meantime an archival inventory might be published. Anyone familiar with the language of the Vatican could have predicted what happened. The inventory was not published and the promised edition of conciliar documents proved to be mostly a convenient excuse for continuing to withhold the archival material of Vatican I from researchers, and for preventing anyone from getting an overview of the documents on hand. The way in which Roman Prelate Francesco Dolinar has gone about implementing the papal announcement thus far makes one question the seriousness of the desire to produce a comprehensive critical edition. It has simply become harder to get at the documents.

Other portions of the archives dating back to the days of Pius IX have been tidied up for public use. Confidential material from the pope's personal papers, such as medical evidence concerning his epilepsy, has wandered off into an unnumbered box and thus become unobtainable.

The condition of the sources looks even more uncertain, when one recalls the oft ignored fact that two central organs of the Roman Curia—the Congregation for Extraordinary Church Affairs, which handled the most explosive questions, and the Congregation of the Faith, the successor to the Holy Inquisition —keep all their nineteenth-century archives closed. Since both of these "dicasteries" played such a vital role in the Council, especially in the story of the submissions made by the bishops, much is bound to remain shrouded in darkness for a long time to come.

8

Social and Religious Repercussions

*Can Papal Authority
Change Public Opinion?*

The Infallibilists exaggerated the significance of the new definition: They actually believed that by raising the pope's authority
to its upward limit they could gradually break society of its liberal and democratic habits. The Council, in the view of Archbishop Victor Dechamps, was to be "the rainbow after the
Flood." Bishop Félix Dupanloup outlined his opponents' position
this way: "The great evil of our day is that the principle of authority lies prostrate. Let us strengthen it in the Church and we
shall save society." On May 25, 1870, the Ultramontane newspaper *Unità Cattolica* wrote, "The infallible pope must counteract and cure the prevailing abuses of unbridled freedom of the
press, thanks to which journalists daily spread lies and calumny.
Every day the pope can teach, condemn, and define dogma—
and Catholics will never be permitted to question his decisions."

At first the Infallibilists complacently entertained the hope
that their goal was achieved. Bishop Claude Plantier said they
had succeeded in bringing about the apotheosis of authority.
This was for him the most important result of the Council. The
Roman pontiff's new authority, it was hoped, would also benefit

the Papal States. But only two months after the definition of infallibility such expectations were cruelly disappointed. The day after the Council ended the Franco-Prussian War broke out. Shortly thereafter the last French troops left the papal harbor of Civitavecchia and the Italian Government in Florence was finally free to settle the problem of Rome. On September 20, 1870, the forces of a newly united Italy, under General Raffaele Cadorna, stormed the Porta Pia. To the very end Pius IX had thought it impossible that the Piedmontese would ever tread upon Roman soil. As in other matters, here, too, the pope believed, in his mystical extravagance, that he had been granted a special divine illumination: There is no other way of explaining the imperturbable confidence of his statements during those last days. Full of inner contentment, he could even find the time to work out a rebus which was quite popular then. But finally he or-

The breach in the walls of Rome at the Porta Pia on September 20, 1870

dered his general, Hermann Kanzler, to put up a token resistance—which nevertheless caused seventy human lives to be sacrificed to *raison d'état*. (During fighting at the city walls, forty-nine soldiers were killed on the Italian side, while twenty died on the papal side.) But this symbolic protest against violent and unjustified Italian aggression could not prevent the loss of Rome once and for all. The situation was not without a certain irony: The dogma of infallibility, which was supposed to prop up the secular power of the pope, only hastened the process of its disintegration. The new doctrine irritated the governments of Europe and made them apprehensive of church interference in their affairs. Neither France nor Austria nor Germany displayed any willingness to lift a finger to win back his lost territories for the pope. The whole episode reveals how completely the Infallibilists had lost their sense of political reality.

The capture of Rome would not be their only disappointment. In many countries where relations between Church and State were already strained, the definitions of Vatican I led

Hermann Kanzler, general of
the papal army

to a crisis situation. A few weeks after the Council ended, Austria abrogated the concordat it had signed with the Holy See in 1855 on the grounds that the new dogmas had altered the nature of the other party to the contract.

In Germany the Vatican decrees triggered the Kulturkampf, most notably in the provinces of Prussia, Hessen, and Baden. At the root of this conflict lay the tension, which had been building up for decades, between modern liberal society and the reactionary impulses of Catholicism. After the Council, more than ever before Bismarck and the National Liberals came to look upon the Catholic Center Party as the focal point of the *grossdeutsch* opposition, hostile to Prussia and the new *kleindeutsch* Empire. Hence, in the years from 1871 to 1875 the Prussian state tried to restructure its relationship with the Church through a series of laws (the "Pulpit Article," prohibition of the Jesuit Order, state supervision of all schools, legal conditions governing the appointment of Catholic clergy, introduction of obligatory civil ceremonies for marriage), and to subject the Church to strict regimentation. These hostile measures backfired: The Catholic Center Party grew stronger. After the death of Pius IX, the new pope, Leo XIII, worked out a step-by-step reconciliation between the Vatican and Germany. In Switzerland, too, the Council exacerbated Church-State troubles, especially in the cantons of Solothurn, Bern, Basel, and Geneva. Some Swiss bishops and priests were forced to leave the country.

Closely bound up with the Kulturkampf was the creation of the Old Catholic Church. Many Catholics, including a particularly large number of professors of theology and history, could not, in conscience, accept the new dogma. They wanted to hold on to their old Catholic faith—hence their name. But the bishops insisted that they recognize the new dogma, and the schism that people had feared at last took place. In Germany, Austria, and Switzerland various communities were founded (with some encouragement from the government) independently of Rome. In the years after the Council they grew to about two hundred thousand members. But the movement never caught on. Today Old Catholic churches in German-speaking countries number about one hundred thousand believers.

In France the Vatican decrees deepened the alienation between Church and Society. The tension became so great that in 1906 Church and State were permanently separated. One of the crucial factors in this development was the Dreyfus affair. In 1894 Alfred Dreyfus, a French officer of Jewish extraction, was condemned for treason on the strength of forged documents and was sent to Devil's Island. The discovery of this scandal rallied the Left, which viewed the Catholic Church as the mainstay of the nationalistic Right. As early as 1870 the French bishops belonging to the conciliar opposition had feared that the Vatican definitions might provoke the separation of Church and State.

This did not occur in Italy, but Catholics there excluded themselves from political life. Mortally offended by the loss of the Papal States, the papacy boycotted the newly unified state of Italy and with its *Non expedit* forbade Catholics to vote or run for office. Pius IX even refused to take note of the laws passed by the Italian Parliament, which recognized him as a secular monarch and guaranteed all his rights. He wanted no partnership with Italy. The dogma of infallibility eased the ghetto existence of Italian Catholics by reinforcing their feelings of self-sufficiency. Such political abstinence, which lasted for decades, would prove dangerous to democracy in Italy, as the trials it faced after World War I showed only too clearly.

The Church might have dealt differently with the movement for Italian unity. This was demonstrated by such cardinals as Girolamo Marchese d'Andrea and Vincenzo Santucci,[26] by bishops, theologians, and laymen who had long felt that the Papal States were an anachronism. And the Roman populace left no doubt as to the enormous hatred and resentment it had stored up towards the papacy, when the body of Pius IX was taken from St. Peter's to the Church of San Lorenzo fuori le mura on the night of July 13, 1881. "The pope's coffin was raised," writes Catholic historian Joseph Schmidlin, "verified, covered with a rich pall, and transported, in a four-in-hand funeral coach built just for the occasion, from St. Peter's over the Bridge of Sant'Angelo through the city to the Campo Verano. Four carriages for prelates from the papal court went along in the procession, followed by two hundred for the members of Roman society. The houses along both sides of the route were illuminated, and people threw flowers down onto the casket. But

A vision of the reconciliation between Pius IX and the king of Italy, Victor Emmanuel II

at St. Peter's mobs had already gathered, crying out, 'Viva l'Italia! Morte al Papa! Morte ai Preti! Al fiume il Porco! Al Tevere la carogna!' [Long live Italy! Death to the Pope! Death to the Priests! Throw the pig in the river! Throw the beast in the Tiber!]. All along the way crowds insulted the participants and showered them with stones. They had, in fact, every intention of hurling the corpse into the river. Six of the demonstrators were penalized for 'disturbing a religious function,' but otherwise the police let them have their way. So much so that Leo XIII, in his allocution of August 4, and the Secretary of State, in a note dated July 13, rightly protested to the government against this outrage to the former pope and to the papal dignity."[27]

Pius IX would not have been the first pope thrown into the Tiber by the Roman people. In the year 897 Pope Stephen VI (896–97) had the corpse of Formosus (891–96), his predecessor on the Chair of St. Peter, removed from the grave, set up in the hall of the synod, and solemnly condemned. "The papal garments were ripped off the mummy, the three fingers of the right hand (with which the Latins give the blessing) were cut off, and with a barbaric shout the people dragged the dead man out of the hall, pulled him through the streets, and plunged him into the Tiber amid the press of the howling rabble."[28]

And so the golden age of a society living in accordance with the old order, which so many Infallibilists had hoped to see, never dawned at all. The attempt to change the course of history failed right down the line. Papal infallibility, once thought of as a cure for the ills of the age, instead promoted the advance of an ever more widespread secularism.

Better Success
Within the Church

But weren't the anti-Infallibilists also guilty of gross exaggeration when they had called the new dogma a catastrophe for the Church? They had believed that the Church would lose its credibility on account of this definition, which had no basis in either Scripture or tradition. Beyond that, they had feared that the extraordinary increase in papal power would downgrade the bishops to mere lackeys of Rome, thereby upsetting the divinely willed order of the Church. Did these fears come true?

As a matter of fact, the First Vatican Council came as a shock to Catholics who were anxious to harmonize science and faith. The resistance to infallibility on the part of so many pro-

The pope's worldly empire is laid to rest

fessors, particularly in Germany, is an eloquent example of this. How could the new dogmas accord with the findings of historical research? It was no accident that Catholic historians suffered through the greatest crisis of conscience over the definition, or that a substantial number of them turned their backs on the Church.

The Council's disregard for history was pregnant with consequences. The Church not only missed its chance for a rapprochement with the scientific scholarship of the day but began more and more to look like an obstacle to cultural evolution and an enemy of the unprejudiced search for truth.

It is hard to deny the justice of such complaints—the way the dogma came to be defined would be proof enough. But the anti-Infallibilists had a still more pointed objection: The dogma of infallibility was not just one more doctrine among others. It took a comprehensive position on the issue of truth. It involved a very broad claim, namely, that the pope could pronounce on questions of faith and morals with guaranteed certainty. The truth was no longer to be brought to light by laborious research and investigation but by the determination of an infallible authority.

Naturally, these implications were not clearly perceived at first. The Curia pressed forward its efforts at centralization with a gentle hand. The first item on the agenda was simply to get everyone to accept the new dogma, to win over the many members of the opposition who had spoken out explicitly at the Council and who later continued to resist in silence.

Modernism:
Trying to Break Out
of the Ghetto

On December 8, 1864, in his encyclical *Quanta cura,* Pius IX had listed eighty contemporary errors and condemned them. The document culminated in the anathema laid upon the thesis that the pope had to reconcile himself to progress, liberalism, and modern culture. This catalog of modern errors, the famous (or notorious) *Syllabus,* was taken to be the opening battle of the Church's war against the *Zeitgeist* and created serious difficulties for many Catholics. For in this same encyclical the pope also denounced "the proponents of freedom of conscience and freedom of religion," as well as "all those who assert that the Church may not use force." In an encyclical letter dated August 15, 1854, Pio Nono had already declared, "The absurd and erroneous teachings, or rather twaddle, presented in defense of freedom of conscience are an extraordinarily pernicious mistake —a plague which the state must fear above all others."

Unlike the pope, many other people were interested in making peace between Catholicism and modernity. But if such attempts faltered before Vatican I, they collapsed afterwards when the Council resulted in a total victory for the Ultramontanes.

In any case, the problems caused by infallibility were only covered up, not solved. That would become evident by the time of Leo XIII. Pope Gioachino Pecci, in contrast to his predecessor, was bent on compromise—up to a point—with modern culture. Thus, along with his social encyclicals (above all *Rerum novarum,* promulgated on May 15, 1891) he also worked for a revival of philosophy and theology without, of course, wishing to disturb the existing structure of doctrine. Rather, in his letter of instruction *Aeterni Patris* he proposed Thomas Aquinas (ca. 1225–74), the greatest Western Doctor of the Church, as its intellectual model. The question of history and the scientific study of history, however, was not even mentioned. For Leo XIII there was simply no problem here. In 1881 he made the resources of the Vatican archives available for general use. "Non abbiamo paura della pubblicità dei documenti" (We are not afraid of the documents' being published), he declared in 1884 to a group of historians in Rome.[29] Leo XIII was convinced that the sources, provided they were studied without prejudice, would always support the papacy.[30] But the pope underestimated the range and significance of historical research. It was precisely the application of modern historical methods to the Bible and early Christianity which, by the end of Leo's pontificate, increasingly threatened to rock the doctrinal edifice of the Catholic Church.[31]

Some Catholics, such as the Dominican exegete Albert Marie Joseph Lagrange and the historian Louis Duchesne, also made important contributions to this field. The French theologian Alfred Loisy, in his noted book *L'Évangile et l'Église (The Gospel and the Church)* from the year 1902 was merely airing a general feeling of discontent when he asked how the Church's dogmas could still be justified in the light of the findings of modern research. By now it had become obvious to many people that there was no direct path from Jesus to the Church. "Jesus proclaimed the coming of the Kingdom," Loisy observed, "but what came was the Church." And yet the Church still remained oriented to the messianic vision of salvation. It had, as it were, institutionalized the expectation for the Kingdom of God. On the basis of this situation, Loisy—called by many "the father of modernism"—tried to explain the rise of dogmas. He understood them as an adaptation to the variable conditions of time and place. Since the Church was compelled to establish itself—when the end of the world did not occur—it had fashioned for itself a doctrinal system (dogmas), hierarchical institutions, and sacramental rites. Building on such historical facts, and drawing upon contemporary philosophical trends, Loisy saw the essence of Christianity not in some solid core but in the process of becoming. This approach left room for new developments: The Church's dogmas would merely reflect the point in its evolution where it found itself. But this also meant that any substantial change in the scientific view of the world might necessitate a "new interpretation of the old formulas," especially since "dogmas are not truths dropped down from heaven" but only symbols of the divine truths. Loisy hoped such considerations might point the way for the Church to deal with dogmas which, in his eyes, had become untenable owing to historical scholarship. He was thinking, among other things, of such doctrinal items as the founding of the Church by Jesus, the Virgin birth, and Jesus' divine sonship.

A number of Catholics appreciated Loisy's concerns and the merits of his work; they believed they had found in him a sheet anchor to save them from rationalist criticism. "He is a true Noah, and the Church will be glad to have his ark," wrote the French theologian Henri Bremond, speaking of Loisy, in a letter (May 23, 1904) to Maurice Blondel.[32] But the majority of Catholic theologians, particularly the representatives of the magisterium, were soon branding Loisy's writings as damnable heresy. They were unwilling to allow historical criticism so wide a scope. In fact, the task of historical research as Loisy saw it was to furnish the essential building blocks for a kind of Christianity which could make sense in today's world without recourse to the Church's teaching authority.

The leading English theologian, George Tyrell, cast the conflict between scientific criticism and the magisterium into still sharper relief. In his book *The Church and the Future* (1903) he attacked the Roman Curia as a system of concentrated despotic authority. The Church, he thought, had no business being an official Institute of Truth. It simply ought to translate the inspirations wrought in the hearts of the faithful by the divine life into certain formulas, which would always be provisional.

From these few examples it becomes obvious that the main point at issue in the highly complex modernist movement was the relationship of science, above all the science of history, to the Church's magisterium. Do science and its representatives enjoy autonomy even within the Church or must they remain forever subordinate to the magisterium? And what should be done in case of conflict? Who and what decides when science has come up with unequivocal results which contradict the doctrine or decisions of the Church?

The reader is by now familiar with these questions. They had already been raised at the First Vatican Council during the debate on infallibility. At that time the controversy was settled in an authoritarian manner: The magisterium had its way. And now, a generation later, the situation was not about to change. Leo XIII, who was more inclined to a conciliatory stance, had exercised restraint, but the same could not be said of his successor, Pius X. Even before his election as pope, Giuseppe Sarto had been extremely disturbed over the sorts of theological discussions going on then, especially in France. This was not surprising for a pope who, in 1899, had extolled the dogma of Mary's Immaculate Conception, the First Vatican Council, papal infallibility, and the miracles of Lourdes and Pompeii as the "greatest events of the nineteenth century."[33] In the very first months of his pontificate, Pius X had the major works of Loisy put on the Index. In 1904 he issued warnings in two encyclicals against innovators who were calling into question the history of early Christianity with a grand display of learning. In the years that followed, the papal admonitions took on a harsher tone, and the Vatican began to make visitations of seminaries and schools of theology. The Curia went after various professors it suspected of modernist errors and had them dismissed.

In 1907 the storm burst with full force. On July 17, after issuing a few more denunciations and warnings, the pope bade the Holy Office (later called the Congregation of the Faith) publish a decree condemning sixty-five theses. This new *Syllabus* dealt with most of the doctrinal issues facing the Church. Its chief target, however, was the erroneous teachings which curtailed the authority of the Church and, above all, the papal magisterium, and which cast doubts on the historical value of Holy Scripture and of certain dogmas. On September 8 of the same year the encyclical *Pascendi gregis* was published, in which Pius X banned the whole modernist movement. According

Pius X

to the pope's diagnosis, the root cause of all these errors was the philosophy of immanence and its view that religious truths merely grew up in response to human needs. Dogmas, it claimed, were just the expression of a subjective state of consciousness—with no "objective correlative" in reality.

Just as revealing as the pope's analysis of modernism was the series of practical measures he introduced to protect believers from the poison of this new heresy. He called for the supervision of all professors in church-run institutions and the dismissal of anyone who taught new theories. Candidates for the priesthood had to be chosen with scrupulous care. All those who showed signs of intellectual pride were to be turned down. Attendance at state universities was, for all practical purposes, forbidden, and censorship of all writings published under church auspices was intensified. Congresses of the lower clergy were no longer to hold meetings. Finally, the pope ordered the creation of a special commission for each diocese to investigate modernist errors and make periodical reports to Rome.

Three years later, in 1910, Pius X decreed in *Sacrorum*

antistitum—a *motu proprio* (an ordinance laid down "on his own initiative")—that everyone who preached or taught in an official capacity had to take a special oath abjuring all the errors of modernism. He further declared a general prohibition against the reading of newspapers by all seminarians and theological students, specifically adding that this rule also applied to the very best journals.

There was one area of theology which Rome felt was in need of particularly sharp surveillance: biblical scholarship. From 1906 to 1915 the papal commission on the Bible issued yearly decrees aimed at immunizing Catholics against higher criticism. By defending positions which had long since become outdated, it forced many exegetes into a conflict with their consciences. Others lost their teaching posts and consequently their only means of support.

All these precautionary arrangements can only be understood as an attempt to set up an impregnable shield against scientific research and scholarly criticism. Exchanging opinions with the modern world struck the Vatican not only as superfluous but dangerous and harmful as well. This constrictingly defensive attitude was not limited to theology. It affected other cultural realms, such as philosophy and literature, denying them even relative independence.

The Spy Ring of
Monsignore
Umberto Benigni

These papal condemnations and disciplinary regulations, however, do not tell the whole story of the battle against modernism. All modernists did not submit. Some left the Church while others took refuge in anonymity and continued to publish their thoughts in hopes of reforming the Church from within. For this reason, the Roman Curia lived for years on end in an atmosphere of panic. It believed there was a conspiracy operating inside the Church against the foundations of Christian faith. It is only too easy to see why, in his morbid anxiety over heresy, Pius X welcomed the help of the "integral Catholics," who had proclaimed themselves the authorized defenders of the faith.

These new guardians of religion called themselves integral Catholics because they wished to affirm "the integrity of their Romanism," that is, their complete "Roman Catholicism (doctrine and practice) and nothing else."[34] They were prepared to put orders from the pope, even concerning altogether mundane affairs, ahead of everything and everyone.[35] In this spirit, the integrists, as their enemies dubbed them, began hunting for heretics. Their goal was to wipe out heresy root and branch. They also kept an eye out for the more subtle forms of deviation from Roman orthodoxy. In fact, they wound up discovering symptoms of spiritual disease in all the more important theologians of the day: There was scarcely one who was not suspect. Even cardinals and bishops were not spared. A full-scale campaign of denunciation was launched, ultimately poisoning the whole atmosphere of the Church.

The center of the integralist conspiracy was the Italian prelate Umberto Benigni, "a fat little man with a wary expression, perpetually on the go." He had founded a secret society called the Sodalitium Pianum to combat cryptomodernism in all its forms. The task of its members was to scrutinize all statements of opinion by Catholic laymen and clergy—up to and including bishops and cardinals—and to forward all information and accusations to Rome. A member of the Sodalitium Pianum, according to its program, was supposed to be "'papalist,' 'clericalist,' antimodernist, antiliberal, antisectarian, fully counterrevolutionary, an enemy not merely of the Jacobin revolution and sectarian radicalism but also of religious and social liberalism."[36] Integral Catholics were to fight for the principles of authority, tradition, and order and against liberalism, egalitarianism, interconfessionalism, and neutral syndicalism.[37]

Benigni had been undersecretary for one of the most important curial congregations (the one for Extraordinary Church Affairs) since 1906, and his organization could count on the full support of the pope. Pius X never let up in his encouragement of Benigni. "We exhort in the Lord," Pope Giuseppe Sarto wrote on July 8, 1912, "our beloved sons and daughters of the Sodalitium Pianum, who have deserved so well of the Catholic cause, to go on fighting the good fight for God's Church and the Holy See

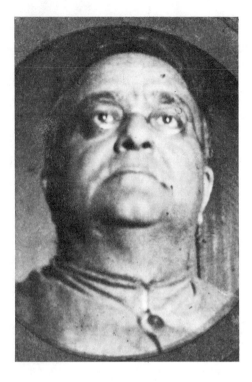

Umberto Benigni,
prelate (ca. 1930)

against their enemies, both without and within."[38] Every year
Benigni received a subsidy of one thousand lire[39] from the pope
—about five thousand dollars in today's money.

Thus, Pius X not only helped to pay for a system of informers and accusers, he also gave his blessing to covert
methods, including espionage. Since the faith of the Church was
threatened, all such means seemed justified. "Pius X," Cardinal
Pietro Gasparri noted for the record at the pope's canonization
proceedings, "approved, blessed, and encouraged a secret organization of spies inside and outside the hierarchy. This organization," Gasparri continued, "spied on members of the hierarchy,
even cardinals. In so doing, the pope was, in essence, approving,
blessing, and encouraging a sort of Freemason lodge in the
Church, something unheard of in the history of the Church. I
am not the only one who felt that this was a grave matter. Cardinal Mercier (he was on the list of suspected persons who were
to be kept under surveillance) thought so too . . . Not only did

Pius X approve, bless, and encourage the Sodalitium Pianum, but the denunciations emanating from it also reveal some disturbing attitudes on the part of Pius X in his administration of the Church, although the Holy Father was doubtless acting in good faith in all this."[40]

Benigni succeeded in building up a network of collaborators that stretched all across Europe, and in founding periodicals to serve the group's ends in all the more important countries. The full-fledged members couldn't have numbered more than one hundred, but there were many more sympathizers. The headquarters in Rome carried on correspondence (often in cipher) with the outposts, and most persons were only mentioned by their aliases. Benigni himself signed with twelve different pseudonyms, such as Charles, Arles, Charlotte, Lotte, Kent, Jerome, Ringer, Amie O., among others. Every day the Sodalitium Pianum sent out detailed confidential reports (i.e., denunciations) to the Roman dicasteries.[41] The identity of the members and their activities were shrouded in deep secrecy. Only the pope and Cardinal Gaetano De Lai from the Congregation of the Consistory had the right to be informed about them.

Once you had been denounced to Rome, it was hard to avoid an official condemnation, which might mean being forbidden to teach and write, the loss of one's teaching post, suspension from church functions, and so forth. There was no possibility of speaking in one's own defense. Unless the accused found a high-ranking advocate in the hierarchy, he had little hope. The pope was often ready to take extreme measures. He came within an inch of removing the entire theological faculty in Freiburg (Switzerland).

The Sodalitium Pianum did not suspend its activities until 1921. During World War I, papers carried by an important member of the Benigni organization, the Belgian lawyer Alphonse Jonckx, were seized by the Germans and later made public. They incriminated Benigni so badly that his group could no longer justify its existence. But the busy prelate did not stop fighting for the cause. In the 1920s he played an active part in the Fascist regime. He became an informant for Mussolini's private secretary and a spy for the Italian Fascist Political Police (OVRA), the equivalent of the Nazi Gestapo.[42]

The secret practices of someone like Umberto Benigni and

his people show—even more clearly than the official measures decreed by the pope—how incapable the Curia was of coping rationally with this conflict in the early years of the century. The anxiety over heresy led to a pattern of hectic, almost compulsive, behavior, of readiness to use every means, fair or foul. In the defensive campaign against modernism, ecclesiastical society displayed clear signs of neurosis. Had not the intransigent party triumphed at the Vatican Council, this condition would never have become as extreme as it did.

*A New Code
of Canon Law:
The Vatican Dogmas
Become Legal Principles*

At Vatican I many of the participants expressed the desire to create a uniform code of canon law for the whole Church. In the existing private digests, applicable law was mixed in with long obsolete regulations, a fact which made it extremely difficult to get one's bearings. Still, it was not until decades later, specifically, on March 18, 1904, that Pius X announced his plan to set about this task.

Vatican I had oriented the Church towards Rome in a strictly centralized fashion. That made it possible to find a centralizing solution to the problem of getting the Church its first unified legal code. In principle, the pope no longer needed to consult with the bishops on any of this. He did have the first preliminary sketches sent out to them for comments, but there was no joint consultation or discussion. "The work of codification went on in strict silence," writes canon lawyer Klaus Mörsdorf.[43] The pope named all the members of the commission. The entire operation, from beginning to end, was directed by Pietro Gasparri, professor of canon law and (from 1914) Cardinal Secretary of State. The new code was promulgated on Pentecost (1917) and went into effect on the same feast day the following year. It made the Church function more smoothly, but, on the other hand, it further tightened the constricting framework of its central government.

The dogmas of the pope's infallibility and his universal jurisdiction, which had gotten through the Council only with difficulty, now became legal principles. There were no more protests from the bishops. It all sounded quite self-evident when people said, for example, that it was the pope's exclusive prerogative to call an ecumenical council, to lead it, to announce its agenda, and to confirm its decisions; or when the power to permit the convening of plenary synods, to direct them through legates, and to review their resolutions was ascribed to the pope alone; or when the pope was presented as the supreme legislative power, with the authority to appoint laws for the Church as a whole and all its parts, to confer privileges, and to grant dispensations and special favors. The impression arose that things had always been this way: The minority's protests and the Curia's harsh coercion in former days were now forgotten.

"Judged in the light of history and of its own presiding spirit," remarked Ulrich Stutz, the historian of canon law from Berlin, "the code is the work of papal absolutism. In it we find a thoroughly papal, thoroughly Vatican kind of church law, both in form and content."[44] He went on to criticize the new code "as the handiwork of primatial authority raised by the Vatican to its highest power."[45] Such assessments, which can hardly be challenged, would suffice by themselves to refute people who try to explain away infallibility by arguing that the dogmas of Vatican I have de facto had almost no practical consequences.

Coming to Terms
with the State

With Pope Benedict XV the antimodernist campaign subsided. Resistance to the grotesque heresy hunt had gradually become too strong even within curial circles. Besides, in the meantime the Church had found other things to worry about. World War I had shaken the fabric of society in various European countries. Totalitarian governments came to power. From the first, the Church had always unambiguously rejected liberalism, and now it adopted a characteristically wavering stance towards totalitarianism. Attempts at close cooperation and broad com-

promise alternated with opposition on specific issues. Both in
Italy and in Germany the Curia took the opportunity to secure
from a dictatorial regime what seemed impossible under parliamentary government, namely, a concordat. Thanks to the cooperation of Benito Mussolini, the Lateran treaties were signed in
Italy in the year 1929, leading to the formation of Vatican City.
In 1933, six months after he came to power, Adolf Hitler concluded the Reichskonkordat with the Holy See. In both cases
Rome was willing to sacrifice Catholic political parties (Partito
Popolare Italiano, Central) whose relative independence had all
too often been a source of awkwardness. On each occasion the
cost of the agreement was a critical weakening of Catholic resistance to totalitarian ideologies.[46] "The 'authoritarian state,'"
noted Ludwig Kaas, the president of the Central Party, "necessarily understood the basic principles of the authoritarian church
better than others had."[47] And Cardinal Michael Faulhaber
wrote to Hitler on July 23, 1933, "What the old parliaments and
parties failed to achieve in sixty years your broad statesman's vision has made a reality of world history in six months. This
handclasp with the papacy, the greatest moral force in the history of the world, signifies a mighty deed full of immense blessing and an increase in German prestige East and West, in the
sight of the entire world."[48]

The Church found fascism compatible in that it was antidemocratic, antiliberal, antisocialist, anticommunist, and an-
tisecular. The Church's sharply defined authoritarian ideal, especially potent after Vatican I, had an affinity with the totalitarian
concept of the Leader. In both cases, power ran exclusively from
top to bottom, responsibility from bottom to top. Order came
before freedom.[49] All this could only encourage the authoritarian
character, which admires authority and submits to it, but at the
same time insists on its own authority and wishes to subject
others to it. "The strong emphasis on authority in the new government," wrote the Catholic theologian Michael Schmaus in
1933, "is something essentially familiar to Catholics. It is the
counterpart, on the natural level, to the Church's authority in the
supernatural sphere. 'Nowhere is the value and meaning of authority so conspicuous as in our holy Catholic Church.' One
need not begin by pointing out the authoritarian nature of the

Church's leadership. One can state it conversely: Today's reawakened feeling for strict authority heightens appreciation for the authority of the Church."[50] And Joseph Lortz, a Catholic professor of church history, never tired of speaking of "the *fundamental kinship* between National Socialism and Catholicism, a kinship which runs amazingly deep, in the face of which we sense, to our shame, how shortsighted we were only yesterday."[51] Lortz saw Catholicism and National Socialism making common cause against bolshevism, liberalism, and relativism. Liberalism, above all, was "the deadly disease of our time" and the "chief enemy of the Church's labors."[52]

Many Catholics, including those in the highest ranks of the hierarchy, agreed with Lortz. "The Catholics who looked upon their faith as a 'total religion,'" writes Kurt Sontheimer, "were more readily attracted to the idea of a total state than to the concept of pluralism. Their respect for the authority of the Church and its leaders—insofar as these leaders recognized the new civil authority—was easily transferred to the authoritarian government. Antidemocratic thinking, which had intellectually outmaneuvered the already weak ideological bastion manned by the liberal democrats of Weimar, was not, to be sure, the sum total of political Catholicism. But it found many adherents among Catholics who felt they had to overcome the parliamentary regime at practically any cost."[53]

Some Catholics even saw a direct line leading from the dogma of infallibility to the führer. In 1933 Robert Grosche, a well-known prelate from Cologne, wrote in *Die Schildgenossen* (a journal edited by Romano Guardini), "When papal infallibility was defined in the year 1870, the Church was anticipating on a higher level the historical decision which has now been made on the political level: a decision for authority and against discussion, for the pope and against the sovereignty of the Council, for the führer and against the Parliament."[54]

This intensification of the principle of authority—which, in some European countries, degenerated into a dictatorship shackling the mind as well as the body—had its counterpart in the Church: the oppressive bureaucratic machine, still operating at full blast, with its visitations and censorship, its Index and antimodernist oath. The whole atmosphere of the period was so

February 11, 1929. Benito Mussolini puts his signature to the treaties of the Lateran. At left, Msgr. Borgongini Duca

unfavorable to scholarship and the critical spirit that the papal magisterium had to intervene only in exceptional cases. Unrest did not break out again among theologians until after World War II. Then it was primarily the French exponents of the *nouvelle théologie* (new theology) who seemed to be assaulting

Italian chaplains give the Fascist salute while parading past the Quirinal Palace (the king's residence) in Rome

the traditional dogmatic system. Leaders of this movement included such men as Marie Dominique Chenu, Yves M. J. Congar, Henri de Lubac, Teilhard de Chardin and, in the German-speaking world, Otto Karrer and Karl Rahner. They were later joined by two Dutchmen, Edward Schillebeeckx and Piet Schoonenberg. All of them got into trouble with Church authorities. On orders from Pius XII, the Holy Office (formerly the Inquisition) set in motion what amounted to purges, with dismissals, banishments, and prohibitions against teaching and publishing. On August 12, 1950, Pope Eugenio Pacelli promulgated the encyclical *Humani generis,* "on certain notions which threaten to undermine the foundations of Catholic doctrine." Among the causes of these "miserable" trends, the pope mentioned the love of novelty, feelings of inferiority towards science, and an overly irenic approach to modern culture. Pius XII accused the theologians of relativizing dogma, failing to recognize the Church's right to have the final say on all questions regarding the sources of the faith, and treating Holy Scripture as a mere historical document. With a clear thrust at Teilhard de Chardin, the pope rejected any theory of evolution which did not distinguish between matter and spirit, and which denied the

Pius XI and Secretary of State Cardinal Eugenio Pacelli (Pius XII)
at the offical opening of the Vatican radio station on February 12,
1931. Between them is the inventor of wireless telegraphy and Nobel
Prize–winner Guglielmo Marconi

biblical doctrine that Adam and Eve were the first parents of humanity (monogenesis).

With a single stroke Pius XII deprived the theologians of any possible excuse by adding that encyclicals had the same binding force as *ex cathedra* decisions and could resolve any doctrinal controversy with definitive authority. In the wake of *Humani generis* there was a great deal of discussion, during which many theologians asserted that even the pope's ordinary magisterium could lay claim to infallibility. On the whole, papal infallibility was construed in the most sweeping terms. Some maintained that the pope was also infallible whenever he canonized saints or approved the rules of religious orders. A characteristic feature of Vatican policy at this time was the reactivation of the pontifical biblical commission, which once again began to enforce its previous decisions, now long since outdated. Only with the publication of the encyclical *Divino afflante Spiritu* on September 30, 1943, did this intense pressure slacken.

The effects of such a broad interpretation of the magisterium were felt in the everyday political sphere. Like the other Piuses of the nineteenth and twentieth centuries, Pope Eugenio Pacelli tried to extend the Vatican's jurisdiction and, in particular, to widen the laity's conscientious obligation to obey the hierarchy. In Italy these efforts took on a special virulence from the fact that the Catholic Democrazia Cristiana, at first under the leadership of Alcide De Gasperi, controlled the government. Like Pius X, Pius XII demanded obedience on specific political and social questions. He reserved his strongest disapproval for cooperative efforts between Catholic politicians and non-Catholics for fear of doctrinal contagion. In opposition to De Gasperi, who wished to work together with the parties of the Left, Pius XII favored an anticommunist Center-Rightist (Centro-Destra) front.[55]

Under Pius XII this situation never changed. Only after the election of Pope John XXIII and the announcement of the Second Vatican Council were theologians and Christian political leaders able to breathe more freely.

*The New Dogma
of Mary's Assumption:
A Sign of the Times*

Hardly anything could better typify the spirit of Pius XII's pontificate than the proclamation of the new Marian dogma in 1950.[56] In making it, the pope was asserting his position as the supreme teaching authority. For the first time since Vatican I there occurred an infallible *ex cathedra* decision when, in the Apostolic Constitution *Munificentissimus Deus* of November 1, 1950, the pope declared as dogma that "the immaculate Mother of God and ever Virgin Mary was at the end of her life assumed into heaven body and soul."

We can see in this act the consciousness of sovereignty possessed by Pius XII's predecessors, this time displayed in the realm of doctrine. But there are other things which remind us especially of Pius IX. Eugenio Pacelli likewise nurtured a fanatical devotion to the Mother of God and had a peculiar fondness for the Fatima cult. As with Pius IX, there were mystical phenomena such as apparitions and miracles—important prerequisites for the creation of the dogma. The pope's supposed "Fatima vision" (October 30–31 and November 1, 1950), along with his "vision of Christ" (December 2, 1954) stirred up a great sensation in their day. They were, unfortunately, "accompanied by 'mediating' circumstances which only heightened the embarrassment of the whole thing."[57] As in the case of Pius IX, once the doctrine was defined no controversies arose, no heresies had to be repressed. "When we hear calls for the dogmatization from far-flung groups of lay people, that must be the result of deliberate propaganda," wrote the dogmatic theologian Bernhard Poschmann (Münster) in a report drawn up for a German bishop, concluding, "There can be no question of a real demand for a definition."[58] Like the doctrinal definition of 1870, this one, too, was a pious luxury.

Before the pope went ahead with the solemn definition, he made inquiries among the bishops. The majority favored the idea, although some of their arguments were hard to believe. One South American bishop offered the following proof: "Just as

Pius XII proclaims, on November 1, 1950, the new dogma that Mary
was assumed into heaven body and soul

the holy house of Nazareth was transported by angels to Loreto,
and thus was saved from profanation by the infidels, so it is
quite evident, *a fortiori,* that the body of Mary, as the 'Domus
Altissimi' (House of the Most High), must have been preserved
from corruption and taken up into heaven."[59] Some bishops
made known their objections, but most of the opposition came
from professors of theology. The Roman Curia wanted all theological faculties to sign a unanimous petition calling for the dogmatization of Mary's bodily assumption into heaven. Not a single faculty in Germany was willing to do so en bloc, and many
other respected theological faculties outside Germany refused as
well. From the scholarly standpoint, patrologist Berthold Altaner
of Würzburg made the clearest and most pointed case against
the possibility of a definition.[60]

For Altaner the dogma had no basis either in the Bible or
tradition. He found no trace of it in the first five centuries of

Christianity. The first notion of Mary's Assumption was introduced in the sixth century through the fantasies of an apocryphal text, *Transitus Mariae*. This piece has absolutely no historical value—as evidenced by its grotesque accounts of miracles. The story of the *Transitus* runs something like this: "Mary lives in Bethlehem. The archangel Gabriel makes known to her that her end is nigh. At her request all the apostles are brought from all the different countries of the world on a wondrous journey through the clouds to Bethlehem. Numerous miraculous cures take place at Mary's sickbed. Since danger threatens from the Jews, the Holy Spirit carries Mary and the apostles off on a cloud to Jerusalem. During this trip and later in Jerusalem more miracles occur. Jesus appears, surrounded by many bands of angels, on a throne in Jerusalem and proclaims that Mary will be taken up into heaven. There follow speeches and prayers by Mary. Christ and the angels intone a song of praise. Mary blesses each apostle individually and then dies. Christ receives her soul. The apostles carry her holy body on a bier to Gethsemane for burial. On the way a Jew rudely attempts to touch the corpse: Both his hands are cut off by an invisible sword and then immediately miraculously reattached by St. Peter. The Jew becomes a Christian. For three days the voices of unseen angels are heard. When the song ceases, the apostles conclude that the body of the Holy Virgin has been assumed into heaven. At that point Mary's mother, Anne, appears, along with her cousin, Elizabeth, Abraham, David (who sings alleluia), and many angels. They all venerate the tomb in which Mary was laid. The apostles praise God and thank him for the wonderful event which they have witnessed."[61]

According to Altaner, there were no other historical sources for Mary's Assumption. If many theologians later defended this doctrine, they did so on purely speculative grounds. Altaner concluded that "not only do the first five centuries constitute a 'lacuna,' but from that time till the present there is simply no historical tradition to point to. Therefore, if we continue to understand the concept of 'historical and theological tradition' in its original sense, without supplying any new interpretation of it, then there is no possible proof from tradition for this doctrine."[62]

For Altaner, theological arguments for the Assumption based on its "fittingness" were empty. And the appeal to the "sense of the faithful" struck him as presupposing what had to be proved. In the definition he noted "in a certain sense the undermining and devaluation of theology as a science."[63]

Despite such serious objections, the constitution *Munificentissimus Deus* spoke of the "Church's unanimous belief from the earliest times," and of proofs from Scripture, the Fathers, and theologians. Indeed, it claimed that the new dogma had been "clearly elaborated by means of the study, scholarship, and wisdom of the theologians." In the final analysis, the truth of the dogma was guaranteed because it was the Church's teaching at the moment—again a begging of the question.

Once the definition was proclaimed, there was no serious resistance to it. Even theologians like Altaner, who had once found the dogma quite impossible, obediently accepted it. In a discussion held in Stuttgart on January 9, 1971, between Hans Küng and representatives from the German Bishops' Conference concerning Küng's book *Infallible? An Inquiry,* Bishop (later Cardinal) Hermann Volk explained the theologians' motivation in coming to terms with the new dogma: "I just want to describe one scene. Before the Assumption became dogma, we were sitting together with the Evangelicals in the Paderborn circle. They had sent in a resolution of their own stating that the dogma was just not definable. And Söhngen [Gottlieb Söhngen, Catholic professor of theology in Munich] had vehemently insisted that there wouldn't be any definition . . . And Schlink [Edmund Schlink, Protestant professor of theology in Heidelberg] said, 'But what if it *is* defined? What do you do then?' And it got deathly quiet, and Söhngen was silent for a while, and then he said, 'Then I accept it, because I trust the Church more'—I'm giving the sense of what he said—'more than I trust myself.' . . . And that was Söhngen's innermost conviction. I've never heard him say a word against it, as hard as that must have been. But that made a tremendous impression at the time, and I found his answer sublime. That was one concrete situation of someone dealing with an issue that certainly gave us all a lot of grief."[64]

For Karl Rahner, too, the proper attitude under such cir-

Rome, 1950. Crowds await the solemn proclamation of the newest Marian dogma by Pius XII

cumstances is one of "humble reverence for God's possible mystery, a reverence whereby man does not make himself the standard of truth; and unconditional faith in the presence of the Church and its doctrine, a faith in the Church as the necessary medium for understanding our own belief, a faith which is the measure of everything else and can only be measured by itself, not by any of our other criteria."[65] In such a spirit Rahner went through voluble exertions in attempting to win an appreciation of the new dogma. But his manuscript on the subject was still so full of troublesome material that it has not been published to date.

The dogma was met with obedient consent. Of course, not even the pope could manufacture enthusiasm for the new truth of faith. The expected boom in Marian piety never materialized. In theology the problems raised by the doctrine were brushed aside. Ever since 1950 scholars have been waiting for clarification of the historical difficulties surrounding the Assumption, but in vain.

Vatican II Confirms Infallibility Without Discussing It

With his announcement of a great ecumenical council on January 25, 1959, Pope John XXIII aroused a wave of hope and anticipation. The word "ecumenical" led many to believe that this gathering would restore the unity of Christians. The overtures made to other Christians would be matched by overtures to the modern world. Forces that had been dammed up for decades were now breaking through. An immense desire for renewal in theology and practical religious life took hold of many Catholics. It found a symbol in the charismatic figure of John XXIII, who criticized the eternal praisers of the past and prophets of doom, observing that the Church was not a museum. He wanted to throw the windows wide open, to let light and air into the dark and stuffy room. In his inaugural address to the Council he declared that Christian doctrine had to be studied and expounded to meet the needs of the day. "For the *Depositum Fidei*, that is, the truths contained in the venerable body of doctrine, is one thing. The way in which it is preached and presented is something else again."[66]

Anxiety swept through the Roman Curia. More than a century ago the idea of a Council had seemed dangerous, but this was worse. The Curia could bring a broad influence to bear on the preparatory commissions, and it hoped to be able to steer the elections for the conciliar commissions in the "proper" direction. The plan had worked for Vatican I, but this time it failed. Similarly, the Council refused to accept all the schemata worked out by Rome in advance; many of them it rejected outright. And the pope himself was on the side of the reformers. For a while it looked as if they would succeed, as if a thoroughgoing renewal of the Catholic Church was on the way, a reform "in head and members" of the sort that people had been demanding in vain for hundreds of years. Then, in the middle of the Council, Pope John died. Paul VI at first walked in the footsteps of his predecessor. John's prestige was simply too great; his successor had to embrace his legacy. But before long the Vatican began to sing a different tune, issuing warnings, limitations, and prohibitions. The whole process of *aggiornamento* seemed too risky to the pope. He forbade the bishops to debate the most serious questions, such as the law of priestly celibacy, the rules for mixed marriages, and birth control. He intervened against the Council's declaration on the Jews, the declaration on religious freedom, and the decree on ecumenism (which had already been approved). Finally, contrary to the will of the conciliar majority, he proclaimed Mary as the "Mother of the Church," and in his encyclical *Mysterium fidei* went off on a doctrinal course out of keeping with the spirit of the Council.

And so the First Vatican Council was never discussed at Vatican II, not just because the bishops had forgotten their history but because a resurgence of repressive curial tactics prevented it from being discussed. "It didn't seem worth our while," Hans Küng wrote ten years later, "to raise the complex issue of infallibility before the full Council in a ten minute Latin address —or to go looking for a bishop to give it."[67] The Curia effectively managed things so that Vatican I's doctrine of the pope's infallibility and universal jurisdiction was simply rubberstamped by Vatican II. And the pope hardened the terms of the old decrees in an explanatory memorandum which he imposed upon the Council. At Vatican II there was a great deal of talk about collegiality between bishops and pope. Theologians often argued that this was the way to do away with the one-sidedness of the previous Council: fine words with few deeds to back them up. No structural changes were made in the Church. Today there is small cause for Catholics to speak of collegial government—as has been amply demonstrated by the episcopal synods held since the Council.

Despite these early efforts at throttling debate, the Council nevertheless succeeded in issuing documents that signified, to some extent at least, a real opening up to the other Christian churches, the early Christian sources, and the modern world. The conciliar decrees had enough tinder to spark unrest for a whole decade and, consequently, to bring about broad changes in the mentality of Catholics. But in the meantime the reactionary party was again firmly in control.[68]

Once More in the Spotlight

In 1970, one hundred years after the First Vatican Council, one of the liveliest debates of the postconciliar period got under way, the topic once again being the infallibility of the papal magisterium. The papacy had only itself to blame for the fact that the issue came up at all, especially after the Curia had whisked it so adroitly and inconspicuously across the stage at Vatican II. This time the pope went too far. Paul VI had already stirred up a good deal of annoyance among the participants at the Council. In the postconciliar period further reactionary measures were taken: a heavily conservative line in episcopal and curial appointments; the strengthening of the position of the nuncios; the drawing up in secret of a church constitution which violated the spirit of the Council; the reconfirmation of the indulgence system; the return to inquisitorial proceedings against theologians; the campaign against the Dutch catechism; the protest against a reasonable divorce law in Italy; the demand that all priests renew their vow of celibacy on Holy Thursday; the encyclical *Sacerdotalis coelibatus;* the pope's *Credo* (1968); the decree on mixed marriages (1970); the curial reform *Regimini ecclesiae,* in which Paul VI took away power from the old congregations, gave it to the state secretariat, and fostered centralization and bureaucratization in areas where it had been absent.

All this, however, might have been accepted without too

much resistance. The real crisis of authority was first triggered
by the encyclical *Humanae vitae,* in which the pope condemned
practically every form of birth control as morally reprehensible.
As far as Vatican authorities were concerned, it was an open
question whether this was an infallible declaration of the ordinary
magisterium. But for Paul VI there already were infallible declarations of the ordinary magisterium on the books concerning
contraception. And so, unlike the majority of his commission of
experts, the pope felt bound to these declarations by his predecessors. The pope agreed with the petition which the so-called
minority had sent him behind the back of the rest of the commission: "If it should be declared," they wrote, "that contraception is not evil in itself, then we should have to concede
frankly that the Holy Spirit had been on the side of the Protestant churches in 1930 (when the encyclical *Casti connubii* was
promulgated), in 1951 (Pius XII's address to the midwives),
and in 1958 (the address delivered before the Society of Hema-
tologists in the year the pope died). It should likewise have to
be admitted that for half a century the Spirit failed to protect
Pius XI, Pius XII, and a large part of the Catholic hierarchy
from a very serious error. This would mean that the leaders of
the Church, acting with extreme imprudence, had condemned
thousands of innocent human acts, forbidding, under pain of
eternal damnation, a practice which would now be sanctioned.
The fact can neither be denied nor ignored that these same acts
would now be declared licit on the grounds of principles cited
by the Protestants, which popes and bishops have either condemned or at least not approved."[69] Thus, it became only too
clear that the core of the problem was not the pill but the authority, continuity, and infallibility of the Church's magisterium.

In *Humanae vitae,* however, the pope was dealing with an
area of experience where most of his "subjects" knew more than
he did. And his decision had painful implications for all of them.
Many people could not understand Paul VI's reasoning, while
others regarded this papal ban as an arrogant intrusion into their
private lives. Accordingly, Catholics showed little inclination to
obey the pope's command.

And when, a short time after this, the Swiss theologian
Hans Küng raised the issue of papal infallibility, the atmosphere

was just right. Küng's *Infallible? An Inquiry* met with an enthusiastic response.[70] This was not the first public discussion of the
subject in recent years: In 1968 Dutch Bishop Francis Simons
had argued that the Catholic Church's faith in infallibility was
theologically dubious.[71]

More than anything else, Küng asked questions. Is there any
basis for infallible propositions in the Bible or tradition? Does
the Church even need such propositions? Later Küng explained
that the expression "infallible propositions" was his shorthand
for statements which would be true a priori and not subject to
critical scrutiny since they were guaranteed by an infallible authority. Although Küng never dropped this somewhat confusing
terminology—and sometimes created the impression that he
would reject "infallible propositions" primarily because they are
per se impossible—he nevertheless clearly challenged the three
sources of infallible authority: the pope, the councils, and the
Bible. Instead of infallibility, Küng makes a case for the
Church's "indefectibility." The Church, he says, will be preserved in the truth however many errors it may fall into or suffer
through. Küng believed that this alternate proposal did not run
contrary to Vatican I, since that Council had never even entertained such a possibility and therefore had not condemned it.
For all that, his suggestion was bitterly opposed by a large part
of the theological community, in particular by the representatives of the hierarchy. Küng, many Catholics claimed, was
no longer one of them. The German and Italian bishops' conferences went on record against Küng's book, and in Rome disciplinary procedures were started against him. Küng had undoubtedly touched a very sore point, but he also got a great deal of
support from all quarters, since many people had come to doubt
that infallibility could still be justified. After a long debate, during which the Church's leadership made no meaningful concessions and the theologians could reach no consensus, and after a
long quarrel between Küng and the erstwhile Inquisition, the
Congregation of the Faith, the disciplinary procedures were
provisionally dropped. True, the Holy Office did explicitly reject
Küng's opinion: "Any notion which casts the least doubt upon
dogmatic faith in the Church's infallibility, or reduces it to a
fundamental indefectibility of the Church in the truth, with the

possiblity of error in propositions which the magisterium presents as definitively binding, contradicts the teaching defined by the First and confirmed by the Second Vatican Council."[72]

For the moment, however, there were no plans to condemn Küng, as the Congregation of the Faith still hoped he could come around to the official position: "Since in his letter of September 4, 1974, Professor Küng in no way denies that after a suitable period of more careful study he may bring his notions into agreement with the authentic doctrine of the Church's magisterium, this Congregation, despite the gravity of these opinions, at the bidding of Pope Paul VI now admonishes him not to speak any longer on their behalf, and reminds him that the Church's authorities have empowered him to lecture on theology in the spirit of her doctrine, but not to advocate ideas which pervert this doctrine or cast doubt upon it."[73]

Where does the discussion go from here? The question is all the more pointed due to the fact that the most recent research has found still more weaknesses in the dogma of infallibility. The debate over Küng and his book paid practically no attention to how the definition came about in the first place. Our investigation has shown that at Vatican I the dogma was pushed through in the face of considerable resistance and with every conceivable means of manipulation. This was the achievement of a relatively small group of Infallibilists and, still more, of a pope obsessed with the *idée fixe* of getting the definition. And so the validity of the conciliar decision must be disputed. But will the Vatican allow free discussion of this matter? Many observers thought that the truce with Hans Küng meant that the Congregation of the Faith had taken a great step forward. I cannot share this opinion. Küng has been spared for the nonce because his popularity and influence are too widespread. But it is clear what is expected of him—and it ought to be still clearer to all his less-famous contemporary Catholics, especially to theologians who don't have professorial chairs at secular universities. In such cases the apparatus of repression shows its true colors. How, then, can there be a free and unprejudiced discussion within the Church? One thinks immediately of the years after the First Vatican Council. Are there any real fundamental differences between then and now, any signs that we have made progress? Even then, as we saw with the theological faculty of Tübingen, the authorities were willing to settle for a truce, for silence. But what does such a truce mean vis-à-vis the demand for untrammeled scholarly research? What could ever justify such an arrangement?

Küng's alternative proposal, namely, that the Church is indefectible in the truth, gives rise to a further set of questions. This view has the textual support of the New Testament, but it, in turn, makes the ancient Christian confession of faith as given in the New Testament an unimpeachable norm. But isn't this only going halfway? Shouldn't this archaic confession of faith itself be subject to critical testing? Can't we make out in Scripture certain developments which have little to do with Jesus and his *kerygma*? In addition, if the Church always remains fundamentally in the truth, isn't Küng taking the possibility of being wrong much too casually? Doesn't he uphold, after all, the Church's old absolutist claims? Küng's position is undoubtedly much more acceptable than infallibilism because it offers more room for freedom. But is it also more consistent? And are not its critics correct in maintaining that a community such as the Catholic Church can only be held together, sociologically speaking, by a strictly authoritarian management (as in the magisterium's official monopoly in interpreting Scripture and tradition)? Can the Church ever allow unconstrained research if it wishes to avoid the danger of self-destruction?

But at this juncture we confront other, more basic, problems growing out of this investigation: What is the relationship between faith and understanding, scientific study and the Church's magisterium, freedom of judgment and credal obligations? To what extent can scholarship be free and unbiased if the Curia gets on the scholar's back and insists upon orthodoxy? Isn't this dilemma strikingly apparent in Küng's latest documentary effort, *Nothing but the Truth?*

There are many problems related to the Christian religion whose solution would be vitally important for contemporary society. It might halt, to some degree, the growing sense of meaninglessness. The question remains, doesn't the institutional environment in which theology operates directly serve to thwart solutions? Just about everyone who teaches or studies Christianity is bound to some particular confession. Hence, the work they do presupposes a comprehensive commitment both to "biblical revelation" and to the teachings of their denomination. Postulates of this sort, however, have become problematic for most people today. And anyone who is not allowed to ask serious questions about them will lose credit with the general public. Isn't it time to set up more professorships for religious studies and the history of religion, including Christianity, which would be fully independent of the churches and serve as a counterweight to them? This might shed more light on the situation than years of discussion among captive theologians.[74]

9

*The Ideology
of Vatican I*

*Knowledge and
Special Interests*

Judging from the facts already presented and reviewed in considerable detail, the dogma of papal infallibility must be characterized as an ideology. I use this term in the widely accepted sense of a doctrine with no substrate in reality, something which arises out of the needs of interest groups and is spread and protected by them.

Our analysis of the claim that the pope has always exercised an infallible magisterium has shown that this runs contrary to historical evidence. Back in 1870 the conciliar opposition had clearly drawn attention to this point. In their eyes the proofs adduced by the Infallibilists did not hold up and were not strong enough to dispel the difficulties raised by the doctrine. Modern scholarship has fully confirmed this assessment.

The minority's objections also serve to demonstrate that even in those days people might have known better. The decisions made at the First Vatican Council, therefore, lagged behind the current (or potentially current) state of knowledge at the time. This draws our attention to another characteristic of all ideologies: They always constitute a regression in the history of thought. The reason why the truth was never discovered at Vatican I, although it might very well have been, lies primarily in the social interests which dominated the Council. The plan was to enhance the pope's authority as much as possible, not only in hopes of strengthening the old hierarchical order within the Church but, above all, in society at large. The methods employed to achieve this matched the forces that wanted it. The ideology of infallibilism would never have been defined as dogma had there been free, unprejudiced discussion. There would have been no definition had not a group been at work in the conciliar underground, applying all sorts of pressure to force a decision upon the bishops which a goodly number of them had no wish for at all. The pope and the curial machine certainly did more than their share in this regard. But decrees that had not been freely agreed upon had to be pushed through and afterwards defended with the instruments of repression. "The new dogmas have come into being thanks to force and coercion," wrote Ignaz von Döllinger on March 1, 1887, to the archbishop

Ein öconomisches — nicht öcumenisches — Concil.

"An economic, not ecumenical, Council" (caricature from the July 1870 issue of the *Der Industrielle Humorist*)

of Munich, Anton von Steichele. "They will also have to be maintained by the constant use of force and coercion."[75]

Ideologizing Ideology

The new dogma taught that the pope was infallible in matters of faith and morals—a uniquely ideological thesis. This claim extends not to one doctrinal statement but to all of them; it covers every single one. It shields the entire doctrinal structure of the Catholic Church from criticism. Papal infallibility—the formal principle, as it were, of Catholicism—becomes the crowning conclusion of the system. The insurance policy is flawless: There can be no appeal from the pope to any other authority. Infallibility in this context functions as a meta-ideology, the ideologizing of an ideology. The many ideological elements in the system are protected by a single, constitutive, all-encompassing ideology. The aim of all this is stabilization and integration. Presupposing the fundamental principle of infallibilty, the Church's entire operation can run smoothly.

This process of formal legitimization was clearly observable for the first time in the late Middle Ages, when serious criticism of the Church's teaching arose. The magisterium stressed the sanctity and immutability of its own utterances and tried to head off the spread of uncertainty among believers. These efforts reached their apogee at the First Vatican Council.

The Church in a Blind Alley

Was the goal met? There can be no doubt that the thought of infallibility provided many believers with a great sense of religious security all through life. In order to deal with the most important and crucial questions, Catholics were given answers which were beyond dispute and hence imparted stability and freedom from anxiety. The dogma of infallibility went a long way towards relieving emotional pressures and softening the impact of reality—as ideologies often do. From a psychological standpoint, the object of belief is secondary, the fact of belief is what counts. This disburdening function of dogma is probably the best explanation why the Roman Curia was able to win general acceptance for infallibility in such short order, despite heavy resistance from some parts of the Church. There was always the unspoken fear that without infallible authorities there would be no more security, no really binding pronouncements, that everything would somehow be left hanging in the air. In the final analysis, people were afraid of uncertainty—and of freedom.

Nonetheless, it is still an open question whether the quest for security was not carried too far. Even at the Vatican Council some individuals perceived this act of violence—the claim to total truth—as logically impossible and ultimately self-destructive. The papacy, they thought, had gone down a blind alley from whence there could be no escape without a critical loss of authority. "The results of the Vatican decree of 1870 are only now beginning to come to light," the Catholic church historian Franz Xaver Kraus noted in his diary on February 9, 1900. "Rome has locked the door leading to its only way out. There seems to be nothing left but for the whole papal system to break down." The Swiss theologian Hans Urs von Balthasar, who could certainly not be accused of hostility to Rome, followed the same line when he called the Vatican dogmas a "gigantic disaster."

Papal infallibility, as a matter of fact, did go too far. In an attempt to provide complete insurance for the system of doctrine, it overdrew the fund of public credit and thereby risked losing most of it. The dogma, to vary the image, exposed such a broad flank to the attacks of historical criticism that the Church's credibility was threatened. This was precisely what the minority bishops at Vatican I were so worried about. The results of research carried on since then have not served to lessen this concern.

A no less serious problem is the structural impasse which Vatican I maneuvered the Church into. Strictly speaking, the pope can now do everything even without the bishops. The supreme leadership is thus so isolated that the flow of information to it is cramped and sluggish, making it difficult to find adequate solutions to problems. Once again stabilization is pressed too far and the whole process backfires: The papal office is on the way to petrifaction. So far, attempts at reforming it have failed. Indeed, they could only have been set in motion and accomplished by the personal initiative of the popes themselves. But self-reform is an exceedingly rare phenomenon in history. The life expectancy of the popes—materially lengthened thanks to modern medicine—magnifies the opportunities for trouble in all sorts of ways. And we cannot rule out the possibility that in the future it might become necessary to remove a pope from office—but there is simply no structural solution for a case like this.

What can the bishops do against the declared wishes of a pope? This was a burning question at Vatican I—and it still is today. It highlights the real dimensions of the Church's blind alley. The fact that behind the campaign for infallibility, ultimately so self-destructive, stood a pope with the intellectual and psychic qualities of a Pius IX must truly give us pause.

Ideological Presuppositions

The need for security and the fear of uncertainty in matters affecting one's life do not, in themselves, suffice to explain the genesis of the Infallibilist ideology. This sort of thing can only arise when people's thinking is molded by certain specific factors, the most basic of which is the wish to lay claim to universal truth. Such a mentality denies the fragmentary character of every human utterance and absolutizes its own interpretations. The Infallibilists were so positive that they were in possession of the whole truth because their thinking was unhistorical: In their eyes the Church had been in possession of the whole truth from the very beginning. They had only a foggy realization of the extent to which all statements are limited and temporally conditioned. Otherwise they would never have wished to make use of infallibility to insure the Church's dogmatic decisions and make them irrevocable.

A further presupposition for the kind of thinking that can lead to ideology is alienation from experience. "One is much more inclined to pay attention to data that confirm one's ideas than to data that contradict them, because in this way one can avoid undesirable cognitive dissonances."[76] The Infallibilists, in fact, closed their eyes to the historical difficulties their dogma presented. Their misuse of history shows how serious their conflict with reality actually was.

Another important characteristic of ideological thinking is that its real presuppositions are kept hidden. In the case of Vatican I, the foundation on which papal infallibility rested, namely, the Church's witness to itself—or, rather, the pope's witness to himself—never came to light. Instead, the Infallibilists trotted out hundreds of arguments, most of them from history. All this pseudodiscussion ever achieved, however, was a laborious concealment of the actual reasons why they thought as they did.

Strategies of Immunization

The Infallibilist ideology can only perform its most vital function—providing psychic relief—if it is not called into question. Such doubt is, however, an ever-present danger, given the precarious assumptions on which the dogma is based. A whole series of precautionary immunizations thus becomes necessary to ward off any possible criticism.

The immunization strategies began to be worked out when the doctrine of infallibility was first being formulated. When is the pope infallible? The requisite conditions here are framed in such a way that it is almost impossible to say that such and such a decision must qualify as infallible. In particular, the stipulation that only *ex cathedra* decisions of the pope are infallible makes the definition of infallibility meaningless as far as the preceding centuries are concerned.

Since the expression *ex cathedra* was not used until the sixteenth century and was then given various meanings until the nineteenth century, we can never confidently say we have a *ex cathedra* papal decision in any given case. So the definition of infallibility turns out to be empty words because it is compatible with any historical situation whatsoever. Its very lack of content means that it cannot be refuted or falsified—a considerable tactical advantage made possible by the vagueness and indefiniteness of the concept itself. Whatever the pope may have said in the past, whatever doctrinal decisions he may have made, it is never certain that he was speaking *ex cathedra*. The conciliar minority at Vatican I rightfully recognized the evasiveness of such manipulative language and denounced it.

Empty formulas are a useful instrument for governing. "They create—especially among the governed—an impression of the unshakable solidity of supreme principles while in no way hampering the ruling authorities in their concrete decisions."[77]

We can see even more clearly just how elastic the dogma is by the manner in which it expands and contracts: Whenever it seems opportune, infallibility, thanks to its vagueness, can be stretched far beyond the limits of *ex cathedra* decisions. The ordinary papal magisterium now becomes infallible too—a doctrine which, while never raised to the status of dogma, has been defended by many theologians and mantles itself in the prestige of the infallible extraordinary magisterium. In a sense, such "infallible" decisions are much more important to the Curia and the Church's bureaucratic machine than the rare *ex cathedra* declarations. The aura of infallibility counts more than its actual use.

As a further immunization against the science of history, the ecclesiastical (in this case, the papal) magisterium had for centuries been claiming it held a monopoly on the interpretation of Scripture and tradition. Catholics were bound not to the findings of critical study of the past but to the word of the magisterium, as enlightened by the Spirit. The definition of infallibility only strengthened the pope's interpretive monopoly. His obligations to Scripture and tradition became, in effect, obligations to himself. The pope no longer needed the Church's approval—his decisions were beyond appeal.

Often enough the magisterium has allowed varying interpretations of the dogma to coexist—another way of softening opposition. This is a familiar phenomenon to the critics of ideology. Such apparent broad-mindedness was already in evidence in the process of getting the bishops to submit after Vatican I. The main thing for Rome was the acceptance of the formula defining infallibility; what the formula meant was less important. In some tactically significant cases (one thinks of Bishop Joseph Hefele of Rottenburg) the Curia was willing to make sweeping concessions—concessions not made for various professors. In this way it succeeded in winning general recognition of the formula, although there was no factual basis for it whatsoever. The radically divergent opinions could be gathered together under a single linguistic umbrella without endangering the Church's unity or disturbing its ability to function. Such an openhanded policy was, of course, purely for appearance' sake. It was designed as an escape valve for postconciliar pressures. Unity, uniformity, and security were the values that counted.

Even today the Curia has been forced to make far-reaching concessions. The formula that the pope is infallible "in and of himself, without the consent of the Church" strikes many Catholics as highly offensive. Contemporary minds find it difficult to abandon their democratic instincts and accept such an extremely monarchical structure. In this situation a good many thinkers have shown a readiness to make adjustments in the dogma to suit contemporary tastes. They stress the need for a link uniting the pope to the Church and its tradition and maintain that an infallible papal decision without prior consent from the Church is impossible. But the text of the definition says nothing of the sort.[78] In discussing one such reading of the dogma, Fr. Giacomo Martina, S.J., even asserts that yesterday's vanquished—the bishops of the conciliar minority—are today's victors.[79] By construing infallibility in this fashion, theologians try to disguise the changes they have de facto made in the dogma and to uphold the fiction of its formal continuity.

The Dutch theologian A. W. J. Houtepen tries to dilute Vatican I in another way. He claims that the Council "never postulated any absolute inalterability of the dogmatic formula."[80] True enough, the Council did not postulate this explicitly, but the idea was very much present. Vatican I viewed the definition of infallibility as binding for all time. If nothing else, the story of how the bishops submitted after the Council should have been enough to show Houtepen his mistake. The Dutchman would like to limit the meaning of infallibility still further with his thesis that Vatican I was less interested in the question of truth than in the problem of where the ultimate authority in the Church was located.[81] To that extent, the pope was not defined as infallible, he was merely given the final word. But if all this is part of a divine design, then the burden of proof for this argument is just as heavy as it was for infallibilism. Furthermore, Houtepen overlooks the fact that the pope's word was considered binding because it was viewed as infallible.

Rome does not take any drastic steps against such efforts to render the dogma innocuous. On the contrary, the Curia seems to welcome them on several accounts. They calm people down and spread the notion around that Vatican I was a lot better than its reputation suggests. Beyond that, they give theologians a certain amount of freedom to let off steam by practicing their elucidative arts. Apart from this, Rome has not the faintest intention of following any such interpretations, either theoretically or practically.

These immunization strategies grew out of the doctrine of infallibility. They were bolstered by various precautionary measures primarily designed to shield the dogma from thoroughgoing criticism—measures employed before, during, and after the Council. In certain instances the Vatican imposed a ban on speaking engagements and publications. If that did not help, it turned to censorship or put undesirable books on the Index. In stubborn cases it pronounced suspension or excommunication. By this time the Church no longer had at its disposal the option of physical coercion, which ranged from detention to annihilation. It did, however, apply all other means to push through the definition of infallibility. After a while, the devices for screening out scholarly criticism began running smoothly all by themselves. People would no longer touch dangerous material. The continual rewarding of obedience paid off, as outside censorship gave way to autocensorship. The banning of books and archival politics had also helped.

Since then, such goings-on have been repeated in many parts of the Catholic world right up to the present. After the promulgation of the encyclical *Humanae vitae* in 1968, the Church conducted a massive purge of its key personnel wherever it could.

Psychic Disturbances

Why does the Vatican have recourse to so many different

tactics, all intended to thwart an unprejudiced examination of the doctrine of infallibility? Is it that unsure of its case? The various immunization strategies, especially apparent in the devious way the archives are run, can only be understood as a defense mechanism against its own better judgment, which has been choked off but still makes itself felt, not least of all by the bad conscience it causes. If it were not for that, Rome could be more relaxed. Such a policy, however, of shielding oneself from historical criticism has its costs. The Church does indeed gain, at first, in unity and uniformity, but it blocks off its own free access to the real world and ultimately stands in danger of losing touch with reality completely. The value of knowing the truth is diminished and relativized. In the long run this process even jeopardizes unity.

Oskar Köhler speaks of Catholicism's psychic disorders, caused, he believes, by the way Catholics have repressed their own history over the past few centuries.[82] The many symptoms which Köhler enumerates seem to me to be present at Vatican I with special intensity. Despite all the misgivings of the council fathers, the definition took place. But a life lived against the grain of one's better judgment cannot avoid painful friction, and eventually must lead to a mind divided against itself. At this point the tension between knowledge and belief becomes unbearable.

This denial of the past has similarly mixed effects on the Church's position in society. On the one hand, Catholicism gains in uniformity and political muscle; on the other, its conflict with science grows more intense. Its dogmatic commitments make it harder for the Church to adapt to circumstances; they lessen its flexibility and the chances for reform. The Church loses its credibility with many people and draws in on itself. This increases the danger of its stiffening into a sect and forfeiting its potential for creative social renewal. The machine may still remain intact, and the power structure may continue to stand firm, but the life has gone out of it.

10

A Hundred Years
After the Death
of Pius IX

*The Canonization
Proceedings*

Floodlights bathed St. Peter's with brilliance. Thirty cardinals
in their scarlet robes, more than forty bishops and archbishops, and canons and representatives of the cathedral chapter
of St. Peter's added their own luster, along with the diplomatic
corps accredited to the Holy See under the leadership of two
archbishops, Giuseppe Caprio, substitute at the Secretariat of
State, and Agostino Casaroli, Secretary of the Council for the
Church's Public Affairs. Thousands of believers and pilgrims, especially from The Marches—among them the Italian Foreign
Minister, Arnaldo Forlani—filled the great square. The Swiss
Guards were wearing their gala uniforms, the papal cham-
berlains were agleam with medals. Everything was ready for the
Capella papale, the solemn service in which Paul VI would celebrate the memory of his predecessor, Pius IX. The pope was
borne on the *sedia gestatoria* through the central nave, past the
statue of St. Peter. Above the statue an enormous medallion of
Pius IX hung resplendently; on it was noted in letters of gold
that Pope Giovanni Mastai-Ferretti was the first pontiff to surpass
the twenty-five-year reign of the Prince of the Apostles—an event

which struck people back in the 1870s as unheard of and worthy of celebration.

After the singing of the Gospel, Paul VI began his eagerly anticipated address on the hundredth anniversary of the day Pius IX died. In it the Roman pontiff lauded his predecessor, above all, as the pope of Mary's Immaculate Conception and of the First Vatican Council. "For forgetful man, and for the world of religious indifference and rationalism, which met faith and grace with hostility or silence, the pope caused the light of the Virgin Mary to shine forth as a 'great sign' of supernatural beauty . . ." Paul VI praised the two new dogmas of Vatican I as "beacons in the one-thousand-year development of theology," as firm anchors of support in the storm of ideologies which characterize the history of modern thought . . ." With these dogmas Pius IX had erected the girders to uphold that solid ecclesiological super-structure which had later been completed by the Second Vatican Council. Paul VI was not sparing with his commendation. He could not altogether ignore the controversies surrounding Pius IX. But Pope Giovanni Battista Montini felt these were due to a lack of historical perspective, to passionate prejudice, and rash judgment. Once these obstacles were removed, then "the full, human credibility, beaming kindness, and exemplary virtue of this pope's personality would be clear for all to see." On this occasion the pope made no explicit mention of the dogma of infallibility, as he had done previously in his address to the faithful in St. Peter's square on February 5, 1978. Neither did he allude to a canonization in the near future, which dashed many high hopes.

On December 14, 1977, he had spoken in the presence of thousands of pilgrims of "our revered and—we may say—holy predecessor." Immediately after the audience, the prefect of the pope's house, French Bishop Jacques Martin, phoned to congrat-ulate the postulator of the canonization proceedings for Pius IX. This was Monsignore Antonio Piolanti, formerly rector of the Lateran University but for some time now pensioned off because of his reactionary policies.

These remarks by the pope awakened fresh expectations for the favorable progress of Pius IX's canonization, as would the celebration of his centenary three months later. The canoniza-

Paul VI at the memorial service in honor of Pius IX, held on March 5, 1978. In the background is the statue of St. Peter and, above that, the medallion of Pius IX and the inscription stating that he was the first pope to exceed the number of years spent on the throne by St. Peter. The memorial tablet was affixed in 1871, during Pius IX's lifetime

tion proceedings had begun as early as 1907 and had been dragging laboriously onward ever since. Pius IX was awarded the title "servant of God" quickly enough, but the beatification seemed to have bogged down. On October 2, 1962, a preliminary session of the Congregation of Rites (*Congregazione antipreparatoria*) ended with another postponement. Thirteen of the nineteen members demanded further historical investigation. Perhaps the petition opposing the canonization of Pius IX which the Melkite synod had twice submitted had made some impression after all. On May 28, 1963, shortly before the death of Pope John XXIII, who zealously backed the plan to declare Pius IX a saint,[82a] a second preparatory session (*Congregazione preparatoria*) took place. On July 6, 1963, Pope Paul VI confirmed the decision that further study was necessary, and so for the time being the proceedings appeared to be blocked.

But the reaction that set in after Vatican II, involving the rejection of overtures to other Christian confessions and the contemporary world, once again made Pius IX a model for many Catholics. A whole group of conservative prelates gathered under the aegis of Cardinal Pietro Palazzini, the first sponsor (*Promotor*) of the canonization, have come to see Pius IX's condemnation of liberalism as an exemplary attitude towards the spirit of the age, both then and now. They consider the dogma of infallibility an absolutely necessary prerequisite for all ecumenical endeavors and the only effective guard against the blurring of denominational distinctions. Such ideas are not surprising from a man like Palazzini, one of the champions of the radical right-wing church organization Opus Dei. In the last few years, however, his prestige has suffered somewhat. In connection with his close friend Camillo Crociani, general manager at Finmeccanica and a multimillionare, Palazzini got entangled in the Italian branch of the Lockheed scandal.[83]

Even the usually restrained curial lawyer Carlo Snider— who, as a token of the revived interest in Pius IX, has been supervising the canonization proceedings for over a year now—has enthusiastic words for the role played by papal infallibility: "Today we must view infallibility as a precious gift which provides the guarantee, the security needed to march boldly forward, leading the way down the path of historical evolution."[84]

Elsewhere Snider remarks, "This dogma is one of the most beautiful, most beneficial, most necessary dogmas for the Church."[85] According to Snider, Pius IX's desire for the dogma of infallibility was part of his charisma and personal inspiration.

For some years now the "Pius IX committee" has been quite busy: It publishes a journal dealing with the pope and has already held a number of conferences in his honor. The committee identifies itself completely with the spirit of Pius IX and repeatedly makes it known that this pope is still alive today. Panegyrical tones heralding the canonization . . .

This same group of people has been the source of many of the Pius IX devotees, who turned the hundredth anniversary of his death into such a grand display. On February 7, 1978, fifteen cardinals, numerous archbishops and bishops, and a crowd of the faithful met at the tomb of Pius IX in the Church of San Lorenzo fuori le mura to inaugurate his centenary with a splendid service. In his address, Cardinal Pietro Palazzini extolled the pope's break with liberalism. The prayers of intercession implored the glorification of the "servant of God" and "infallible teacher of the faith." The hundredth anniversary of the death of this pope, who sat on the chair of St. Peter longer than anyone else, was also celebrated in other ways with great extravagance: There were commemorative coins and stamps (the Italian postal service issued commemoratives of its own; amusingly enough, it at first forgot to render the same honor to Victor Emmanuel II, the Risorgimento king, who also died in 1878); concerts, lectures, and festivals in Rome, Senigallia, Spoleto, Imola, Naples, Verona, Milan, and St. Louis; exhibits; and many organized pilgrimages to the "holy places" associated with Pius IX. Italian Prime Minister Giulio Andreotti was supposed to conclude the tributes with a festive address on Pio Nono as pope and head of state, but this was cancelled owing to the murder of Aldo Moro, the president of the Christian Democratic Party. Andreotti was a member of the centenary committee, as was Italian Foreign Minister Arnaldo Forlani.

The efforts to get the pope canonized, like the anniversary celebrations, clearly had a lot to do with church politics. Paying homage to Pius IX is a way of expressing full public approval of the former pope's position and of taking an unambiguous swipe

Mosaic at the tomb of Pius IX bearing the inscription, "To the teacher who knows no error the bishops come to offer their obedience and faith." From left to right, back row: Joseph Georg Strossmayer, opponent of infallibility and bishop of Diakovar; John Martin Spalding, archbishop of Baltimore; two unidentified bishops. Second row: Antonius Petrus Hassun, Armenian patriarch of Constantinople (wearing crown); Henry Edward Manning, archbishop of Westminster (bareheaded); Mieczysław Halka of Ledóchowski, archbishop of Gniezno; Joseph Fessler, bishop of St. Pölten (with cross); Cardinal Carlo Luigi Morichini; Cardinal Luigi Bilio. First row, kneeling: Anastasio Rodrigo Yusto, archbishop of Burgos; René François Régnier, archbishop of Cambrai; and Giuseppe Valerga, Latin patriarch of Jerusalem

Cardinal Pietro Palazzini speaking on February 7, 1978, at the hundredth anniversary of the death of Pius IX, held in the Church of San Lorenzo fuori le mura, where the pope is buried

at the progressives. Declaring the pope a saint would give a solemn sanction to his authoritarian principles and the dogmas he successfully promoted—which is just what many people in the Church think must be done to counteract the centrifugal tendencies of the day. At the same time, such measures would serve to restore many conservative elements in the Church to their old positions of power. The First Vatican Council would be revalorized, and any hazardous-sounding statements made by Vatican II would be mitigated. As conservatives see it, all this would lead to a consolidation of the Church's position. Of course, the canonization of Pius IX would also be a great setback for historical truth, the reform of the Catholic Church, and the ecumenical movement—none of which means it is out of the question for the future.

Even the numerous difficulties blocking the canonization of Giovanni Maria Mastai-Ferretti do not mean very much. Along with the pope's role at Vatican I, curial attorney Snider will also have to deal with some other blemishes on Pius IX's record. Until 1870, that is, until Italian troops marched into Rome, the pope kept the Jews locked up in the ghetto. In 1858 he ordered the papal police to take the seven-year-old son of the Mortaras, a rich Jewish family from Bologna, and place him in a Christian boarding school because he had been baptized shortly after birth by a Christian maid. The case of Edgar Mortara unleashed a storm of protest in liberal circles comparable to the one stirred up by the Dreyfus affair several decades later. When, at the customary papal audience with the Jews of Rome on New Year's, the boy's

Edgar Mortara, as a seminarian, kneeling at the feet of Pius IX (contemporary engraving)

parents tried to plead for the return of their son, Pius IX responded with sarcasm: "In the past year you've given a fine example of submissiveness. To turn all of Europe topsy-turvy on account of the Mortara case . . . But let the newspapers, for their part, go on talking all they want . . . I don't care a rap for the whole world!" The pope treated the young secretary of the Jewish community, Sabatino Scazzocchio, with particular cruelty and humiliated him so badly that he suffered a protracted nervous breakdown. Two years later Pius IX displayed Edgar Mortara, now dressed in a seminarian's robe, to the Jews of Rome.[86]

With similar intolerance he recommended the introduction of prison sentences for Protestants trying to spread their faith in Tuscany. In 1868 Pius IX ordered the Italian revolutionaries Monti and Tognetti beheaded in the Piazza del Popolo for attempting to blow up a papal barracks. And just two weeks before Rome was taken by storm, a certain Paolo Muzi was hanged in Frosinone, the last citizen of the Papal States to be executed.

Snider is worried about the decades of collaboration between the pope and his Secretary of State, Cardinal Giacomo Antonelli, a man not overly fastidious in his choice of methods. Then there is the naming of the "notorious concubinizer," Antonio Matteucci, as cardinal.[87] But, above all, Snider is concerned over Pius IX's irrational emotional outbursts. This is understandable, because in order to be declared a saint one must have shown evidence of possessing, in heroic measure, both the three divine virtues of faith, hope, and charity and the four cardinal virtues of prudence, justice, temperance, and fortitude. Still, a holy pope, according to Snider, need not be totally flawless. He sees as the critical point here "the recognition that a special vocation in the Church was entrusted, in keeping with the plan of Providence, to this supreme shepherd."

This same principle, in bygone days, smoothed over many an awkward hitch. Popes as dubious as Pius IX already enjoy the honors of sainthood. In 1606 Pope Paul V canonized Gregory VII because the latter had laid the foundations for papal absolutism with his *Dictatus papae*, "a horrible work," according to the church historian Georg Schwaiger, "judged from the point of view of Holy Scripture and its chief commandment of love."

And Pius X, who was canonized in 1954 by Pius XII, authorized an altogether criminal system of spies and informers to ward off modernist errors.

Defensive Reaction

With this background in mind, it is no wonder that this author's investigation concerning Pius IX and the First Vatican Council (see note 1) met such bitter opposition from Church officials. Just ten days after the second volume of the fuller, scholarly version of this book was published, church historian Walter Brandmüller of Augsburg tried to dismiss its findings in the *Rheinische Merkur* as "old rubbish" and "biased history." The secretary of the German Bishops' Conference broadcast these calumnies inside and outside of Germany by means of a

Execution of Italian revolutionaries Giuseppe Monti and Gaetano Tognetti (contemporary engraving)

special press release. The Catholic News Agency (KNA), which spoke of "Hasler's difficulties with infallibility," and the Church press in general gave greater currency to such slanders in cruder form. This sort of nearsighted apologetics, however, could not prevent the international press, including numerous Italian newspapers with a nationwide distribution, from taking an interest in the results of my research. This, in turn, led *L'Osservatore Romano*, the official organ of the Vatican, to enter the fray, charging me with inaccuracies. At the same time, people at the Vatican attempted to put pressure on Italian journals so that no more would be printed about this controversy and the whole affair would be played down—efforts which were partially successful.

In a long letter to the *Corriere della Sera* Monsignore Igino Ragni, chairman of the committee for the centenary celebration in honor of Pius IX, expressed his astonishment that so much importance had been attached to this author's study. He, Ragni, as a Catholic, an Italian, and a Marchegiano (native of The Marches), had to protest against this attempt to defame and blacken the name of Pius IX. Such a book made a mockery of the Church—just at the moment when it was preparing to honor Pope Giovanni Maria Mastai-Ferretti on the occasion of the hundredth anniversary of his death.[88]

Surprisingly enough, the newspaper published by the German bishops, *Der Rheinische Merkur*, waited almost a year after publishing Brandmüller's attack before once again broaching the issue. In a longish article, Matthias Buschkühl labeled my study Nazi propaganda. Neither the *Rheinische Merkur* nor *L'Osservatore Romano* would allow me an opportunity to reply.

Some Support Nonetheless

Discussion (at times quite violent) of my work on Pius IX only dates from September 1977, but a sizable number of reports, critiques, and comments on it have already accumulated.[89] This makes it possible to draw up an interim balance sheet.

I have never deluded myself with the expectation of getting much support from Catholic theologians. The more closely one

Msgr. Igino Ragni, chairman of the committee for the centenary celebration in honor of Pius IX, at the memorial service in St. Peter's basilica held on March 5, 1978. At extreme right, Italian Foreign Minister Arnaldo Forlani

identifies oneself with the Church's system, the more threatening must the findings of a study like mine appear. I was therefore very happy to meet with an understanding reception from quite a few Catholic theologians.[90] I found even more ready agreement from laymen and non-Catholics, who naturally felt less constrained by the magisterium.[91]

Still, important as such public endorsements are to me, I consider the indirect confirmation of my argument by my critics —some of whom are quite aggressive—as almost equally significant. Apart from the substantial concessions they make, the very violence of their reactions and their defensiveness show, if nothing else, that a rather sensitive nerve has been hit. But even beyond this, some of my critics have retreated from positions which they evidently no longer judge defensible. Thus, for instance, Professors Schatz, Martina, and Kasper wonder how the dogma of infallibility could be saved in the event that the Council really had not been free. They conclude that the definition would still stand, since it was later accepted by the Church.[92]

In the same way theologians have begun to reconcile themselves to the idea that in the first millennium the Church knew nothing of papal infallibility, and that in the centuries that followed there was nothing official laid down about it. But then how can one justify the definition of 1870? Schatz tries to see the dogmatization as one choice made from among many possibilities. (He speaks of its "decisionistic" character.) This means that the Church might have chosen a synodal structure. But in that case the definition would never have occurred.[93] Nothing could better illustrate the embarrassing plight of the defenders of infallibility than this rear-guard action. Have they completely forgotten that the dogmas promulgated in 1870 were supposed to have been divinely revealed?

The foregoing discussion has tried to bring a number of questions into sharper focus. These problems, insofar as they are of general interest, have been treated here in rough outline. A more detailed analysis will have to be undertaken somewhere else.

Which Sources?

Up till now Catholic presentations of the history of Vatican I have been based mainly on the sources supplied by the victors. The losers did not dare, for fear of reprisals, to write down and publish their view of what happened. The same motive caused some bishops and theologians to destroy their notes and letters relating to the First Vatican Council. Since the previous historiography had so seldom done so, I tried in my study to let the anti-Infallibilist—the defeated—side have its say. This put the story in a different light, but that does not warrant my critics' talk of one-sidedness and partisan spirit.[94] One-sidedness is much rather the problem with earlier writing on the Council. Someone, finally, had to show the other side of the coin.

The selective compilation of sources has not only excluded the anti-Infallibilists. It has also, as far as possible, disregarded the Infallibilists' inner circle, men such as the bishop of Regensburg, Ignatius von Senestrey, the archbishop of Westminster, Henry Edward Manning, a member of the staff of *La Civiltà Cattolica*, Giuseppe Giovanni Franco, and the founder of the Assumptionists, Emmanuel d'Alzon. Histories of the Council have preferred to deal with the moderate Infallibilists. But it is precisely the extremists who confirm the accuracy of the version of the events put forth by the anti-Infallibilists—bishops such as Félix Dupanloup, Georges Darboy, Joseph Georg Strossmayer, and Joseph Hefele.

In attempting to clarify these issues, I must once again make emphatic reference to the wholesale manipulation of the truth, which until recently was customary in the writing of conciliar history, and to the Vatican's archival policy, which is as repressive as ever. To this day, the highly informative papers of Archbishop Vincenzo Tizzani are being kept under lock and key —and the Tizzani case is not the only one of its kind.[95]

Closely connected with the problem of sources is the further question of whether historical research ought to advance any sort of thesis.[96] Some people claim that there is a danger here of a procrustean stretching of the facts, something incompatible with a disinterested approach to history. One might reply to this by noting that the historian does not begin his work with ready-made theses: They evolve and take shape in the course of his research. They are, in the final analysis, an attempt to get a grasp on the problems being studied.[97]

Furthermore, from the standpoint of scientific theory I do not think that the origin of theses is so crucial. The important thing is the results they provide. A thesis acquires value not only from the facts which support it but, above all, from the light that it sheds on events. In line with Karl Popper, I understand theses not as the last link in a chain of proofs, and hence literally incontestable, but as statements which always remain subject to falsification (i.e., refutation) and which must be withdrawn when facts can be found to contradict them. To that extent, every thesis is a hypothesis. But if no real objections are raised— I'm still waiting for such objections to be lodged against my work—then there is no reason to abandon any thesis. I believe that theses are necessary for the writing of history. Without them one would have to forego all in-depth analysis and settle for mere description and narration.

With reference to the use I make of the notion of ideology, one writer has postulated that in studying any given epoch historians may only employ concepts familiar to the period in question.[98] This demand is not feasible, as may be seen by the continual use of such terms as "antiquity" and "Middle Ages," which were obviously unheard of at the time. And any historian who wishes to trace developments spanning great periods of time will have to work with comprehensive conceptual tools unknown to the subjects of his investigation. Without such tools the science of history would have to limit itself to isolated moments and could no longer take the long view. Analyses such as those Max Weber undertook of the various forms of government down through history would be unthinkable.

Psychological Profile
of Pius IX

The effort to comprehend the personality of Pope Giovanni Maria Mastai-Ferretti from the psychological and psychiatric point of view presents a whole series of problems. In particular, the case made by two professors of psychology and psychopathology, Paul Matussek and Ludwig E. Pongratz, has provoked the indignation of some critics. Speaking of their diagnosis, Walter Brandmüller writes in the *Rheinische Merkur*, "One's respect for the powers of modern science swells—or shrinks—immensely when one considers what it takes to diagnose a patient who has been dead for one hundred years. Karl Jaspers was much more careful in his day when he warned against such diagnoses in his book on Hölderlin and Swedenborg."[99] Brandmüller is seconded by E. Müller in Bochum, who rates long-distance diagnoses as unscientific.[100] Heinz Joachim Fischer goes so far as to say, in the *Frankfurter Allgemeine Zeitung* of March 31, 1978, "It strikes one as ridiculous, in 1978, to go around collecting medical opinions on Pope Pius IX, who has been dead for exactly one hundred years—despite the fact that the personality of this pope, who made a dogma of his own infallibility, remains, in the nearly unanimous opinion of Catholic historians, highly problematic."[101] In his article in *Orientierung* Victor Conzemius objects that "the expert reports filed by Professors Pongratz and Matussek would have been appropriate in a biography of the pope, but they are out of place here, because the pope's epilepsy has no connection, not even an indirect one, with the Council or infallibility. The evidence submitted is too skimpy to permit a real characterization of the pope. As an 'abnormal' personality Pius IX finds himself in good company with psychically troubled men in history. One need only think of Luther and the numerous interpretive essays (from Grisar to Dalbiez and Erikson) which look past Luther the theologian to his 'abnormal' personality. Hasler, on the other hand, seems to be guilty of discriminating against epileptics, even cured ones."[102]

With such remarks Conzemius tries to reduce Pius IX's psychological problems to epilepsy, as Werner Egli rightly notes in *Orientierung:* "In conclusion, I should just like to say that, regardless of how one views the pope's disease, the critical role played by Pius IX has to be given greater emphasis. Conzemius cannot dismiss so lightly the charge that the pope's personality affected the debate over infallibility, and it is not just a question of epilepsy here. Along with his unhealthy mysticism, it seems to me that both the despotic traits and the insincerity of Pius IX have been sufficiently documented. That is a nuisance only as far as canonization is concerned, but not for a history of the Church!"[103] Werner Küppers also supports a psychohistorical examination of Pius IX: "Why should we not scrutinize this unusual personality, who helped to shape an entire era, as 'ruthlessly' as we do other great popes and men in world history? This would not eliminate the good and legitimate features of Pius IX's pontificate which Roger Aubert has pointed out. It would simply be an instance of the complexity of all human life."[104] In the *Frankfurter Hefte* Regina Bohne likewise considers it "perfectly reasonable" to make such inquiries and raises the further question of whether we can still speak of genuine piety on the part of Pius IX, given his grandiose opinion of himself.[105] Finally, despite all his critical reserve, Peter Stockmeier observes, "The psychological makeup of an individual entrusted with power undoubtedly represents a grave problem for the Church, as it does for all societies, and this holds true even with regard to mystical phenomena."[106]

There can be no disputing the fact, then, that the kaleido-scopic personality of this Roman pontiff raises psychological questions which become especially acute with reference to Vatican I. And since we have these problems on our hands anyway, we would be depriving ourselves of important help in clarifying them if we neglected interdisciplinary collaboration. Or should we interpret resistance to the use of psychohistorical research in church history to mean that people are afraid of giving too much weight to purely human factors?

As we sketch out a psychic profile of Pius IX, some studies which range further afield particularly recommend themselves to our attention. One, for example, by Norbert Wetzel of the Heidelberg University Institute for Fundamental Psychoana-lytical Research and Family Therapy (directed by Professor Stierlin) called my attention to the fact that in order to get a clearer picture of Pius IX's psychic constitution one had, first of all, to look into his family origins. Beyond this, we would have to ask if Pius IX did not overcompensate for his epilepsy by his sense of divine mission, his personal arrogance and, finally, the definition of infallibility. Fr. Giacomo Martina has already pointed out a similar phenomenon: He notes that an inferiority complex growing out of his political fiascos in the years 1846–48 drove Pius IX to reactionary intransigence.[107] Again, the aura of fascination that emanated from the pope merits more exhaustive study, for Pius IX did, after all, attract a group of adherents whose loyalty bordered on fanaticism.

In discussing Pius IX, the basic question remains: What part did the pope have in bringing about the definition of infallibility? Scientific history nowadays takes a very critical view of personalistic approaches and favors explanations based on structures and developmental tendencies. Such factors undoubtedly played a large role in the genesis of the infallibility dogma, a fact which this study has pointed out. Nevertheless, it would be hard to account for the definitions of Vatican I as well as the two Marian dogmas of more recent times without the two popes

Pius. Hence, I think Hans Kühner was fully justified in giving prominence to this personal aspect of the issue in his articles dealing with infallibility.[108]

Were the Councils Free?

Nothing has so stung my Catholic critics as the proposition impugning the freedom of the First Vatican Council. "Whether the Council was free or not is such an important question that to answer it in the negative, without referring to other councils, comes close to recklessness," writes Victor Conzemius in *Orientierung*. "If the standards Hasler applies to Vatican I were to be accepted, then no council of earlier days would be free, since they were all subject to pressure from the imperial, the papal, or some sort of episcopal party."[109] Peter Stockmeier likewise cannot go along with my judgment that Vatican I was not free because, he says, there have been councils which had much less freedom than that.[110] Josef Blank correctly replies to such objections in *Imprimatur*: "This is no counterargument. All it does is plainly show the problems which are involved in this and other dogmatizations and which need fresh clarification."[111] Piet Fransen observes, "It seems to me a frivolous argument to say that if we apply the criteria which Hasler requires for a council to be free, then all councils would come under suspicion, because they were always under pressure in one way or another."[111a] Gerhard Voss is right to ask, "Were not the councils convoked by the emperor in the old days of Christendom freer than Vatican I—and not just to some small degree, but substantially freer?"[112] In this context, Fr. Yves Congar takes particular note of the Council of Ephesus.[113]

This concern is also apparent in an article by Werner Küppers, who argues that anyone who questions the freedom of Vatican I raises the same issue with respect to earlier councils as well. "For freedom from external coercion was generally accepted as one of the prerequisites for a well-run council (a *synodus bene gesta*). Nonetheless, even in the great councils recognized by tradition this freedom was not always clearly present."[114] Küppers would evidently like to drop freedom as an essential condition for a valid ecumenical council. He speaks of "three broad, fundamental conditions: The entire Church must be represented, any decision on matters of faith must be virtually unanimous, and the Church must subsequently recognize and freely accept the conciliar decisions."[115] Küppers (an Old Catholic) lays particular stress on the first condition. He thinks that the entire Church was not represented at Vatican I; to that extent it was therefore only a sectional council. Thus, Vatican I was not ecumenical and its decrees would be subject to alteration. But would Rome be any more inclined to approve this point of view than mine, especially considering that it would allow for the revision of all the councils in the second millennium? Besides, the problem of freedom comes up again anyhow because of Küpper's second and third conditions, neither of which was met: There was no unanimity and the Church's acceptance of the dogma was tainted by manipulation.

Of all my critics it is Klaus Schatz who relativizes freedom in the most radical fashion. For him "conciliar freedom is, historically speaking, a highly relative concept. It is contingent upon the development both of the consciousness of freedom in society as a whole and upon the Church's understanding of itself."[116] He continues, "Thus, one can hardly deny that the influence of secular power, as brought to bear on the councils of the first millennium by the emperors, would, if judged in accordance with the way the Catholic Church sees itself today, wholly invalidate any Council."[117] Schatz undoubtedly wants to do more justice to historical reality than some earlier writers, but precisely because he overextends the category of "historicity" he succumbs to a relativism which understands all and forgives all.

So far no one has brought up any telling objections against my thesis that Vatican I was not free. Of course, there were some bishops who were spontaneously willing to renounce their own rights and agree to the expansion of the Vatican's prerogatives. This is a fact I have never disputed. Their numbers, however, were not large enough to explain how infallibility became a dogma of faith. The initial impetus for it, which came from the outside, and the coercion that followed were more significant than support from within the Council. In addition, the mentality of the bishops of the Latin Church would not permit more than a feeble resistance. The likely critical factor here was that for most of them the truth was only a minor issue.

One can easily see why people find the question of the Council's freedom so disturbing. Should the ecumenicity and validity of the Vatican decrees be overturned, this would have practical consequences. Meanwhile, theologians have fastened upon the notion of "reception" as a way of validating dogmas. Is this because the freedom of so many councils is so dubious? In any case, the important thing, according to the proponents of this theory, is not that a conciliar decision was freely arrived at but that it was subsequently ratified.[118] For Klaus Schatz, S.J., "The reception of a dogma by the whole Church is . . . in itself a theologically relevant fact, even if such acceptance may not have occurred without a good deal of pressure and manipulation."[119] Here the expression "theologically relevant" can only mean that whatever is imposed upon the Church, in whatever way, has to be considered true. And so once again the faith of the Church at any given moment, that is, the version of the faith as presented by the magisterium, is declared to be the norm.

In line with this, Schatz maintains that even a supporter of the dogma of 1870 can deny the Council's freedom. The main thing is that the entire episcopate later accepted infallibility. Here, too, it is only the fact of reception that counts; the use of force and coercion would make no essential difference.[120] Schatz explicitly grounds his thinking in the Church's infallibility, which is in no way dependent upon human performance, since otherwise the dogma would break down in its very core.[121] The difference between such notions and outright cynicism is not very great.

The reception theory leads Schatz to believe that the crucial point is not how a text was originally understood but how it was interpreted when finally accepted. Whatever Schatz's intentions, this looks like the old defensive strategy: The Church can define any text any way it likes. Because I read the statements of Vatican I in the sense in which they were taken at the time—and as they were clearly meant to be taken—Schatz accuses me of adopting a much too rigid position.[122] But, now as ever, I hold to the opinion that a text must first of all be understood as its author intended it. And I cannot see how an interpretation may be called correct when it runs completely counter to the original and natural sense.

Theology and History

Up till now my critics have barely addressed themselves to the fact that the Infallibilist arguments for the new dogma have already been soundly refuted—as early as 1870 by the conciliar minority. And this refutation has been fully confirmed by recent research. This obliviousness is all the more surprising since all the issues raised by the anti-Infallibilists lie at the heart of my research; without dealing with them it is impossible to do justice to any of the other related questions. For example, when all is said and done, Rudolf Pesche completely evades the difficulties created by infallibility in his article in *Publik-Forum*.[123] For Pesche, the findings of biblical research represent a "contribution to the history of the reception" (*Rezeptionsgeschichte*) accorded the dogma of infallibility. Once such contorted language is straightened out, this can only mean that biblical scholarship not only does not cast doubt on papal infallibility but confirms it. This is as novel as Pesche's claim that research historians have complete freedom today in the Catholic Church.[124] Anyone who challenges the Vatican definitions on the basis of modern exegesis, he says, is obviously thinking "unhistorically." Such thinking only makes sense if we take into account the ambiguous concept of history it implies. Any developments which have actually occurred, writers like Pesche suggest, bear within themselves their own justification. Peter Stockmeier is more cautious. He speaks of results that are "in flux," and suggests that discussion of these questions is still going on among scholars.[125] Klaus Schatz has already begun to reflect on ways to defend the dogma of infallibility should its foundation in church history give way.[126]

Josef Blank has done a useful service in clearly framing the issues at stake here: "What is the status of a dogma whose historical rationale—as the conciliar minority knew then and as modern exegesis and church history know now—is so very shaky? Here Hasler boldly exposes a problem which, as the whole Küng discussion shows, is far from solved. Furthermore, what are we to make of the fact (if it is one) that this dogma could only be passed with the help of direct manipulation and a good deal of pressure?"[127]

The closer we look, the more the relationship of dogma to history begins to emerge as the central issue. "This problem," writes Blank, "has been with us since the nineteenth century, but it has yet to receive a convincing theological answer. What is the theological significance of arguments based on a critical reading of history? A twofold concept of history, as everyone knows, offers no honest way out. Above and beyond that, as long as theology views history as a necessary element of belief in biblical revelation and as an account of the role played by that belief through the ages, it can never dispense with the task of elucidating historical truth. In the posing of historical questions, a biased a priori infallibility makes little sense."[128] In confronting these problems, can a more dynamic and, to some extent, "pneumatological" understanding of tradition help us to forge ahead, as Harding Meyer proposes in the *Lutherische Rundschau?*[129] Not as far as I can see. The concept of a dynamic church tradition has been far too profoundly influenced by dogma and doctrinal authority instead of by historical science, critical evaluation of sources, and empirical facts.[130] Even the strict distinction which Torrell postulates between history and tradition only helps someone who already believes. He maintains that "historically doubtful evidence takes on an altogether different value through the faith of the Church, acquiring an undreamt of clarity and power."[130a]

Klaus Schatz makes a distinction between historical and dogmatic statements. A tenet which is elevated to dogma today need not have been professed in the past in any formal way: The doctrine might be present *in germine* or inchoately. In a way, Schatz goes beyond Ignaz von Döllinger in his use of modern hermeneutics and his perception of the fundamental historicity of all dogma.[131] Manfred Weitlauff has a more perceptive view of the situation when he says, with reference to the great theologian from Munich, "Unfortunately we find that . . . the question of the historicity of the infallibility dogma as it was defined in 1870 has yet to receive a satisfactory solution."[131a] Yet,

although Schatz continually talks about "historicity," his suggestions evidently constitute a massive retreat from history. Characteristically, he asserts that the definition cannot be interpreted
retroactively, that is, no pope before Pius IX ever laid claim to
an infallible magisterium.[132] Naturally, if one abolishes the link
between religion and history one may defend any doctrinal thesis at all. But does Schatz manage to explain why the popes suddenly became infallible teachers with the arrival of Pius IX?

In contrast to such evasive positions, Yves Congar takes the
relationship between theology and history to be of decisive importance, and calls for the rethinking of the delicate distinction
between dogmatic tradition and historical documents.[133] Pope
Honorius I presents a special problem for Congar. But the
French Dominican is unwilling to smooth over the condemnation of this pope by the Sixth Ecumenical Council. On the
contrary, he turns the tables on the orthodox: "The dogma
proclaimed on July 18, 1870, teaches that the papal magisterium
is infallible—something which must be shown to be consistent
with cases like that of Honorius."[134] But shouldn't the question
be: Does the condemnation of Honorius in any way permit the
definition of an infallible papal teaching office? The condemnation was possible only because at that time no bishop even
dreamed of the pope's infallibility.[135] When Schatz observes that
no one at the Third Council of Constantinople (the Sixth Ecumenical Council) was even remotely thinking "in specific terms
of the infallibility of *ex cathedra* papal decisions"—and so the
judgment passed on Honorius says nothing against Vatican I[136]
—he is guilty of a logical lapse. The question still remains:
Can something be defined in 1870 if the Church in the seventh
century had no idea of it? In comparison with that, the problem
of what value to assign the letters of Honorius is of little consequence.

But, the objection is occasionally heard, wasn't the dogma
of infallibility, after all, a majority decision? This would seem to
remove any grounds for agitation, especially since, as Hansjakob
Stehle says in *Die Zeit*, it would be a complete mistake to sup-
pose that "in church politics, unlike the worldly kind, you have
to do your cooking not with water but with holy water."[137] But
Stehle quite forgets that a conciliar definition is not just another

political decision. It claims to be truth and must be accepted under pain of damnation. "The great burden which, to this day, still weighs down the definition," Blank observes pointedly in *Una Sancta*, "is *the problem of majority decisions and the question of truth*."[138] To repeat, since truth—the truth that the dogma obliges Catholics to believe—is at stake here, the machinations of the Roman system, including its practices and policies, take on a rather different meaning from the one they would have in an ordinary secular context.

The uncertain relations between dogma and history have had a much greater impact on the discipline of church history than Victor Conzemius would like to admit when he writes, "The attitude of the magisterium towards my research and my judgments as a church historian does not interest me in the slightest."[139] Conzemius may feel that way subjectively, but would he deny the manifold unconscious ties of dependence which can lead to a thoroughgoing autocensorship? Or the innumerable cases (e.g., Modernism) where the Church's magisterium has intervened to punish transgressions, real or imaginary —something it is still prepared to do even today? Vatican I is only a particularly vivid instance of the tension between religious faith and free scientific research.[140]

Revise the First Vatican Council?

The value and significance of the dogma of infallibility have been assessed very differently by different writers. While Margiotta-Broglio sees in it one of the roots of the discord between the Church and the modern world,[140a] for Hansjakob Stehle the dogma seems to be a bit of stage decoration from the "Vatican cabinet of antiquities," a curiosity which has long since lost any practical meaning. Is the wish the father to the thought here? The dogma of infallibility continues to have palpable effects even now. We have already shown how much Pope Paul VI's decision against the pill owed to the ideology of infallibilism. The encyclical *Humanae vitae* is the bond linking the infallible pope with the population explosion in Latin America.

More helpful than Stehle's remarks are some notes by Victor J. Willi on the cultural and sociological side of this issue. He argues that infallibility is one thing north of the Alps and another to the south: "Italians typically make no connection between recognizing an authority as such and obeying it unconditionally or, still less, identifying themselves totally with it. There are many indications that southern Europeans have never taken the Church's doctrinal opinions as seriously as the northerners are forever doing."[141] This feature of the Italian mentality, Willi says, expresses itself in a deep skepticism, in a different sort of relationship to truth. "Everywhere one turns throughout the peninsula one encounters the fact that in their system of likes and dislikes Italians have a very high appreciation of pliancy, diplomacy, and the arts of survival, and a correspondingly low opinion of confessing to the truth. The impression grows that the Italian, at bottom, has no real, unconditional belief in anything. Not only no faith in God, but not even in his fellow man, the state, or himself. Nihilism may well be more widespread in Italy than anywhere else in the world, and this does not just date from the rise of the welfare state."[142] If this is the case, one may wonder whether the dogma of infallibility hasn't become a sort of fence one can slip under at will. Needless to say, it can never be officially abandoned, but one comes to terms with it. Belief in it is unnecessary.

All this may be fine for Italians, but not for Christians all over the world, as Willi rightly stresses. The dogma of infallibility still represents one of the greatest obstacles to church reform and the ecumenical movement. In the final analysis, however, this is a battle between the spirit of authority and the spirit of freedom—which is why so many Catholics have gotten so heated up over it. They see danger threatening the principle of authority and, consequently, the foundations of their own inner security as well. For the same reason even Protestants may find a study like mine distinctly uncomfortable, as Harding Meyer emphasized in the *Lutherische Rundschau*.[143] In recent days we have frequently seen the churches supporting each other's authoritarian system.

If many Protestants have shown little interest in a more open exchange of views, the situation is still worse among Catholics. Writing in the *Basler Zeitung,* Hans Kühner warns of the possibility that "the dialogue we shall soon be having may be shifted towards such things as the laity, faith, the magisterium, and so forth, and thus deflected from the only topics that matter: historical reality and truth."[144] Others, too, are as ready as ever to grapple with weighty unresolved problems posed by infallibility. "Hasler's book," Hans Küng remarks in *Time* magazine, "only underlines the fact that the debate over infallibility is not over yet. The Church cannot sidestep this issue."[145] Yves Congar goes still further than Küng. He wants to see a "re-reception" of the papal dogmas defined by the First Vatican Council.[146] This complicated-sounding word basically means a revision. The questions discussed at Vatican I, he says, will have to be weighed and reformulated once more by Catholics and groups from other churches working together. Congar further insists that the "re-reception" take into acount not only the recent uses to which the papal magisterium has been put but also the exegetical, historical, and theological scholarship of the last few decades, as well as ecumenical exchanges on infallibility. Werner Küppers likewise proposes, in the *Schweizerische Kirchenzeitung,* that this question be dealt with in an ecumenical setting, perhaps in the Study Group on Faith and Church Constitutions of the World Council of Churches. For the immediate future, he suggests "an ecumenical symposium of experts . . . which would provide plenty of opportunities for face-to-face conversation—and controversy. The issue is too important and has been around for too long to let it get bogged down in published speeches and published replies."[147]

It is becoming increasingly obvious, in fact, that the dogma of papal infallibility has no basis either in the Bible or the history of the Church during the first millennium. If, however, the First Vatican Council was not free, then neither was it ecumenical. And in that case its decrees have no claim to validity. So the way is clear to revise this Council and, at the same time, to escape from a situation which both history and theology find more and more indefensible. Is this asking too much of the Church? Can it ever admit that a council erred, that in 1870 Vatican I made the wrong decision?

Actually, why couldn't John Paul II be the last infallible

pope? If he really takes the collegiality of bishops seriously, then it is time to have the Third Vatican Council straighten out the mistakes of the First. And what about the loss of authority this would imply? Would it not make any revision simply unthinkable? Would it not be much wiser to go on reinterpreting the dogma and to adapt it to changing circumstances? But then doesn't the Church have a lot more to lose this way? A revision would have the great advantage of being honest.

Let us hope that infallibility gets the unprejudiced review so many people have wanted, so that the truth—the whole truth—may be brought to light. For only of the truth is it said that it makes us free.

From *Publik-Forum,* no. 14, July 11, 1980

Open Letter from August Bernhard Hasler and Georg Denzler
to Pope John Paul II
The Truth Is at Stake!
Holy Father:

On May 15, 1980, you sent a letter to the German Bishops'
Conference praising and confirming the decision by the Congregation of the Doctrine of the Faith that is supposed to put
an authoritative end, once and for all, to the debate on papal
infallibility (now over a decade old). You have done this,
mindful of your responsibility to keep the faith secure. For
although you concede that it ranks rather low in the "hierarchy
of the truths revealed by God and confessed by the Church,"
you are nonetheless convinced that the doctrine of infallibility
"is in a certain sense the key to the certainty with which the
faith is confessed and proclaimed, as well as to the life and
conduct of the faithful. For once this essential foundation is
shaken or destroyed, the most basic truths of our faith likewise begin to break down." Your concern in this matter is understandable, but we must call your attention as plainly as
possible to the fact that you have in no way responded to the
questions that for some time now people have been asking with
increasing urgency, and that more and more cause trouble for
countless Catholics:

1) How can the dogma of the infallibility of the papal
magisterium be justified from the Bible and the tradition of the
Church?

As early as the First Vatican Council an unusually large and highly trained minority of 140 bishops fell prey to the most severe crisis of conscience on account of the evidence from the Bible and tradition. Even back then this group refuted the arguments proposed for papal infallibility and, with the best will in the world, could not see how the new dogma could be compatible with church history. More recent research has only aggravated this problem.

2) How can the decision of the First Vatican Council be considered valid when it was reached by flying in the face of the best information available and through the use of all sorts of pressure?

The infallibility debate will not quiet down until both these questions get a satisfactory answer. Hence we find it highly regrettable that you, Holy Father, have not made even the slightest attempt to address openly the real problems besetting many Christians today. Furthermore, you have not thought it worthwhile to accept repeated suggestions that an ecumenical commission, both interdisciplinary and international, launch an unprejudiced investigation into this complex issue.

In view of this, we find it hard to comprehend how you wish to defend the truth—which you count in your letter among the fundamental rights of the human being. How can this statement be squared with your attempt to silence theological and historical scholars without offering even the sketchiest arguments on the matter at hand? What is the point of Catholic theology anymore, we anxiously wonder, if its representatives are constantly being admonished to "stand loyally by the Church's doctrine" and not publish any research that runs counter to it out of respect for current norms in dogmatics and the Church's magisterium, which alone makes doctrinal decisions? It was quite wrong of you to commend the German Bishops' Conference for its "careful attention and goodwill," for as far as the dogma of infallibility is concerned, the Conference did not say a single word in response to the biblical and historical questions at issue.

It causes us grave concern to note how little understanding and esteem you display for historical truth, the truth from which the Church, in the words of Pope Leo XIII, has nothing to fear. How can you assert, for example, that Jesus had to confer infallibility upon Peter and his successors "because man is fallible"? We find in the Bible no mention at all of Jesus' furnishing the papacy with infallibility. Your appeal to Bishop Irenaeus (d. ca. 202) is also unfounded, for he in no way understood the Roman Church as the exclusive norm for all other Christians. Rather, he expressly attributed the same role as Rome's [Church] to other churches of Apostolic origins as well. Your claim to be defending the truth becomes even less credible in light of the fact that in your very own purview you have not taken it upon yourself to remove at long last the numerous obstacles blocking scholarly study of the First Vatican Council. The archives of the most important curial bodies remain closed for that period, just as they were before.

Holy Father, in your letter you also manifest the wish to work for church reform in the sense of the Second Vatican Council. But when you quote texts from this Council, you always pick out the passages that stress the unchanging elements in the Church. In so doing, you give no help of any sort to all those Catholics affected by the difficulties of living in and with the modern world, especially in the field of the sciences. Here, too, the question of truth is at stake. How is a church to appear credible and to be capable of self-reform when it cares so much for the structures of power—of course, you prefer to use the word "service" instead—and so little for the victory of divine truth?

You continually protest that you want to work for the unity of all Christians. But all this remains mere lip service as long as you are not prepared to tackle the main issues raised by the First Vatican Council. Nowadays the dogmatic definitions of this Council represent virtually the only important barrier to the reunion of Christians. Just recently, on April 28, 1980, in a joint communiqué issued after fruitful discussions in Odessa, Roman Catholic and Russian Orthodox theologians mentioned, among the differences that would be difficult to surmount, "the dogmatic formulation of the First Vatican Council concerning the primacy and infallibility of the bishop of Rome."

On the subject of ecumenicity you have repeatedly said how necessary and vital dialogue is. But anyone who listens carefully soon recognizes that you don't mean *real* dialogue. For you preclude any alteration of your own position and you see no possibility of responding to the arguments of the other side in such a way that your own point of view might be called into question.

In conclusion, we would like to assure you that we have written this letter out of genuine concern for the growth of freedom in the Church and in society. And so we urgently beg you to give disinterested attention and energetic assistance to all matters related to papal infallibility, so that the problems we have mentioned may be objectively studied—and solved.

Bamberg–Munich, June 27, 1980

August Bernhard Hasler was born in 1937 in Aadorf, Switzerland. He studied in Fribourg, Geneva, Paderborn, Tübingen, and Rome. In 1965 he received a doctorate in Catholic theology. In 1966 he was appointed by Cardinal Bea to the Vatican Secretariat for the Unity of Christians, where he handled relations with the Lutheran, Reformed, and Old Catholic churches until 1971. In 1976 he was awarded a doctorate in modern history and scientific theory. He died on July 1, 1980.

Georg Denzler, Professor of Church History in Bamberg, is the editor of the series "The Popes and the Papacy" (Hiersemann Verlag, Stuttgart), in which August B. Hasler's dissertation (1977) appeared as volume 12 under the title *Pius IX (1846–1878), Papal Infallibility, and the Imposition of an Ideology.*

Appendix

The *Rheinische Merkur*, the German Bishops, and Infallibility.
The Controversy over *Pius IX (1846–1878), Papal Infallibility,
and the First Vatican Council*

1. Walter Brandmüller writes the first review in the *Rheinische
Merkur* (no. 35, Sept. 2, 1977).

Found in the Junk Shop:
A Warped History of Pius IX
and the First Vatican Council

Some time ago a Swiss writer named August Hasler, along
with another author,* published a book entitled *The Vatican:
An Inside View* under the pseudonym "Hieronymus." The title
in itself was fairly revealing. Now Hasler has followed it
up—this time writing by himself and without the pseudonym—
with a two-volume work, *Pius IX (1846–1878), Papal Infallibility,
and the First Vatican Council: Dogmatization and Imposition of
an Ideology* (Anton Hiersemann, 2 vols., 300 DM). And once
again the title tells us something, although this book lays claim
to scholarly rigor and earned the author a doctorate from the
Philosophical Faculty of the University of Munich.

A thirty-three-page bibliography, previously unpublished
material from thirty-eight archives, and a topic like that—it all

---

* The other author was Dr. Helmut Herles, former Roman correspondent for *Publik*, now in the Bonn office of the *Frankfurter Allgemeine
Zeitung*.

promises a scholarly sensation. But as we read it, expectation turns into disappointment. For at bottom this is just a copy of the old objections first proposed by the anticonciliar movement from 1869 to 1871 and now decked out a bit modishly as a critique of ideology.

The core of Hasler's assertions is that the Council was manipulated by a small, determined party of fanatics and pseudomystics, theologically poverty-stricken and mostly Jesuits or their associates; that the Council was subjected to massive pressure by Pius IX and was therefore not free. Given this lack of freedom, the Council's decrees can lay no claim to truth.

Since it has long been open season on Pius IX, one is not surprised when this book goes on to maintain that Pius IX was paranoid and at least partly not in his right mind at the time of the Council—and morally corrupt besides (liar, hypocrite, despot, illegitimate father). No wonder that such a monster of a pope could only produce such a monstrous dogma like infallibility. Must not all of Catholicism be monstrous, too, if to this very day Catholics (apart from a few critically enlightened spirits) have to believe this dogma? This is doubtless the unspoken conclusion which Hasler would like to suggest to his readers.

One cannot avoid the impression here that "historical material is being stockpiled for a campaign, à la Küng, against infallibility." The positions Hasler takes, as has already been said, are for the most part not new, nor is his method—about which one finds it hard to say whether it is merely bad or cunningly perfidious. One thing is certain: It is only scientific in appearance, in superficial appearance.

Hasler contends that without Pius IX there never would have been a dogma of infallibility, and that except for Pius IX's epilepsy he never would have become a priest—or pope. Such statements are enough to startle anyone with a little experience in historical methodology.

But there is more. There are glaring contradictions in this book. Hasler writes, "Despite intensive efforts by the Roman Curia and the leaders of the Ultramontane movement, on the eve of the Vatican Council the doctrine of papal infallibility was by no means generally accepted . . ." But two pages later we read, "The Curia's attitude towards papal infallibility was still more guarded (i.e., than towards the idea of convoking the

Council)." One cannot help wondering what things were really like. First the Curia is exerting itself tremendously, then it holds back. Hasler obviously failed to notice this contradiction. And he makes the same mistake in a different context. He affirms that Pius IX urged Archbishop Scherr of Munich to adopt sanctions against Döllinger. Later on he says, ". . . even in the case of Döllinger, Rome would probably have been satisfied with his silence had not Archbishop Scherr forced him to take an unequivocal stance." Who, then, was doing the urging, Pius IX or Archbishop Scherr? It is precisely at this point that we see the methodological error which characterizes the entire book. Certainly Hasler has uncovered and made use of an immense abundance of sources, some hitherto unknown. But he was incapable of critically assessing the significance of the individual sources and of fitting the individual statements into an organic unity. He relies blindly on his informants and occasionally edits his quotations to suit his purposes. He uncritically accepts accounts of episodes, general feelings, and spontaneous remarks by the pope and council fathers without asking who is writing to whom with what intention in such and such a way. He neglects to ask who is reporting this, who is keeping silent on that, and so forth, as the historical method would have demanded. Without making any distinctions, he capitalizes on the remarks and judgments of notorious enemies of the pope and the Church (especially from diplomatic circles), treating them as fully conclusive. He does the same with impromptu statements by the bishops of the minority, as they vented their annoyance at conciliar opponents. The historical quality of these diplomatic reports may be gauged from the fact that, to take one example, the Prussian envoy von Arnim, whom Bismarck didn't take very seriously anyway, actually wrote: "The story is making the rounds that . . . as he was passing by the Church of the Trinitate [*sic* Brandmüller] the pope bade a cripple who was lying out in front, 'Rise up and walk!' But the experiment failed." Hasler admits that this sounds incredible, but he nonetheless infers from it that Pius IX impressed people as suffering from megalomania. Rumor-mongering and Roman backstairs gossip are not, however, serious sources, even if they turn up in reports from diplomats or in the Roman diary of Gregorovius. In this fashion Pius IX even acquires a son: the Dominican Cardinal Guidi. This is documented by several letters filed with the Piedmontese Government by a Polish count named Kulczycki, who styled the cardinal a "fils naturel" of the pope. Hasler further claims that during the famous "la tradizione sono io" audience Guidi spoke up for a formula limiting papal infallibility, whereupon the pope replied, "Tu quoque fili mi" (you, too, Brutus my son). This quotation is actually taken to be a confession that the pope was the cardinal's father—as if Brutus had been Caesar's physical son!

While the critical apparatus for some passages of the book swells to gigantic proportions, the only "proof" provided here is the following statement: "No one denies that the pope, before he entered the priesthood, was involved in love affairs. In the literature on Pius IX there is mention here and there of his having fathered children. A tradition to this effect has persisted in Rome." There is no reference to the writers who said this, nor any indication where this Roman tradition is supposedly expressed.

That is the sum total of the hard historical evidence . . . but it's enough for Hasler to reconstruct, at least hypothetically, the stormy audience and turn it into a tragic father-son conflict. It's as easy as that.

In the very same way we get a portrait of a pope who is overmastered by unhealthy mysticism, displays repulsive despotic traits, has lost touch with reality, shocks us by his intellectual shallowness. Then there are the eccentricities and the mental lapses. (Hasler uses some of these notions as chapter titles.) On these grounds he reaches his diagnosis that the pope suffered from paranoia, intense ego-fixation, and narcissistic disturbances. As a final touch, all this is confirmed by Professors (of psychopathology and psychology) Matussek and Pongratz, based on the "material so carefully and reliably assembled" by Hasler. One's respect for the powers of modern science swells—or shrinks—immensely when one considers what it takes to diagnose a patient who has been dead for one hundred years. Karl Jaspers was much more careful in his day when he warned against such diagnoses in his book on Hölderlin and Swedenborg.

Even as he draws this psychological profile of the pope as a pathological case, a further characteristic of Hasler's method leaps into view: Whenever the facts are inconvenient, he sweeps them under the rug. He is a master of the art of leaving things out (an art which has produced some great works—but not of critical history). Yet, one asks oneself, in view of this papal monster, what sort of college of cardinals did it take to elect such a man the supreme shepherd of the Church? Furthermore, no pope in the last one hundred years, not even Pius XII, enjoyed such an overwhelming measure of sympathy, veneration, and profound respect as Pio Nono—and not by any means exclusively among undiscriminating Ultramontane fanatics. On the occasion of the pope's golden jubilee as a priest, even such liberal journals as the *Neue Freie Presse* in Vienna and the *Augsburger Allgemeine Zeitung* painted relatively sympathetic portraits of his personality. And there can be no doubt that the bishops of the minority themselves respected and revered Pius, though they may have disagreed with some of his actions. If Hasler couldn't bring himself to believe this, he ought at least to have discussed it thoroughly—for up till now these positive features have had broad historiographical currency.

At other points in the text the author shows himself to be very poorly read. Has he really studied everything which he quotes? It is, for example, generally acknowledged that Karl Joseph von Hefele, that highly critical opponent of the infallibility definition, was, in his role as a conciliar consultant in Rome, assigned the task of drafting an agenda for the Council on the basis of documents from Trent. His proposal was put into effect by Pius IX, with trifling alterations, in the decree *Multiplices inter*. Nevertheless, Hasler unblinkingly goes along with him when Hefele (God knows why) writes that he was fobbed off with the assignment of making excerpts from the Tridentine ceremonial.

Again, Hasler writes of the bishops at Trent: "Compared with Vatican I, the procedural rules they established for themselves were much freer. For this reason the Tridentine regulations—there was a copy in the Vatican secret archives—were kept under lock and key." Doesn't Hasler see the contradiction here? But enough of this for now.

A more probing confrontation with Hasler's book will have to ensue in the learned journals dealing with church history. As a precaution, the author chides Catholic church historians for their ideologically motivated "only fragmentary" acceptance of the critical impulses of modern historical science. Of course, when Ebeling calls for "the radical critical destruction of everything which in the course of history has gotten between us and Christ," Hasler gladly complies; indeed, he makes the demand his own. But the Catholic church historian can never regard either the pope or the Church as a barrier between himself and Christ, as an obstacle to be destroyed. If anyone wants to do that, then let him, but not, at least, the way Hasler does.

2. On September 8, 1977, August B. Hasler urgently requested permission of the *Rheinische Merkur* to publish a reply—even in the form of a letter to the editor—to the article by Walter Brandmüller. This request was not granted. *Publik-Forum* (no. 22, Oct. 28, 1977) printed in its entirety the text which the *Merkur* had refused.

Dogma Instead of History:
A Response

Barely ten days after the appearance of the second volume of my book (which runs to over 640 pages), Walter Brandmüller has plunged into a passionate attack against it. One must wonder how the church historian from Augsburg mastered such a large-scale work in such a short time. And why the hurry, since in Brandmüller's eyes my arguments are such tired old stuff? But these and other rhetorical flourishes—such as his disappointment over the book's failure to live up to its promise as a scholarly sensation—are only designed to cover up his own uneasiness. At bottom he finds my thesis deeply disturbing—although he has come up with precious little to refute it.

First of all, Brandmüller objects to the title. The concept of ideology, which is clearly defined in the text later on, is not to his liking. While ostensibly preferring a more matter-of-fact approach, in his own titles he throws out such terms as "Junk Shop" and "Warped History."

Then there's the question of my method, which is alleged to be "bad," "cunningly perfidious," "only scientific in appearance, in superficial appearance." Why? Because for once I have let the defeated side, the losers, say their piece and at length—insofar as the sources have not already been destroyed or withheld from me. For Brandmüller these materials don't count. Is it necessary for me to point out how convenient it is for him to discredit in advance a whole series of documents as scandal-mongering and Roman backstairs gossip because they don't jibe with his viewpoint? Brandmüller rules out of court the reports of Prussian Ambassador Arnim and the historian Gregorovius. He very wisely avoids coming to grips with the diaries of Dupanloup, Darboy, Icard, the notes of Maret, the letters of Foulon, and so forth, not to mention the testimony of the Infallibilists—Senestrey, Franco, d'Alzon, Manning—which bolsters the minority's case. Who is uncritical here? Who picks and chooses the sources to suit his purposes?

The ellipses marking omissions in the Dupanloup quotations are from Dupanloup, not me, as Brandmüller might have realized had he read page 541. But reading is precisely what Brandmüller has not been doing. Indeed, he didn't have to because his scathing critique was prepared well in advance. It always looks good if you can point out logical inconsistencies, and after skimming the book Brandmüller discovers "manifest contradictions." I have no desire to go into them here: As any vigilant reader can see, such contradictions dissolve by themselves.

What obviously irritates Brandmüller the most are my detailed analyses of Pius IX. First he exaggerates the drift of my remarks so that the pope becomes a monster. Then he takes on a tone at once threatening and pedantic and calls attention to the respect widely accorded the pope. He deliberately overlooks the fact that I never denied Pius IX's positive qualities—his piety, his personal charm, his vibrant humanity, his sense of humor. But contemporary reports on the darker side of this pope are too numerous, too believable, too consistent to ignore. And Brandmüller has not even attempted to deny Pius IX's epileptic disease.

As Brandmüller sees it, I am a master of the art of leaving things out. But the charge rebounds back onto him. His presentation of my work could have hardly been more one-sided. He says not a word about the main problem dealt with in my study: how the definition of infallibility could have come about in 1870. He says almost nothing about the second and longest part of the book (the arguments for and against papal infallibility) and absolutely nothing about the third part (the story of how the minority made its submission to Rome). I would have been interested in hearing from Brandmüller about, say, archival politics. It strikes one as grotesque to have one's research faulted for incompleteness while on the other side the Church's archives remain closed or purged. And, to top it all off, Brandmüller quotes me incompletely and out of context. The sentences thus pieced together are then "enough to startle anyone with a little experience in historical methodology." But enough of this.

At the end of his article Brandmüller finally lets the cat all the way out of the bag. What should not happen did not happen. The ideological constraints binding Catholic church historians of Brandmüller's stripe could not have been better expressed than by his maxim, "The Catholic church historian can never regard either the pope or the Church as a barrier between himself and Christ, as an obstacle to be destroyed." In the very last line of his article Brandmüller states that he simply doesn't like my criticism. In reality, though, he thinks there should be no criticism at all on the fundamental issues facing the Church and the faith. Can someone who thinks this way make any claims about the scientific method? Or is church history, in the final analysis, not a science at all? In that case, of course, the subject would have no business being taught at universities.

3. On September 12, 1977, the News Service of the Secretariat of the German Bishops' Conference (Immediate Release, no. XXII/77, Dr. Joseph Homeyer, Prelate) circulated Brandmüller's review, with the following introductory paragraph:

Der Spiegel Dredges
Up Old Charges

With reference to an article in the latest edition of *Der Spiegel* (no. 38, Sept. 12) entitled "Sick in the Head," which attempts to present Pius IX as a sick man and not completely in his right mind, the News Service wishes to draw attention to a piece which has already appeared in the Sept. 2 issue of the *Rheinische Merkur,* and which we enclose here for your information. Other periodicals as well have come out with critical assessments of the charges now published in *Der Spiegel*.

4. On October 28, 1977, *Publik-Forum* (no. 22) published a letter to the editor from Georg Denzler. The *Rheinische Merkur* had refused to print an earlier letter from Denzler to the same effect.

Liberating Truth: A Comment on "Case History of a Pope, or Rummaging in the Junk Shop?" (no. 20/77)

As editor of the series of scholarly books entitled "The Popes and the Papacy" (A. Hiersemann, Stuttgart, 1971–), which includes the work by Dr. August B. Hasler, priest of the diocese of St. Gall, entitled, *Pius IX (1846–1878), Papal Infallibility, and the First Vatican Council: Dogmatization and Imposition of an Ideology,* I was not a little surprised by the press release from the Secretariat of the German Bishops' Conference. I find it astonishing, to begin with, that the Secretariat should pay any serious attention to the extremely one-sided and biased presentation of the book in *Der Spiegel* (Sept. 12), and could feel obliged to take a stand on it. But I find it even more amazing that in its blanket condemnation the Secretariat—surely not a single one of its members can have read this 632-page book, with its extraordinarily large critical apparatus, scarcely a week after the publication of the second volume—supports its case by appealing to the article by Walter Brandmüller, a church historian from Augsburg, which appeared in the *Rheinische Merkur*. Brandmüller's piece is unscholarly, full of anger and resentment, and written in the spirit of a sixteenth-century Catholic apologetic. Significantly, the editors of the *Rheinische Merkur* denied Hasler the chance to print his side of the question.

Thank God the Church's problems these days can no longer be brushed aside with cheap defamations and hasty denials. Precisely in the field of the theological sciences the prevailing norm must be the biblical one, "The truth will make you free."

5. Almost a year later, on July 14, 1978, the *Rheinische Merkur* started up a new campaign with the following review by Matthias Buschkühl.

Based on a Nazi Work:
August Bernhard Hasler's Book on Pius IX

In a first review of August Bernard Hasler's *Pius IX (1846–1878), Papal Infallibility, and the First Vatican Council: Dogmatization and Imposition of an Ideology* (Stuttgart, 1977), Walter Brandmüller aptly characterized this work as "warped history." While working on my dissertation, which deals with relations between England and the Vatican during the reign of Pius IX and with the English role at Vatican I, I had occasion to look into Hasler's study in considerable detail.

Up till now no one has noticed that Hasler relies on Nazi propaganda. In his bibliography he annotates a book, "E. Schmidt. *Bismarck's Battle with Political Catholicism, Part I: Pius IX and the Period of Mobilization, 1848 to 1870.* Hamburg, 1942." Typically, Hasler does not write out the author's given name even though the surname is a common one—probably to hush the whole thing up. "E. Schmidt" is none other than SS-Obersturmbannführer Erich Schmidt. In a commentary on this work (*Historical Yearbook,* 83, 1963, p. 217f., under the heading "Problems of *Kulturkampf* Research"; references are also given to the many other reviews of it) written on the occasion of the reissue of the second part (this time under the name "Schmidt-Volkmar") in 1962, Rudolf Morsey pointed out that in 1940 Schmidt informed the Foreign Ministry: "My position as educational director of a National Political Training Institute and as an SS leader should be a sufficient guarantee that I am undertaking the task of studying the records with an appropriate awareness of my political responsibility." (Quoted ibid.) The Nazism in Schmidt's work comes out in the foreword and in the advertisement for volume I of the series in which Schmidt's study appears, which deals with the "Jewish question." Hasler only refers to Schmidt's book in his bibliography, but there are so many striking points of agreement between remarks made by

SS-Obersturmbannführer Schmidt and those of Hasler that Hasler must have borrowed the ideas from Schmidt (without footnoting them).

On page 27 Schmidt takes up the beginnings of Ultramontanism in France, alluding to "the Savoyard and Jesuit, Count de Maistre" (p. 27f.), Bonald and Lamennais (p. 28). Hasler treats the same topic on page 14f., naming Count Louis de Bonald, "the Savoyard Count Joseph de Maistre" (p. 14) and Félicité Robert de Lamennais (p. 15). Schmidt writes on page 17f. of the origins of Ultramontanism in Germany, of "religious circles" in the province of Münster (p. 17f.), the group surrounding the "half-Czech Klemens Maria Hofbauer" in Vienna, and in Munich (p. 18). Hasler writes on page 15 of the spread of Ultramontane ideas in Germany through the groups surrounding Klemens Maria Hofbauer and Schlegel in Vienna, and "analogous circles in Münster and Munich."

The most important overlapping area, however, is between Hasler's section "Part One: The Manipulation of the Infallibility Debate. III. At the Time of the Council Was Pius IX of Completely Sound Mind? 2. The Personality of Pius IX. A. Unhealthy Mysticism" (pp. 130–35), in which Hasler charges Pius IX with "near morbid piety" and a "belief in miracles bordering on superstition," and Schmidt's comments on pages 45 to 47. SS-Obersturmbannführer Schmidt writes, "Thus, his [Pius IX's] actions often appear to be less the result of careful thought by a responsible personality than the outpouring of transcendental inspirations. Various incidents offer proof of this fanatical trait" (p. 45; there follow a page and a half of examples). "Even though such reports may not have always mirrored the whole situation, one thing they do clearly show is that in the depth of his soul Pius IX was a religious enthusiast" (p. 46). "This is the same source which fostered the notion of the suprapersonal power of the pope's official charisma. Because of it he made decisions more on instinct than from any thorough study of the facts, for he was utterly convinced that God spoke directly through him, the privileged bearer of divine charisma. He placed himself on a level with God, applying to himself Christ's statement, 'I am the truth and the life.' The conviction of the magical power of his office led him to deify his own person . . ." (p. 47).

Anyone who has read Hasler's book must recognize that Hasler fully adopts and takes as his point of departure what ·Schmidt writes on page 290: "The Council of 1869–70 was primarily a personal achievement of Pius IX, the organic conclusion of the policy he followed from the day he first ascended the throne . . . By his systematic selection of new members, Pius IX had shaped the College of Cardinals into a compliant tool. The Pius cult, the intensely devout veneration of Mary as the sinless Queen of Heaven, and the heralds of Ultramontanism, using the instruments and theories of democracy, had trained the masses to follow the papal line. The form in which the dogma of Mary's Immaculate Conception was announced had constituted the first attack upon the position of the episcopacy, and the *Syllabus* the definitive challenge to the modern state. Thus, in the course of his reign one block was laid upon another to build a structure of absolute power. The dogmatization of papal infallibility represents only the conspicuous crowning cupola of the monumental effort. In 1869, when he was congratulated by the Belgian ambassador on the anniversary of his ascent to the throne, Pius IX said, 'They will bestow infallibility on me—I don't need it at all. Am I not infallible already? Did I not some years ago establish the dogma of the Virgin's Immaculate Conception on my own? . . .' Pius IX experienced his identity as a successor of Peter and the representative of God so strongly, and felt the transcendental roots of his office so immediately, that there was no room for rational misgivings or considerations of opportuneness."

Hasler even brings in the report of the Belgian ambassador (p. 98). In fact, he merely fills in Schmidt's skeletal framework, modishly decking out the end result with a little critique of ideology. But Hasler adds something which even SS-Obersturmbannführer Schmidt thought too petty to be used against the Church. Hasler puts Pius IX on the psychiatrist's couch and finds him partially *non compos mentis* (to the point of violent outbursts) on account of his epilepsy, from which Hasler thinks —contrary to the judgment of serious researchers—the pope still suffered in his later years. As Helen Young of "North London Action Epilepsy" says in the *Catholic Herald* (Feb. 17, 1978), Hasler's thesis strikes the experts as absurd. The assumption that epilepsy produces mental lability or violence is outmoded.

On the strength of the information I provided, the *Catholic Herald* instructed its Roman correspondent to confront Hasler with my charges. Hasler responded by claiming that the Schmidt he listed in his bibliography and SS-Obersturmbann-führer Erich Schmidt were not the same person. He made this assertion despite the fact that in his bibliography (p. 570) he gives the full title and subtitle of Schmidt's book. Why did Hasler come out with such a clumsy and easily refutable claim? Was he speculating that Schmidt's propagandistic work would not be available in England? Is he embarrassed by the intellectual affinity between his line of argument and that of SS-Obersturmbannführer Schmidt?

6. On August 17, 1978, August B. Hasler sent the following reply to Matthias Buschkühl's article, to the *Rheinische Merkur,* which again refused him any space in its columns.

**The Dogma of Infallibility
and Nazi Propaganda:
A Comment on Matthias Buschkühl's
"Based on a Nazi Work," in
the *Rheinische Merkur,* no. 28, July 14, 1978**

Last year Walter Brandmüller did me the honor of commenting extensively on my study, *Pius IX (1846–1878), Papal Infallibility, and the First Vatican Council: Dogmatization and Imposition of an Ideology,* barely ten days after the publication of the second volume. This review, published in the *Rheinische Merkur,* was the very first to appear. In it Brandmüller whetted readers' appetites with such expressions as "warped history" and "found in the junk room." Scarcely a year later the respected Catholic weekly has, astonishingly, renewed the honor. In accord with Brandmüller, Matthias Buschkühl characterizes my work in the *Rheinische Merkur* as Nazi propaganda. He accuses me of borrowing my most important points from SS-Obersturm-bannführer Erich Schmidt, merely filling them out somewhat and garnishing them with a critique of ideology.

I advise Herr Buschkühl to try and patent his method as a formula for liquidating literary enemies. It ought not to be hard for him to convince the examiners at the patent office how the system operates in each and every case. Depending upon circumstances and the needs of the moment, all one need do is find a Communist, Jew, Freemason, Baptist, Jesuit, Fascist, Nazi, and so forth, who has already done work in the same area as one's adversary. Then any congruences which emerge—for Buschkühl even the names of major historical figures will do—must simply be characterized as deliberate borrowing. Thus, for Buschkühl the chain of proof is closed.

Buschkühl further maintains that I tried to gloss over my dependence on SS-Obersturmbannführer Schmidt, and for this reason I did not write Schmidt's first name in the bibliography. He ought to have said that I abbreviated *all* the given names in the thirty-four-page bibliography so that no one could discover the SS-Obersturmbannführer among the many authors.

Finally, Buschkühl was taken in by a canard when he wrote that I denied that SS-Obersturmbannführer Schmidt and the E. Schmidt named in the bibliography were identical. He speaks of a "clumsy claim" on my part, but the facts were quite different. Some months ago the Roman correspondent of the *Catholic Herald*, Michael Wilson, called me up and asked me whether I had quoted an SS-Obersturmbannführer Schmidt in my book, which I denied. Wilson in no way confronted me with Buschkühl's accusations. I made no sense of the question from the *Catholic Herald* and Wilson could give me no further help on the matter.

I said no to his question because there are no quotations from anyone named Schmidt in my study. I came across Erich Schmidt's book only when I was finishing my research. But I found no new angles in it for my topic and saw no reason to make any special reference to it—though I included it in the bibliography for completeness' sake. Besides, at the time I was asked the question I did not know that Schmidt was an Obersturmbannführer in the SS. This is not evident from his book. I was quite aware, however, that it was a Nazi work. By quoting so extensively from it, Buschkühl has now given it ample publicity.

7. On August 18, 1978, the *Rheinische Merkur* published a letter to the editor from Georg Denzler, commenting on Buschkühl's review (no. 33), but with two characteristic deletions that are included here in square brackets.

A Slanderous Attack

Whoever this Buschkühl may be—I've never even heard his name before—he has so disgraced himself as a scholar with his article, as stupid as it is shameful, that his Ph.D. mentor (Buschkühl, as he himself stresses, is writing a dissertation of English-Vatican relations during the reign of Pius IX) has really no choice but to show him the door.

The things Hasler writes in his summary treatment of Ultramontanism can be found in any textbook of church history. He had no need of the book by the "SS-Obersturmbannführer"— a term that Buschkühl uses five times.

Hasler's assertions concerning the personality of Pius IX, unlike those of E. Schmidt, are abundantly documented. Any serious critic of his book must come to terms with Hasler's sources —and not as a self-defensive ideologue but as an unbiased historian. [Since I agree with Hasler's characterization of the pope, Buschkühl probably classifies me as a Nazi.]

Buschkühl has been corresponding with Helen Young. But her opinions on epilepsy are radically contradicted by leading physicians and psychologists. That Pius IX was an epileptic in the period before his ordination is beyond doubt. The controverted point is whether he was ever totally cured of the disease. In any case, Hasler is guarded in his judgments on this question and leaves the verdict to two prominent psychologists (Professor Matussek of Munich and Professor Pongratz of Würzburg).

Bad as Buschkühl's yellow journalism is, I find it still more regrettable that the *Rheinische Merkur* was prepared to publish such an irrelevant and slanderous attack on Hasler's book. [A paper such as the *Rheinische Merkur* should not stoop this low.]

Anyone interested in a thorough, extremely critical, but well-informed and consistently fair discussion of Hasler's book—

so that he can make up his own mind—may read what Dr. Klaus Schatz, S.J., of Frankfurt, an outstanding expert on Vatican I, has written in *Theologie und Philosophie* (no. 2, 1978). That's what I call historical-theological science.

8. On September 1, 1978 (no. 35), the *Rheinische Merkur* granted Matthias Buschkühl space to "correct" Georg Denzler.

A "Correction" of Denzler

In a letter to the editor (*Rheinische Merkur*, no. 33) Herr Denzler taxes me, or, rather, my article ("Based on a Nazi Work," *RM*, no. 28) with being "stupid," "shameful," and an instance of "yellow journalism." He bids my doctoral mentor "show me the door" and reproaches me—unjustly—for making an "irrelevant and slanderous attack" on Hasler. At one point in particular, namely, his provocative remark directed at my mentor, it becomes clear that he aims to destroy my existence and to prevent me from ever publishing my views on all the interrelated themes Hasler touches on. Herr Denzler takes me to task for calling Erich Schmidt an "SS-Obersturmbannführer" five times in two hundred lines and charges me with ideological prejudice. All this reminds me that Professor Morsey, after he published the letter Schmidt wrote to the Foreign Office in 1942 (which I allude to in my article), was labeled by Schmidt as a "Christian scribbler riding a wave of prosperity." (See *Historical Yearbook*, 83, 1963, p. 218, n. 6.)

I must also reject the accusation of being a narrow-minded apologist. The subject of my article was Hasler's method and one aspect of his work on Pius IX, not Pius IX himself. On the contrary, as Fr. Klaus Schatz, S.J., writes in his review of Hasler (*Theologie und Philosophie*, no. 2, p. 276), the danger of the book lies in the fact that, in counterreaction to Hasler, any critical assessment of the policies of Pius IX might now be "disqualified as uncritical and a threat to the faith." On the basis of my newspaper article Herr Denzler denies my scholarly credentials. I must therefore point out that Hasler, whom he defends so unscrupulously, published a *chronique scandaleuse* before doing his dissertation. It was called *The Vatican: An Inside View;* Hasler wrote it (together with somebody else) under the pseudonym "Hieronymus." Hasler has dragged what used to be objective discussion of Pius IX's policies down to the level of Döllinger's inflammatory journalism (written, as Professor Conzemius puts it, out of "hate-filled antipapalism," at first anonymously and later under the pseudonym "Janus") and Friedrich's Old Catholic polemics. Arguments concerning the policies of Pius IX must be pursued on the level of scientific history and not by means of articles in *Der Spiegel.*

Typically, Herr Denzler's letter says nothing about my charge that Hasler got the idea for the section where he censures Pius IX's unhealthy mysticism (pp. 130–35) from the work by SS-Obersturmbannführer Schmidt (pp. 45–47), and that Hasler took Schmidt's remarks on page 290 as the point of departure for his book. I had expressly stated that Hasler "fills in Schmidt's skeletal framework." Herr Denzler's objection, therefore, that Hasler "abundantly documents" his case is wide of the mark. As far as the evidential value of Hasler's sources goes, not only Professor Brandmüller of Augsburg (*Rheinische Merkur,* no. 35, 1977) but also Professor Martina, S.J., of Rome (*L'Osservatore Romano,* Feb. 8, 1978, p. 6), who is working on a critical biography of Pius IX, has had many negative things to say. With regard to the way Hasler uses his sources, Professor Conzemius of Lucerne wrote in his review (*Orientierung,* 41, 1977, p. 207), "To begin with, one must take exception to the careless hermeneutical utilization of published and unpublished sources." Herr Denzler would have been better advised not to recommend the review by Fr. Klaus Schatz, S.J., which I am well acquainted with, as a defense of Hasler. Dr. Schatz finds that Hasler's selection of sources is remarkably one-sided (p. 258), and that "Hasler cannot escape the blame for his very frequently partisan and uncritical use of sources by arguing that he . . . brings in Senestrey and Franco by way of supplement" (p. 259). Fr. Schatz also writes that "Hasler's description (of Pius IX) doesn't add up" (p. 261).

I cannot imagine why Herr Denzler spreads the story that I

"have been corresponding" with Mrs. Helen Young. I neither know her personally nor do I correspond with her. In my article I cite Helen Young's statement in the *Catholic Herald* that Hasler's repetition of the obsolete medical opinion that epileptics are violent is a calumny against hundreds of thousands of people. It is. It seems especially disturbing to me that Herr Denzler continues to defend Hasler's procedure of trying to turn his comments on the pope into a diagnosis of a man who has been dead more than one hundred years. This sort of thing is too amateurish for a historical dissertation. Fr. Schatz calls the reports filed by Hasler's experts simply "worthless" (p. 250).

Although in my article I don't at all go into the question of whether Pius IX was an epileptic in his youth, Herr Denzler lectures me: "That Pius IX was an epileptic in the period before his ordination is beyond doubt." I must conclude from this that Professor Georg Denzler, S.T.D., is unacquainted with the work by A. Serafini, *Pio Nono: Giovanni Mastai Ferretti* . . . , vol. I (subseq. vols. have not appeared), 1792–1846 (Rome, 1958). Serafini has an altogether different view of the nervous disturbances which Giovanni Mastai-Ferretti suffered from in the years after puberty. In an article entitled "How Sick Was Pius IX?" published in *Orientierung* (no. 41, 1977), Professor Martina summarized his findings as follows: "In his youth Mastai had violent nervous disturbances whose nature has not been explained."

Finally, I must stress that my article, as is obvious from the first sentence, was intended merely to round out one aspect of Professor Brandmüller's review. As a professor himself, Herr Denzler knows that one may not publish any part of a dissertation in advance, and that therefore I could not undertake a substantial discussion of Hasler's position. That was the only reason why I referred to my doctoral dissertation.

9. On November 10, 1978, the *Rheinische Merkur* (no. 45) opened its pages a third time for an attack on Hasler's book, as Ulrich Horst, O.P., defended his fellow Dominican, Guidi, and Pius IX.

Father-Son Conflict

Was Cardinal Guidi the illegitimate son of Pius IX, as August B. Hasler suggests in his book *Papal Infallibility and the Vatican Council?* Ulrich Horst, O.P., replies.

Anyone who takes in hand A. B. Hasler's book *Pius IX* (*1846–1878*), *Papal Infallibility, and the First Vatican Council* (Stuttgart, 1977) and reads the subtitle (*Dogmatization and Imposition of an Ideology*) as well as some of the chapter and section headings ("The Manipulation of the Infallibility Debate," "Was Pius IX Still Fully in His Right Mind at the Time of the Council?" "Bishops under Physical and Moral Pressure") can guess what motives led the author to his conclusions and what method he chiefly applies. The language gives the game away. Or does one merely imagine this? For, after all, Hasler commands a knowledge of the sources and of the historical literature that might surprise even a specialist. But one should not let oneself be overwhelmed by the profusion of quotations: Sometimes they feign a degree of certainty which doesn't stand up to criticism. One would be glad to pass over certain features of this book with indulgence if it had been written in a more modest tone.

One might have surmised that Hasler would bring up the speech that Cardinal Guidi, archbishop of Bologna, gave at the Council, and the stormy argument which took place between Guidi and the pope on the evening of June 18, 1870—in the course of which the famous remark, "*I* am tradition," was supposedly uttered—in connection with the "manipulation of the infallibility debate." But Hasler also knows how to spice up familiar material. He tries to make the scene take on an exemplary character in order to expose the papal system. The dramatic section heading proclaims it: "Pope Pius IX and Cardinal Guidi—A Father-Son Conflict?" That *is* news. In any case, Hasler's psychological interpretation of the quarrel based on this suspicion seems more solid than the reports from his two professional experts, which attest that the pope was not entirely of sound mind. Hasler writes, "This would shed a still more lurid light on the most oppressive scene from the Council: the moment, so pregnant with symbolism, when the pope flings at his son the line, 'I am tradition, I am the Church.' And then a son who takes a stand against his father, appealing to the testimony of tradition, swearing that it runs completely counter to his father's ambitions." Nothing, in fact, would be more revealing than this struggle at night, which, assuming all the suppositions are true, lays bare the moral and theological reprehensibleness of the man who is said to have manipulated the debate on infallibility.

Hasler does admit that his thesis has "not yet" been proved, but the reader gets the impression that this is more than a conjecture originating with a Polish count. Especially since the very spare biographical records suggest that a systematic effort has been made to cover the cardinal's traces. Guidi was "practically passed over in silence." Since we allegedly don't know where he was born, this makes Hasler's suspicions of a dark, mysterious illegitimacy almost a certainty.

Place of Birth

The truth is simpler, though of course less "impressive." And Hasler ought to have known about it. For, one year before his book appeared, I. Casoli [sic], an archivist in Bologna, discovered Guidi's birthplace, San Biagio d'Argenta. The entry I have before me from the baptismal register of his home parish (San Biagio) leaves no room for doubt that his birth was legitimate. And so the "father-son conflict" bursts like a soap bubble.

Hasler also should have been more careful with his dramatic reconstructions for other reasons. As is clear from the position paper which he submitted to the Council (along with the general of the Order and the other Dominican bishops), Cardinal Guidi was a pronounced supporter of infallibility. To reject the doctrine would have been to contradict the tradition of Thomistic ecclesiology in general and the teaching of Rome's Minerva College in particular. Thus, Guidi's placet in the solemn final vote was not out of character. Likewise, a close analysis of his speech (which Hasler strangely fails to undertake) shows that Guidi supported infallibility as a matter of principle, invoking Thomas and the Thomists as he did so.

To interpret this conciliar episode properly, one must be familiar with its background. A *memoria* composed by P. Pellegrinetti, O.P., fills us in about this. (Hasler mentions it, but he dismisses it—without discussing its contents—as "apologetical.") In it we learn that among the Dominican bishops residing in the Convent of S. Maria sopra Minerva there were three fathers (Guidi being one) who wanted to see certain restrictions placed on the definition of infallibility. In particular, they were concerned about the pope's obligation to consult with the rest of the Church. This little group intended to work out a compromise between the two conciliar parties by offering a middle ground. The text of the speech in the original version comes from Pellegrinetti, who, he says, prepared the manuscript in two days. This is surprising because the cardinal was himself a respected theologian. But it is probably best not to press the question of authorship, since the most important ideas were worked out in common.

Everyone who was directly involved in the affair probably knew that the speech by the Italian cardinal, who wanted to mediate between the two sides, would stir up attention, but we may presume that no one foresaw the explosion that actually resulted. There was sharp criticism for the canon condemning the view that in a definition the pope acted as he saw fit, on his own, independently of the Church, and not "on the advice of the bishops, who bear witness to the tradition of the Church." The spokesman for the Commission on Faith even said that Guidi was worse than a Gallican. In truth, the cardinal's thesis was anything but Gallican, rather, it was in keeping with the fundamental principles of sixteenth- and seventeenth-century Thomistic ecclesiology, which holds that on matters of faith the pope has a strict duty to consult the bishops. Guidi undoubtedly knew of these Thomistic theologians. From the reaction to his speech it became evident that the position of the great Dominicans from bygone days had come under suspicion as pro-Gallican. People now feared that every condition binding a definition would conjure up the danger of an appeal to the Council (against the pope) or doubts about the compulsory nature of the decision.

I Am Tradition

On the very same evening, Pius IX, who had been given at least partly false or inadequate information about the speech, summoned the cardinal. A proposal for mediating the dispute over infallibility struck the pope—with all his recollections of past discussions—as utterly out of place. Even serious historians find it believable that during the meeting the pope cried out, "*I am tradition*," but one notes with some surprise that so far nobody has bothered to trace the history of how this remark was handed down. The only thing we know for certain is that we cannot simply assume it to be authentic, as Hasler, among others, does. The first thing that stands out is that no one who reports it mentions Guidi himself telling it. If we had statements from individuals vouching for the story, it would be easier to silence our doubts, for at the time of the incident some people thought it was just court gossip. One should also consider that many of the details associated with the scene and events that followed are so contradictory in themselves that the whole thing does not gain in credibility. Furthermore, in the earliest accounts grave errors of fact are detectable. It does not speak for the authenticity of the anecdote that the details of the interview and the controversial sentence only became known after June 21. Since the saying created an immediate sensation, it would most likely have been making the rounds on the day after the meeting at the latest.

The earliest records we have of the episode give us a hint which is perhaps important. If one accepts the dates in their journals as accurate, Dupanloup and Darboy were the first to write down the remark—without giving its source—but, oddly enough, it took two or three days to spread it around Rome. Did it possibly originate in anti-Infallibilist circles, along the same lines as "L'État, c'est moi"? Given the tradition as we now have it, this is no more than a hypothesis. The only thing certain is the fact that for the moment the traces of "*I* am tradition" come to an end in the diaries of the two French bishops.

10. Horst's article appeared shortly before this book went to press. It was therefore not possible to debate him in the pages of the *Rheinische Merkur*. Besides, judging from previous experience, it would have probably been excessively optimistic to expect the journal to publish a reply. Hence, a few brief remarks are appended here.

For Ulrich Horst "the father-son conflict bursts like a soap bubble." He believes he has proved that Cardinal Guidi can in no way be the son of Pius IX. For evidence he adduces an entry in the baptismal register of the parish of San Biagio d'Argenta. This is enough for him to sweep away any doubts that Guidi's birth was legitimate. It's so simple. It was to be assumed that the father would be named Guidi. But in the case of a cardinal who later became so famous, one would really have to know much more than his father's Christian name. And I have never doubted that Guidi was baptized.

Horst goes on to write that I. Casoli, an archivist from Bologna, discovered the entry a year before the appearance of my book, in other words, quite independently of my research. Horst does not speak of this information being published—and rightly so—for a notice in the clerical register of the archdiocese of Bologna cannot actually count as a form of publication. He completely missed the fact that as early as 1976 Professor Georg Denzler published news of the pope's son on the basis of my investigations (see *Das Papsttum und der Amtszölibat*, vol. 2 [Stuttgart, 1976], p. 293, n. 12a). I. Casoli therefore accidentally found Guidi's baptismal records just at the time when both the particular controversy surrounding this prelate and the report of the pope's being a father were gradually becoming known. And, on the other hand, is it not remarkable that up till now other authors could only come up with quite inaccurate data, and that it took so long to determine where this cardinal had been baptized?

Horst goes much further than I do when he speaks of the "moral and theological reprehensibleness" of Pius IX, if the supposition of his illegitimate son should prove correct. I see no reason for such intolerance. I would care precious little about Pius IX's proving to have an illegitimate child if Polish Count Wladislaw Kulczycki had not been so emphatic (not a mere speculation, as Horst suggests) in his astonishing statement that the one Roman cardinal to come out against the definition of infallibility was, of all people, the son of the pope.

I feel grateful to Horst for the support he gives me through his interpretation of Guidi's speech. The question of whether the pope had a relative or an absolute obligation to consult the bishops was, after all, *the* burning issue of the Council. This may be seen with all the clarity one could wish in the concluding remarks of Bishop Vinzenz Gasser (Mansi 52, 1215 CD), speaking in the name of the Commission on Faith. In this sense, Guidi's compromise proposal brought him down squarely on the side of the minority; hence, the anger of the pope and the Infallibilists needs no detailed explanation.

In his conclusion Horst advances the hypothesis that the saying, "*I* am tradition," was invented by the group surrounding Bishops Georges Darboy and Félix Dupanloup in order to discredit the pope. But if that were the case, would the bishops have confided these words—allegedly coined by them but attributed to the pope—to their diaries only a few hours after the event? One could wish that the sayings of Jesus had been so well preserved by tradition: Decades passed before they were first written down. Besides, Darboy and Dupanloup, as leaders of the opposition, didn't have to write expressly that the report came from Guidi, since the minority bishops were, after all, in contact with him from the beginning of the Council. (Horst overlooks this.) It is also not particularly surprising that the pope's dictum did not appear immediately in diplomatic dispatches and the letters of other bishops, for neither the ambassadors nor the council fathers sent out daily reports. The meeting between Pius IX and Cardinal Guidi took place on a Saturday evening. The council fathers did not meet again till the following Monday.

Notes

[1] August Bernhard Hasler, *Pius IX* (*1846–1878*), *Päpstliche Unfehlbarkeit und 1. Vatikanisches Konzil. Dogmatisierung und Durchsetzung einer Ideologie,* 2 vols. No. 12 in the series Päpste und Papsttum (Stuttgart: Verlag Anton Hiersemann, 1977).

[2] Among the most recent publications since the appearance of my study of Pius IX and Vatican I, I should like to make special reference to the following: Ignatius von Senestrey, *Wie es zur Definition der päpstlichen Unfehlbarkeit kam. Tagebuch vom 1. Vatikanischen Konzil,* edited with a commentary by Klaus Schatz. No. 24 in the series Frankfurter Theologische Studien (Frankfurt am Main, 1977); Franz-Xaver Bantle, *Unfehlbarkeit der Kirche in Aufklärung und Romantik. Eine dogmengeschichtliche Untersuchung für die Zeit der Wende vom 18. zum 19. Jahrhundert.* No. 103 in the series Freiburger Theologische Studien (Freiburg, 1976); P. G. Camaiani, "Castighi di Dio e trionfo della Chiesa: Mentalità e polemiche dei cattolici temporalisti nell'età di Pio IX," *Rivista Storica Italiana,* vol. 88 (1976), 708–44; Christoph Weber, *Kardinäle und Prälaten in den letzten Jahrzehnten des Kirchenstaates. Elite-Rekrutierung, Karriere-Muster und soziale Zusammensetzung der kurialen Führungschicht zur Zeit Pius' IX,* 2 vols. No. 13 in the series Päpste und Papsttum (Stuttgart, 1978); R. Aubert, M. Gueret, and P. Tombeur, *Concilium Vaticanum I. Concordance, Index, Listes de fréquence, Tables comparatives* (Louvain, 1977); Walter Brandmüller, *Ignaz von Döllinger am Vorabend des I. Vatikanums. Herausforderung und Antwort.* No. 9 in the series Kirchengeschichtliche Quellen und Studien (St. Ottilien, 1977); Karl Josef Rivinius, "Bischof Wilhelm Emmanuel von Ketteler und die Infallibilität des Papstes. Ein Beitrag zur Unfehlbarkeitsdiskussion auf dem 1. Vatikanischen Konzil," in *Europäische Hochschulschriften* XXIII, 48 (Bern and Frankfurt, 1976); Ivo Sirić, *Bishop J. G. Strossmayer: New Light on Vatican I* (Rome and Chicago, 1975).

[3] Rudolf Zinnhobler, "Pius IX. in der katholischen Literatur seiner Zeit. Ein Baustein zur Geschichte des Triumphalismus," in G. Schwaiger (ed.), *Konzil und Papst. Historische Beiträge zur Frage der höchsten Gewalt in der Kirche. Festgabe für Hermann Tüchle* (Munich/Paderborn/Vienna, 1975), pp. 387–432.

[4] Roger Aubert, *Le Pontificat de Pie IX* (Paris, 1952), pp. 302ff.

[5] Zinnhobler, "Pius IX. in der katholischen Literatur," pp. 420ff.

[6] Ibid., p. 425.

[7] Giovanni Bosco, *Meditazioni*, vol. I (Turin, n.d.), pp. 89–90. Quoted in Giancarlo Zizola, *Quale Papa? Analisi delle strutture elettorali e governative del papato romano* (Rome, 1977), p. 22.

[8] Jacques Martin, "Pie IX vu par le 'Saint Homme de Tours,' Léon Dupont," *Pio IX: Studi e ricerche sulla vita della Chiesa del settecento ad oggi*, vol. 5 (1976), 403–8.

[9] Zinnhobler, "Pius IX. in der katholischen Literatur," pp. 414–18.

[10] Ignatius von Senestrey, *Wie es zur Definition der päpstlichen Unfehlbarkeit kam*, pp. 77ff.

[11] Ibid., pp. 63ff.

[12] Cuthbert Butler and Hugo Lang, *Das Vatikanische Konzil. Seine Geschichte von innen geschildert in Bischof Ullathornes Briefen* (Munich, 1933), p. 152.

[13] Joseph Hajjar, "Die katholischen orientalischen Kirchen," in *Geschichte der Kirche*, vol. V, no. 2: *Vom Kirchenstaat zur Weltkirche* (Zurich/Einsiedeln/Cologne, 1977), p. 229.

[14] See also the description given by Robert Hotz of the same incident, but using a different source: "Hajjar does mention [cf. the article cited in note 13] that the Melkite Patriarch Gregor Youssef also earned the displeasure of the pope by his genuinely ecumenical activities at the First Vatican Council (1870), but it would be very much worthwhile to mention further the way in which Pius IX expressed his rage. As Youssef performed his obeisance, the pope placed his foot on the neck of the Melchite patriarch and said, 'Mala testa.' The enormity of this humiliation can only be fully appreciated if one knows that in the East all the patriarchs consider each other as equals in rank. Patriarch Gregor Youssef departed and broke off all contact with Rome until the death of Pius IX. But he did not break with the Church. He even kept totally silent about the incident so as not to give occasion for a schism, for most of the Melkites would hardly have approved this humiliation of the supreme head of their church. Only when Leo XIII pressed him did Youssef give him an account of the episode. Many Eastern Christians truly paid a high price for their union with Rome!" ("Das 'Malaise' der Unierten. Nachwort zur *Woche der christlichen Einheit*," *Orientierung*, 42 [1978], 17.)

[15] For Wladislaw Kulczycki, see the article by Jerzy Zdrada in *Polski Stownik Biograficzny 1971*, vol. 14, pp. 135–36; Bronislaw Biliński, "Władysław Kulczycki e le sue corrispondenze romane negli anni 1870–1871," in Biliński (ed.), *Incontri polacco-italiani a Porta Pia: J. I. Kraszewski, W. Kulczycki, M. Konopicka* (Wroclaw/Warsaw/Cracow/Gdansk, 1971). This is no. 49 in a series of lectures published by the Polish Academy of Sciences for the centenary of Rome as the capital of Italy; cf. also Kulczycki's reports after 1870 to the Italian Foreign Minister, Emilio Visconti Venosta, which are reprinted in *I Documenti diplomatici italiani*, second series (1870–1896) (Rome, 1960).

[16] For the court prelates serving Pius IX, see also Weber, *Kardinäle und Prälaten*, I, 192–98.

[17] G. Martina, *Pio IX (1846–1850)*, vol. 38 of *Miscellanea Historiae Pontificiae* (Rome, 1974), p. 531f.

[18] See Weber, *Kardinäle und Prälaten*, I, 259: "No one disputes the fact that Pius IX believed in the inspirations which he believed had been given him from on high . . ."

[19] See Otto Weiss, *Die Redemptoristen in Bayern (1790–1909). Ein Beitrag zur Geschichte des Ultramontanismus.* Dissertation im Fachbereich Geschichte und Kunstwissenschaften (Munich, 1977), pp. 968–1205, 1615f., 1685–1728.

[20] For Cardinals Santucci and D'Andrea, see Weber, *Kardinäle und Prälaten*, I, 317f. Weber mentions "parallel accounts of the deaths of the extremely conservative Cardinals Massimo (1848) and Della Genga Sermattei (1851). Both were so furious over a certain change in papal politics, and particularly over their own sudden loss of power because of this, that in a manner of speaking there was nothing left for them but to die" (ibid.).

[21] Carl Mirbt, *Quellen zur Geschichte des Papsttums und des römischen Katholizismus* (Tübingen, 1934), p. 465.

[22] *The Letters and Diaries of John Henry Newman*, ed. Charles Stephen Dessain (London, 1961), vol. 25, p. 262.

[23] *Ignaz von Döllinger. Lord Acton: Briefwechsel 1850–1890*, ed. V. Conzemius, 3 vols. (Munich, 1963–71), II, 353.

[24] Weber, *Kardinäle und Prälaten*, I, 315, n. 47.

[25] D. Milburn, "Impressions of English Bishops at the First Vatican Council: Letters of Bishop Chadwick of Hexham and Newcastle to the President of Ushaw," *The Wiseman Review*, no. 493 (1962), 231.

[25a] Xavier de Montclos, *Lavigérie le Saint-Siège et l'Église de l'avènement de Pie IX à l'avènement de Léon XIII (1846–1878)* (Paris, 1965), p. 596.

[26] For liberal trends among the cardinals, see especially Weber, *Kardinäle und Prälaten*, I, 306ff.

[27] J. Schmidlin, *Papstgeschichte der neuesten Zeit*, vol. II: *Papsttum und Päpste gegenüber den modernen Strömungen. Pius IX und Leo XIII (1846–1903)* (Munich, 1934), p. 104.

[28] Ferdinand Gregorovius, *Geschichte der Stadt Rom im Mittelalter* (Stuttgart, 1890), III, 220.

[29] Schmidlin, *Papstgeschichte*, II, 400.

[30] The letter *Saepenumero* of August 18, 1883, to various cardinals (*Acta Leonis*, III, 259–73).

[31] In connection with the remarks on modernism which follow, see Roger Aubert, "Die modernistische Krise," in H. Jedin (ed.), *Handbuch der Kirchengeschichte* (Freiburg/Basel/Vienna, 1973), VI/2, 435–500; Émile Poulat, *Histoire, dogme et critique dans la crise moderniste* (Tournai/Paris, 1962); idem, *Intégrisme et catholicisme intégral. Un Réseau secret international antimoderniste: La "Sapinière" (1909–1921)* (Tournai and Paris, 1969); idem, *Catholicisme, démocratie et socialisme: Le Mouvement catholique et Mgr Benigni de la naissance du socialisme à la victoire du fascisme* (Tournai and Paris, 1977); idem, *Église contre bourgeoisie: Introduction au devenir du catholicisme actuel* (Tournai and Paris, 1977); R. Aubert, "Mgr Benigni, un intégriste aux antécédents progressistes: Une interprétation nouvelle du 'catholicisme intégral,'" *Revue Théologique de Louvain*, 8 (1977), 461–68; idem, "Henri Bremond et la crise moderniste: Lumières nouvelles," *Revue d'Histoire Ecclésiastique*, 72 (1977), 332–48; (F. Antonelli and G. Löw), *Disquisitio circa quasdam obiectiones modum agendi servi Dei Pii X respicientes in modernismi debellatione* (Vatican City, 1950); Lorenzo Bedeschi, *La Curia romana durante la crisi modernista: Episodi e metodi di governo* (Parma, 1968); idem, *Interpretazioni e sviluppo del modernismo cattolico* (Milan, 1975); Gottfried Maron, "Die römisch-katholische Kirche von 1870–1970," in K. D. Schmidt and E. Wolf (eds.), *Die Kirche in ihrer Geschichte* (Göttingen, 1972), vol. 4, pp. 197–328; Oskar Schroeder, *Aufbruch und Missverständnis. Zur Geschichte der reformkatholischen Bewegung* (Graz, 1969); Erika Weinzierl (ed.), *Der Modernismus: Beiträge zu seiner Erforschung* (Graz/Vienna/Cologne, 1974); Norbert Trippen, *Theologie und Lehramt im Konflikt. Die kirchlichen Massnahmen gegen den Modernismus in Jahre 1907 und ihre Auswirkungen in Deutschland* (Freiburg/Basel/Vienna, 1977); Peter Neuner, *Religion zwischen Kirche und Mystik. Friedrich von Hügel und der Modernismus* (Frankfurt am Main, 1977); idem, *Religiöse Erfahrung und geschichtliche Offenbarung. Friedrich von Hügels Grundlegung der Theologie* (Munich/Paderborn/Vienna, 1977).

[32] *Henri Bremond-Maurice Blondel: Correspondance*, I, 494. Quoted by Aubert in "Die modernistische Krise," p. 455.

[33] Weinzierl, *Der Modernismus*, p. 238.

[34] Statement made by the Agence internationale Rome (AIR) on June 19, 1913. Quoted in Poulat, *Intégrisme*, p. 132.

[35] Statement appearing in the magazine *La Vigie* on May 12, 1912.

[36] *Disquisitio*, p. 262.

[37] Ibid., pp. 263ff.

[38] Ibid., p. 240.

[39] Ibid., p. 234.

[40] Ibid., p. 10.

[41] Ibid., p. 213.

[42] Poulat, *Catholicisme, démocratie et socialisme*, p. 459.

[43] *Codex Iuris Canonici*, in *Lexikon für Theologie und Kirche* (Freiburg, 1958), II, 1245.

[44] Ulrich Stutz, *Der Geist des Codex iuris canonici. Eine Einführung in das auf Geheiss Papst Pius X. verfasste und von Papst Benedikt XV erlassene Gesetzbuch der katholischen Kirche* (Stuttgart, 1918), p. 50.

[45] Ibid., p. 50; cf. p. 155f.

[46] See, especially, Klaus Scholder, *Die Kirchen und das Dritte Reich*, vol. I: *Vorgeschichte und Zeit der Illusionen 1918–1934* (Frankfurt am Main, 1977).

[47] Ludwig Kaas, "Der Konkordatstyp des faschistischen Italien," *Zeitschrift für auslandisches offentliches Recht und Völkerrecht*, III/1 (1933), 517; quoted in Scholder, *Die Kirchen*, p. 210.

[48] Gerhart Binder, *Irrtum und Widerstand. Die deutschen Katholiken in der Auseinandersetzung mit dem Nationalsozialismus* (Munich, 1968), p. 184.

[49] See, in this connection, Heinrich Lutz, *Demokratie im Zwielicht. Der Weg der deutschen Katholiken aus dem Kaiserreich in die Republik 1914–1925* (Munich, 1963), esp. p. 120f.

[50] Michael Schmaus, *Begegnungen zwischen katholischem Christentum und nationalsozialistischer Weltanschauung* (Münster, 1933), p. 9.

[51] Joseph Lortz, *Katholischer Zugang zum Nationalsozialismus kirchengeschichtlich gesehen*. Reich und Kirche, no. 1 (Münster, 1933), p. 9.

[52] Lortz, *Katholischer Zugang*, p. 9; see also Franz von Papen, *Der 12. November, 1933 und die deutschen Katholiken* (Münster, 1933); Franz Taeschner, *Der Totalitätsanspruch des Nationalsozialismus und der deutsche Katholizismus* (Münster, 1934); Josef Pieper, *Das Arbeitsrecht des Neuen Reiches und die Enzyklika Quadragesimo anno* (Münster, 1934).

[53] Introduction to Hans Müller, *Katholische Kirche und Nationalsozialismus. Dokumentation 1930–1935* (Munich, 1963), p. xix.

[54] Grosche, "Die Grundlagen einer christlichen Politik der deutschen Katholiken," in *Die Schildgenossen* [Catholic bimonthly magazine], 13 (1933–34), 48.

[55] See G. Martina and E. Ruffini, *La Chiesa in Italia tra fede e storia* (Rome, 1975); L. Kaufmann and G. Palo, "'Kaiser und Papst' in Italien," *Orientierung*, 40 (1976), 124–31.

[56] On this and related points, see Eduard Stakemeier, *Das Dogma der Himmelfahrt Mariens. Die Apostolische Konstitution vom 1. November 1950 und die Theologie der Verherrlichung Mariens* (Paderborn, 1950); *Evangelisches Gutachten zur Dogmatisierung der leiblichen Himmelfahrt Mariens* (Munich, 1950); Berthold Altaner, "Zur Frage der Definibilität der Assumptio B. M. V.," *Theologische Revue*, 44 (1948), 129–40; 45 (1949), 129–42; 46 (1950), 5–20; Josef Ternus, *Der gegenwärtige Stand der Assumptafrage* (Regensburg, 1948); Hermann Volk, *Das neue Mariendogma* (Münster, 1956); Karl Rahner, "Mariologie" (on Mary's bodily assumption into heaven; typewritten manuscript), Innsbruck, 1959.

[57] Georg Schwaiger, "Pius XII. in der Kirchengeschichte," in Herbert Schambeck (ed.), *Pius XII. zum Gedächtnis* (Berlin, 1977), p. 760, n. 107.

[58] Altaner, "Zur Frage der Definibilität der Assumptio B. M. V.," *Theologische Revue*, 46 (1950), 17.

[59] Ibid., 45 (1949), 140f.

[60] Ibid., 44 (1948), 129–40; 45 (1949), 129–42; 46 (1950), 5–20.

[61] Ibid., 44 (1948), 135f.

[62] Ibid., p. 140.

[63] Ibid., 46 (1950), 19.

[64] A typewritten transcript of the conversation (pp. 37–38) may be found in the archives of the Institute for Ecumenical Research at the University of Tübingen.

[65] Rahner, *Mariologie*, p. 18.

[66] Pope John XXIII, inaugural address to the Second Vatican Council, in *Acta Apostolicae Sedis*, 54 (1962), 792.

[67] Hans Küng (ed.), *Fehlbar? Eine Bilanz* (Zurich/Einsiedeln/Cologne, 1973), p. 320.

[68] See Gerd Hirschauer, *Der Katholizismus vor dem Risiko der Freiheit. Nachruf auf ein Konzil* (Munich, 1966); Fritz Leist, *Der Gefangene des Vatikans. Strukturen päpstlicher Herrschaft* (Munich, 1971).

[69] *Herderkorrespondenz*, 21 (1967), 436; for the latest developments, see Ludwig Kaufmann, "Zehn Jahre Enzyzklika 'Humanae Vitae,'" in *Orientierung*, 42 (1978), 151–56.

[70] Hans Küng, *Infallible? An Inquiry* (Garden City, N.Y., 1971);

idem. (ed.), *Fehlbar? Eine Bilanz* (Zurich/Einsiedeln/Cologne, 1973).

[71] Francis Simons, *Infallibility and the Evidence* (Springfield, Mass., 1968).

[72] Walter Jens (ed.), *Um nichts als die Wahrheit. Deutsche Bischofskonferenz contra Hans Küng* (Munich, 1978), p. 143.

[73] Ibid., p. 144.

[74] See Matthias Gatzemeier, *Theologie als Wissenschaft?* 2 vols. I: *Die Sache der Theologie*. II: *Wissenschafts-und Institutionenkritik* (Stuttgart and Bad Cannstatt, 1974–75); Rütger Schäfer, *Die Misere der theologischen Fakultäten. Dokumentation und Kritik eines Tabus* (Schwerte [Ruhr], 1970); idem, "Die theologische Fakultät—ein staatskirchliches Relikt," in G. Szczesny (ed.), *Club Voltaire. Jahrbuch für kritische Aufklärung IV* (Reinbek bei Hamburg, 1970), pp. 286–98.

[75] J. J. Ignaz von Döllinger, *Briefe und Erklärungen über die Vatikanischen Dekrete 1869 bis 1887*, ed. F. H. Reusch (reprint; Darmstadt, 1968), p. 141.

[76] Hans Albert, *Plädoyer für kritischen Rationalismus*, Piper series no. 10 (Munich, 1971), p. 23.

[77] Ernst Topisch, *Sozialphilosophie zwischen Ideologie und Wissenschaft* (Neuwied, 1961), p. 75f.

[78] See, e.g., Klaus Schatz, *Kirchenbild und päpstliche Unfehlbarkeit bei den deustchsprachigen Minoritätsbischöfen auf dem 1. Vatikanum* (Rome, 1975), pp. 84, 221, 333; Heinrich Fries, "'Ex sese, non autem ex consensu Ecclesiae,'" in R. Bäumer and H. Dolch (eds.), *Volk Gottes. Zum Kirchenverständnis der katholischen, evangelischen und anglikanischen Theologie. Festgabe für J. Höfer* (Freiburg/Basel/Vienna, 1967), p. 491.

[79] Giacomo Martina, *Pio IX: Chiesa e mondo moderno*. No. 18 in the series Nuova Universale Studium (Rome, 1976), p. 198.

[80] A. W. J. Houtepen, *Onfeilbaarheid en hermeneutiek. De betekenis van het infallibilitas-concept op Vaticanum I* (Bruges, 1973), p. 374f.

[81] Ibid., pp. 326f., 344f., 376.

[82] *Bewusstseinstörungen im Katholizismus* (Frankfurt am Main, 1972), pp. 16, 25.

[82a] Loris Francesco Capovilla, "Pio IX nel pensiero e sul cuore di Giovanni XXIII," in *Pio IX nel primo centenario della sua morte* (by various hands) (Vatican City, 1978), p. 751f.

[83] See Hans Kühner, "Der Kardinal und die Moral," *Die Weltwoche*, no. 17 (April 1976), 28.

[84] *National Catholic News Service* (Rome), January 31, 1978.

[85] "La causa di beatificazione di Pio IX: Intervista con il Procuratore della causa, avvocato Snider," in *Pio IX—la sua terra, la sua gente. A cura dei Comitati Marchigiani di Roma a di Senigallia per le Celebrazioni Centenarie* (Rome, 1978), p. 6.

[86] Bruno di Porto, "Gli ebrei di Roma dai Papi all'Italia," in *1870: La Breccia del Ghetto. Evoluzione degli ebrei di Roma* (Rome, 1971), p. 58f.

[87] Weber, *Kardinäle und Prälaten*, I, 273.

[88] *Corriere della Sera*, February 15, 1978.

[89] Walter Brandmüller, "Aus der Trödelkammer. Eine Geschichtsklitterung um Pius IX und das Erste Vatikanische Konzil," *Rheinischer Merkur*, no. 35, Sept. 2, 1977, p. 20; "Krank im Kopf," *Der Spiegel*, no. 38, Sept. 12, 1977, pp. 60–63; *Pressedienst des Sekretariats der Deustchen Bischofskonferenz*, no. 28, Sept. 12, 1977; *Katholische Nachrichten Agentur, Aktueller Dienst Inland*, no. 212, Sept. 13, 1977, p. 1; *Katholische Nachrichten Agentur, Informationsdienst*, no. 38, vol. XXV, Sept. 15, 1977, p. 2; "Angriffe aus der Trödelkammer," in *Kirchenzeitung für die Diözese Augsburg*, Sept. 25, 1977; A. M., "Krankengeschichte eines Papstes oder Griff in die Trödelkammer?" *Publik-Forum*, no. 20, Sept. 30, 1977, pp. 16–17; Hans Kühner, "Ein kranker Papst setzte das Unfehlbarkeitsdogma durch. Ein Schweizer Theologe und Historiker untersucht das Persönlichkeitsbild Pius' IX," *Luzerner Neueste Nachrichten*, no. 240, Oct. 14, 1977, p. 5; Hanspeter Oschwald, "Historische Argumente gegen Unfehlbarkeit des Papstes," *dpa-brief*, Nov. 3, 1977, pp. 1–3; Victor Conzemius, "Erstes Vatikanum und Unfehlbarkeit. August B. Haslers provokative Thesen zu Pio Nono," *Orientierung*, 41 (1977), 207–9; "Was Vatican I Rigged? How the Pope Became Infallible," *Time*, Nov. 14, 1977, p. 52; Hanno Helbling, "Kunst des Weglassens. August Bernhard Haslers Arbeit über die Unfehlbarkeitserklärung," *Neue Zürcher Zeitung*, out-of-town edition no. 264, Nov. 11, 1977, p. 35; article by R. Mols in *Nouvelle Revue Théologique*, 109 (1977), 897–98; Hansjakob Stehle, "Aus dem vatikanischen Antiquitäten-Kabinett. Die 'Ideologisierung einer Ideologie,'" *Die Zeit*, no. 53, Dec. 23, 1977, p. 13; Werner Egli, "Zuschrift zu 'Erstes Vatikanum und Unfehlbarkeit,'" *Orientierung*, 41 (1977), 247–48; "Kirchengeschichte und profanhistorische Kritik. Diskussion um 'Erstes Vatikanum und Unfehlbarkeit,'" *Orientierung*, 41 (1977), 259, 262; *L'Osservatore della Domenica*, no. 1, Jan. 1, 1978, p. 9; Vincenzo Mantovani, "Fu truccato il Concilio di Pio IX? Secondo uno storico tedesco, Papa Mastai ottenne con la prevaricazione il dogma dell'Infallibità," *Paese Sera*, Jan. 4, 1978; "Infallible per forza," *Panorama*, Jan. 10, 1978, pp. 60–61; Herbert Kolbe, "War Pius IX. noch zurechnungsfähig? Neue Attacke gegen das Unfehlbarkeitsdogma von 1870," *Neue Ruhr-Zeitung*, Jan. 29, 1978; "Pio IX contestato: Paolo VI lo diffende parlando ai pellegrini," *Il Messagero*, Feb. 6, 1978, p.

2; Paolo Giuntella, "Papa Mastai oltre la polemica," *Il Popolo*, Feb. 7, 1978, p. 5; Giacomo Martina, "Giustificate riserve su una recente opera," *L'Osservatore Romano*, Feb. 8, 1978, p. 6; Lamberto Furno, "Pio IX, un papa tra polemiche ed esaltazioni," in *La Stampa*, Feb. 8, 1978, p. 2; Fabrizio De Santis, "Ancora polemiche su papa Mastai. Scontro Vaticano-Hasler per Pio IX," in *Corriere della Sera*, Feb. 8, 1978, p. 6; "Fu Pio IX a imporre l'infallibilità papale. Le tesi del sacerdote svizerro Bernhard Hasler—Il dispotismo di Papa Mastai," *Corriere del Ticino*, Feb. 8, 1978, p. 3; " 'Story in schwarz und weiss —ohne Sinn für Nuancen.' Vatikanzeitung kritisiert Haslers Studie über Papst Pius IX," *Katholische Nachrichten Agentur*, no. 34, Feb. 9, 1978; "Kirchengeschichte macht Schlagzeilen," *Die Ostschweiz*, Feb. 9, 1978; "Kritik an Publikation über Pius IX," *Die Ostschweiz*, Feb. 10, 1978; Michael Wilson, "Vatican Hits Back at Pius IX Book," *Catholic Herald* [London], Feb. 17, 1978, p. 1; Helen Young, "Papal Epilepsy Slur," *Catholic Herald* [London], Feb. 17, 1978, p. 4; "August Bernhard Hasler: Pio IX, il Papa dell'infallibilità," *Il Giorno*, no. 40, Feb. 18, 1978, p. 4; " 'Story in Schwarz und Weiss.' Prof. Martina kritisiert Haslers Studie über Papst Pius IX.," *Kirchenzeitung der Diözese Augsburg*, Feb. 19, 1978, p. 7; Lamberto Furno, "Perché Hasler 'ridiscute' L'infallibilità del Papa," *La Stampa*, no. 44, Feb. 22, 1978; Josef Blank, "Pius IX und das Unfehlbarkeitsdogma," *Imprimatur*, vol. 11, no. 2, Feb. 28, 1978, pp. 56–59; Marco Politi, "La pantofala infallibile," *Il Messagero*, March 5, 1978, p. 3; Giacomo Martina, "Pope Pius IX: Justified Reservations on a Recent Work," *L'Osservatore Romano, Weekly English Edition*, March 9, 1978, p. 10; Hans Kühner, "Explosivstoff Unfehlbarkeit," *Basler Zeitung*, March 17, 1978; article by Harding Meyer in *Lutherische Rundschau*, 27 (1977), 656–57; idem, *Lutheran World*, 24 (1977), 492–93; Martin Ros, "Het drama van Pio Nono," *De Tijd*, March 17, 1978, pp. 16–17; Heinz-Joachim Fischer, "Verschlungene Wege zur göttlichen Wahrheit. Wie es zur päpstlichen Unfehlbarkeit kam. Eine historische Studie und ein zeitgenössisches Zeugnis," *Frankfurter Allgemeine Zeitung*, no. 63, March 31, 1978, p. 11; Josef Blank and Gerhard Voss, "Pius IX.—Päpstliche Unfehlbarkeit—Erstes Vatikanisches Konzil. Uber eine Untersuchung von A. B. Hasler," *Una Sancta*, 33 (1978), 72–82; Werner Küppers, "Infragestellung des Ersten Vatikanums in heutiger alt-katholischer Sicht. Anstössig oder Anstoss?" *Schweizerische Kirchenzeitung*, 146 (1978), 190–94; "Ehre der Altäre," *Der Spiegel*, no. 17, April 24, 1978, pp. 193–96; Yves M. J. Congar, "Bulletin d'Ecclésiologie: Premier Concile du Vatican," *Revue des sciences philosophiques et théologiques*, 62 (1978), 85–88; Victor J. Willi, "Fehlbare Unfehlbarkeit?" *Vaterland*, no. 84, April 12, 1978, p. 5; idem, "Fehlbare Unfehlbarkeit? Dogma des Vaticanum I im Kreuzfeuer einer schonungslosen kirchengeschichtlichen Untersuchung. Vermittelnde geschichtssoziologische Erklärung," *Schweizer Rundschau*, 77 (April 1978), 15–18; Otto Weiss, review in *Zeitschrift für bayerische Landesgeschichte*, 41 (1978), 329–33; Klaus Schatz, "Totalrevision der Geschichte des I. Vatikanums? Zur Auseinandersetzung mit den Thesen von August B. Hasler," *Theologie und Philosophie*, 53 (1978), 248–76; Peter Stockmeier, "Geschichte und Unfehlbarkeit. Zu einer Neuerscheinung über die Debatte auf dem Ersten Vatikanischen Konzil," *Münchener Theologische Zeitschrift*, 29 (1978), 189–99; Matthias Buschkühl, "Einer NS Schrift aufgesessen. Zu August Bernhard Haslers Buch über Pius IX," *Rheinischer Merkur*, no. 28, July 14, 1978; Francesco Margiotta-Broglio, "Pio IX nell'armadio. Il Dogma dell'infallibilità," *La Nazione*, August 3, 1978; Max Seckler, article in *Das historisch-politische Buch*, 26 (1978), 234; Regina Bohne, "Die Forderung: Glaube als Gehorsam," *Frankfurter Hefte*, 33 (1978), 73–76; H. Ewald Kessler, article in *Alt-Katholische Kirchenzeitung*, 22 (1978), 24, 32; Ulrich Horst, "Vater-Sohn-Konflikt," in *Rheinischer Merkur*, no. 45, Nov. 10, 1978, p. 31; Piet Fransen, "Een recente studie over Pius IX en de onfeilbaarheid van de Paus," *Bijdragen*, 39 (1978), 447–56; Robrecht Boudens, "Nieuw licht op de pauselijke onfeil-baarheidsverklaring?" *Collationes* (1978), 359–62; review by Josef Imbach in *Laurentianum* (1978), 490; by Ronald J. Ross in *The American Historical Review*, 83 (1978), 999–1000; *Elseviers*, vol. 34, no. 49, Sept. 12, 1978, p. 172; by Gert Haendler in *Deutsche Literaturzeitung*, 99 (1978), 770–73; by Georg Franz-Willing in *Zeitschrift für Religions- und Geistesgeschichte*, 30 (1978), 382–84; and by Francesco Margiotta-Broglio in *Storia Contemporanea*, 9 (1978), 769–71; Klaus Schatz, S.J., "Storia contro dogma? Discussione delle tesi di A. B. Hasler sul Concilio Vaticano I," *La Civiltà Cattolica*, 130, no. 3087 (1979), 245–58; Giacomo Martina, "Pio IX e il Vaticano I, di A. B. Hasler—Rivlievi critici," *Archivum Historiae Pontificiae*, 16 (1978), 341–69; Giacomo Martina, "Giustificate riserve su una recente opera," *Pio IX*, 8 (1979), 103–7; Andreas Lindt, "Zwei Päpste—zwei Konzilien. Bermerkungen zu zwei neuen Büchern," *Reformatio*, 28 (1979), 115–18; Joseph Hoffmann, "Histoire et dogme: la définition de l'infaillibilité pontificale à Vatican I: À propos de l'ouvrage de A. B. Hasler," *Revue des sciences philosophiques et théologiques*, 62 (1978), 543–57, and 63 (1979), 61–82; Otto Hermann Pesch, "Wie frei war das 1. Vatikanische Konzil? Zu August Bernhard Haslers Buch über die Unfehlbarkeit von Pius IX," *Deutsches Allgemeines Sonntagsblatt*, no. 10, March 11, 1979, p. 20; see supplement for August 1979; review by Walter Tanner in *Kirchenblatt für die reformierte Schweiz*, 135 (1979), 74; Franco Molinari, "Riesaminata dopo cent'anni la personalità di Papa Mastai," *Corriere della Sera*, February 14, 1979, p. 15; review by C. Roses in *Studia Monastica (Abadía de Montserrat)* [Barcelona], 20 (1978), 74; Piet Fransen, "Pius IX und die päpstliche Unfehlbarkeit," *Theologie der Gegenwart*, 22 (1979), 43–49; review by

Peter Stadler in *Schweizerische Zeitschrift für Geschichte,* 28 (1978), 582–83; Brunero Gherardini, "Pio IX e l'infallibilità," *Pio IX,* 8 (1979), 243–44; review by N. E. in *Irenikon,* 52 (1979), 157; John T. Ford, "Current Theology—Infallibility: A Review of Recent Studies," in *Theological Studies,* 40 (1979), 273–305, esp. 298ff.; review by W. Klausnitzer in *Zeitschrift für katholische Theologie,* 101 (1979), 86–88; review by Brian Tierney in the *Journal of Ecclesiastical History,* 30 (1979), 396–97; Konrad Rudolf Lienert, "Geschichte eines fatalen Konzils, A. B. Haslers Arbeit zur Frage der Unfehlbarkeit des Papstes," *Tagesanzeiger,* Sept. 29, 1979, p. 65; Jean-Pierre Torrell, O.P., "Tradition, histoire et idéologie à Vatican I. À propos d'un livre récent," *Revue Thomiste,* 79 (1979), 51–72; Otto Hermann Pesch, "Bilanz der Diskussion um die Vatikanische Primats- und Unfehlbarkeitsdefinition," *Papsttum als ökumenische Frage* (Munich and Mainz: Arbeitsgemeinschaft ökumenischer Universitätsinstitut, 1979), pp. 159–211; review by Manfred Weitlauff in *Zeitschrift für Kirchengeschichte* (1979).

[90] Particular mention should be made of Congar, Küng, Seckler, Hoffmann, Fransen, Weitlauff, Blank, and Denzler.

[91] Cf., for example, the reviews by Stehle, Willi, Politi, Kühner, Bohne, Oschwald, Weiss, Küppers, Meyer, Ross, Margiotta-Broglio, Haendler, Lindt, Franz-Willig, Stadler, and Otto Hermann Pesch. I should also not wish to forget all the professors who made it possible for me to publish my study in the "Päpste und Papsttum" series put out by Hiersemann Verlag.

[92] Schatz, "Totalrevision," p. 256; Martina, "Pio IX e il Vaticano I, di A. B. Hasler," pp. 357–58; Walter Kasper, "Deinst an der Einheit und Freiheit der Kirche. Zur gegenwärtigen Diskussion um das Petrusamt in der Kirche," *Catholica,* 32 (1978), 6.

[93] Schatz, "Totalrevision," p. 257, n. 18.

[94] See the reviews by Brandmüller, Conzemius, Helbling, Martina, Schatz, Boudens, and Torrell.

[95] The Vatican also bought the unpublished biography of Pius IX by a professor of church history named Joseph Clementi, thus preventing historians from making any use of it. Not even Fr. Giacomo Martina, S.J., the Vatican's official biographer of Pius IX, got to see it, although he asked about it several times. On this whole problem, see the review by Max Seckler in *Das historisch-politische Buch,* 26 (1978), 234.

[96] See Hanno Helbling, "Kunst des Weglassens," *Neue Zürcher Zeitung,* out-of-town edition, no. 264, Nov. 11, 1977, p. 35; Schatz, "Totalrevision," p. 258f.

[97] See August Bernhard Hasler, "Pius IX und die päpstliche Unfehlbarkeit. Eine Antwort," *Neue Zürcher Zeitung,* out-of-town edition,

no. 293, Dec. 15, 1977, pp. 39–40.

[98] See Helbling, "Kunst des Weglassens," p. 35.

[99] Brandmüller, *Rheinischer Merkur*, no. 35, Sept. 2, 1977, p. 20.

[100] "Ferndiagnose unwissenschaftlich," *Publik-Forum*, no. 22, Oct. 28, 1977, p. 23.

[101] Fischer, *Frankfurter Allgemeine Zeitung*, no. 63, p. 11.

[102] Conzemius, "Erstes Vatikanum und Unfehlbarkeit," p. 208. Schatz writes, "The psychiatric reports cited there are worthless in my opinion because the negative features of Pius IX on which they are based do not—even though they are carefully documented in themselves—amount to a complete picture of the pope's personality" ("Totalrevision," p. 250, n. 12). Why does there have to be a total picture of an individual (and what constitutes such a thing?) in order to determine the presence of abnormalities?

[103] Egli, "Zuschrift zu 'Erstes Vatikanum und Unfehlbarkeit,'" *Orientierung*, 41 (1977), 248.

[104] Küppers, "Infragestellung des Ersten Vatikanums in heutiger alt-katholischer Sicht," *Schweizerische Kirchenzeitung*, 146 (1978), 192.

[105] Bohne, *Frankfurter Hefte*, 33 (1978), 76.

[106] Stockmeier, "Geschichte und Unfehlbarkeit," 192; Weitlauff also agrees.

[107] Roger Aubert and Giacomo Martina, *Il Pontificato di Pio IX* (Turin, 1970), II, 846.

[108] Kühner, "Ein kranker Papst setzte das Unfehlbarkeitsdogma durch . . ." *Luzerner Neueste Nachrichten*, no. 240, Oct. 14, 1977, p. 5; "Explosivstoff Unfehlbarkeit," *Basler Zeitung*, March 17, 1978.

[109] Conzemius, "Erstes Vatikanum und Unfehlbarkeit," p. 208.

[110] Stockmeier, "Geschichte und Unfehlbarkeit," p. 193.

[111] "Pius IX und das Unfehlbarkeitsdogma," 58.

[111a] Fransen, "Pius IX und die päpstliche Unfehlbarkheits," p. 44.

[112] Voss, "Pius IX.—Päpstliche Unfehlbarkeit—Erstes Vatikanisches Konzil," 81.

[113] Congar, "Bulletin d'Écclésiologie," p. 87.

[114] Küppers, "Infragestellung des Ersten Vatikanums," p. 193.

[115] Ibid.

[116] Schatz, "Totalrevision," p. 264.

[117] Ibid., p. 264, n. 39.

[118] See esp. Kasper, "Dienst an der Einheit," p. 6.

[119] Schatz, "Totalrevision," p. 256.

[120] Ibid. In a similar fashion, Otto Hermann Pesch, in his review in the *Allgemeines Sonntagsblatt*, considers the actual reception of the dogma as more crucial than a free conciliar decision.

[121] Ibid.

[122] Ibid., p. 256f.

[123] Pesche, "Parteiischer Anwalt. Zu August B. Haslers Papst- und Dogmenkritik," *Publik-Forum*, no. 6, March 24, 1978, pp. 16–17.

[124] See Regina Bohne, "Freiheit gewahrleistet," *Publik-Forum*, no. 8, April 21, 1978, p. 22.

[125] Stockmeier, "Geschichte und Unfehlbarkeit," p. 197.

[126] Schatz, "Totalrevision," p. 257.

[127] Blank, "Pius IX und das Unfehlbarkeitsdogma," *Imprimatur*, no. 2, Feb. 28, 1978, p. 58.

[128] Blank, "Pius IX.–Päpstliche Unfehlbarkeit–Erstes Vatikanisches Konzil," *Una Sancta*, 33 (1978), 80.

[129] Meyer, article in *Lutherische Rundschau*, 27 (1977), 656–57.

[130] See Otto Weiss, in *Zeitschrift für bayerische Landesgeschichte* 41 (1978), 330.

[130a] Torrell, "Tradition, histoire et idéologie à Vatican I," p. 61f.

[131] Schatz, "Totalrevision," p. 265f.

[131a] Review by Manfred Weitlauff in *Zeitschrift für Kirchengeschichte* (1979).

[132] Schatz, "Totalrevision," p. 267.

[133] Congar, "Bulletin d'Écclésiologie," p. 88.

[134] Ibid., p. 87.

[135] See Stockmeier, "Geschichte und Unfehlbarkeit," p. 194f.

[136] Schatz, "Totalrevision," p. 267.

[137] Stehle, *Die Zeit*, no. 53, Dec. 23, 1977, p. 13.

[138] Blank, "Pius IX.–Päpstliche Unfehlbarkeit–Erstes Vatikanisches Konzil," *Una Sancta*, 33 (1978), 76.

[139] Conzemius, "Erstes Vatikanum," *Orientierung*, 41 (1977), p. 262.

[140] See F. Margiotta-Broglio, "Pio IX nell'armadio: Il Dogma dell'infallibilità," *La Nazione*, August 3, 1978; idem, review in *Storia Contemporanea*, 9 (1978), 771.

[140a] Idem, *Storia Contemporanea*, 9 (1978), 769.

[141] Willi, "Fehlbare Unfehlbarkeit?" *Schweizer Rundschau*, 77 (1978), 17.

[142] Ibid.

[143] Meyer, *Lutherische Rundschau*, 27 (1977), 657.

[144] Kühner, *Basler Zeitung*, March 17, 1978.

[145] Küng, "Was Vatican I Rigged? How the Pope Became Infallible," *Time*, Nov. 14, 1977, p. 52.

[146] Congar, "Bulletin d'Écclésiologie," p. 88.

[147] Küppers, "Infragestellung des Ersten Vatikanums," p. 193f.

Select Bibliography

I. Sources

J. D. Mansi. *Sacrorum conciliorum nova et amplissima collectio.* Newly edited and expanded by L. Petit and J. B. Martin. 60 vols. Paris, 1899–1927; Arnhem, 1923–27; reprint, Graz, 1960–61, (vols. 49–53 deal with the First Vatican Council).

Collectio Lacensis. *Acta et Decreta Sacrorum Conciliorum Recentiorum.* Edited by the Jesuits of Maria Laach. Vol. VII. Freiburg im Breisgau, 1890.

E. Cecconi. *Storia del Concilio Ecumenico Vaticano scritta sui documenti originali.* 4 vols. Rome, 1872–79.

E. Friedberg. *Sammlung der Aktenstücke zum ersten vaticanischen Concil mit einem Grundrisse der Geschichte desselben.* 2 vols. Tübingen, 1872–76.

C. Mirbt and K. Aland. *Quellen zur Geschichte des Papsttums und des römischen Katholizismus.* Vol. I: *Von den Anfängen bis zum Tridentinum.* Tübingen, 1967.

H. Denzinger and A. Schönmetzer. *Enchiridion symbolorum, definitionum et declarationum de rebus fidei et morum.* Barcelona/ Freiburg/Rome/New York, 1967.

Centro di Documentazione, Istituto per le Scienze Religiose, ed. *Conciliorum oecumenicorum decreta.* Bologna/Basel/Barcelona/ Freiburg/Rome/Vienna, 1962.

I. von Döllinger and Lord Acton. *Briefwechsel, 1850–1890.* Edited by the Kommission für Bayerische Landesgeschichte; rev. ed. by V. Conzemius. 3 vols. Munich, 1963–71.

I. von Döllinger. *Das Papsttum* (rev. ed. of "Janus": *Der Papst und das Concil,* edited by J. Friedrich). Munich, 1892.

———. *Briefe und Erklärungen über die Vatikanischen Dekrete 1869 bis 1887.* Edited by F. H. Reusch. Darmstadt, 1968 (reprint).

I. von Senestrey. *Wie es zur Definition der päpstlichen Unfehlbarkeit kam. Tagebuch vom 1. Vatikanischen Konzil.* Edited and with a commentary by K. Schatz. Frankfurter Theologische Studien, no. 24. Frankfurt am Main, 1977.

G. G. Franco. *Appunti storici sopra il Concilio Vaticano.* Introduced and revised by G. Martina. Miscellanea Historiae Pontificiae, vol. 33. Rome, 1972.

A. Tamborra. *Imbro I. Tkalac e l'Italia.* Istituto per la Storia del Risorgimento Italiano, Biblioteca Scientifica, vol. XXIV. Rome, 1966.

N. Blakiston. *The Roman Question: Extracts from the Despatches of Odo Russell from Rome, 1858–1870.* London, 1962.

J. Gadille. *Albert du Boÿs: Ses "Souvenirs du Concile du Vatican, 1869–1870." L'Intervention du gouvernement impérial à Vatican I.* Bibliothèque de la Revue d'Histoire Ecclésiastique, vol. 46. Louvain, 1968.

II. History of the Papacy and the Doctrine of Infallibility

F. X. Seppelt. *Geschichte der Päpste von den Anfängen bis zur Mitte des 20. Jahrhunderts.* 5 vols. Munich, 1954–59.

F. X. Seppelt and G. Schwaiger. *Geschichte der Päpste. Von den Anfängen bis zur Gegenwart.* Munich, 1964.

J. Haller. *Das Papsttum. Idee und Wirklichkeit.* 3 vols. Stuttgart, 1934–45; reprint, 5 vols. Munich, 1965.

E. Caspar. *Geschichte des Papsttums von den Anfängen bis zur Höhe der Weltherrschaft.* 2 vols. Tübingen, 1930–33.

H. Kühner. *Das Imperium der Päpste. Kirchengeschichte, Weltgeschichte, Zeitgeschichte. Von Petrus bis heute.* Zurich and Stuttgart, 1977.

B. Tierney. *Origins of Papal Infallibility, 1150–1350: A Study on the Concept of Infallibility, Sovereignty and Tradition in the Middle Ages.* Studies in the History of Christian Thought, vol. 6. Leiden, 1972.

F. X. Bantle. *Unfehlbarkeit der Kirche in Aufklärung und Romantik. Eine dogmengeschichtliche Untersuchung für die Zeit der Wende vom 18. zum 19. Jahrhundert.* Freiburger Theologische Studien, no. 103. Freiburg, 1976.

H. J. Pottmeyer. *Unfehlbarkeit und Souveränität. Die päpstliche Unfehlbarkeit im System der ultramontanen Ekklesiologie des 19. Jahrhunderts.* Tübinger Theologische Studien, vol. 5. Mainz, 1975.

Y. M. J. Congar. *Die Lehre von der Kirche. Von Augustinus bis zum Abendländischen Schisma.* Handbuch der Dogmengeschichte, 3, 3c. Freiburg im Breisgau, 1971.

III. First Vatican Council

J. Friedrich. *Geschichte des Vatikanischen Konzils.* 3 vols. Bonn, 1877–87; reprint, Hildesheim, 1971.

T. Granderath. *Geschichte des Vatikanischen Konzils von seiner ersten Ankündigung bis zu seiner Vertagung. Nach den authentischen Dokumenten dargestellt.* Edited by K. Kirch. 3 vols. Freiburg im Breisgau, 1903–6.

C. Butler and H. Lang. *Das Vatikanische Konzil. Seine Geschichte von innen geschildert in Bischof Ullathornes Briefen.* Munich, 1933; 2nd edn., 1961.

R. Aubert. *Vaticanum I.* Mainz, 1965.

R. Aubert, J. Beckmann, P. J. Corish, and L. Lill. "Die Kirche zwischen Revolution und Restauration," in *Handbuch der Kirchengeschichte,* edited by H. Jedin. Vol. VI/1. Freiburg/Basel/Vienna, 1971.

A. B. Hasler. *Pius IX. (1846–1878), päpstliche Unfehlbarkeit und 1. Vatikanisches Konzil. Dogmatisierung und Durchsetzung einer Ideologie.* Päpste und Papsttum, no. 12. Stuttgart, 1977. (Contains extensive bibliography)

F. Heyer. "Die katholische Kirche von 1648 bis 1870," in *Die Kirche in ihrer Geschichte. Ein Handbuch,* edited by K. D. Schmidt and E. Wolf. Vol. IV/1. Göttingen, 1963.

R. Aubert. *Le Pontificat de Pie IX (1846–1878).* Histoire de l'Église depuis les origines jusqu'à nos jours, vol. 21. Paris, 1963.

R. Aubert and G. Martina. *Il Pontificato di Pio IX.* Storia della Chiesa dalle origini ai nostri giorni, vols. XX/1 and 2. Turin, 1970.

K. Schatz. *Kirchenbild und päpstliche Unfehlbarkeit bei den deutschsprachigen Minoritätsbischöfen auf dem 1. Vatikanum.* Miscellanea Historiae Pontificiae, vol. 40. Rome, 1975.

G. Adriányi. *Ungarn und das. 1. Vaticanum.* Bonner Beiträge zur Kirchengeschichte, vol. 5. Cologne, 1975.

J. Hennessey. *The First Vatican Council: The American Experience.* New York, 1963.

F. J. Cwiekowski. *The English Bishops and the First Vatican Council.* Bibliothèque de la Revue d'Histoire Ecclésiastique, vol. 52. Louvain, 1971.

E. Weinzierl, ed. *Die päpstliche Autorität im katholischen Selbstverständnis des 19. und 20. Jahrhunderts.* Forschungsgespräche des internationalen Forschungszentrums für Grundfragen der Wissenschaften (Salzburg), no. 11. Salzburg and Munich, 1970.

V. Conzemius. *Katholizismus ohne Rome. Die altkatholische Kirchengemeinschaft.* Zurich/Einsiedeln/Rome, 1919.

IV. Current Discussions of the Papacy and Infallibility

F. Simons. *Infallibility and the Evidence.* Springfield, Mass., 1968.

H. Küng. *Unfehlbar? Eine Anfrage.* Zurich/Einsiedeln/Cologne, 1970.

H. Küng, ed. *Fehlbar? Eine Bilanz.* Zurich/Einsiedeln/Cologne, 1973.

K. Rahner, ed. *Zum Problem Unfehlbarkeit. Antworten auf die Anfrage von Hans Küng.* Quaestiones Disputatae, no. 54. Freiburg/Basel/Vienna, 1971.

W. Jens, ed. *Um Nichts als die Wahrheit. Deutsche Bischofskonferenz contra Hans Küng.* Munich and Zurich, 1978.

F. Leist. *Der Gefangene des Vatikans. Strukturen päpstlicher Herrschaft.* Munich, 1971.

G. Denzler, ed. *Das Papsttum in der Diskussion.* Regensburg, 1974.

———. *Papsttum heute und morgen. 57 Antworten auf eine Umfrage.* Regensburg, 1975.

K. H. Ohlig. *Braucht die Kirche einen Papst? Umfang und Grenzen des päpstlichden Primats.* Mainz and Düsseldorf, 1973.

H. Stirnimann and L. Vischer. *Papsttum und Petrusdienst,* with additional contributions from G. Gassmann, H. Meyer, D. Papandreou, K. Stadler, A. Stoecklin, including documents. Ökumenische Perspektiven, no. 7. Frankfurt am Main, 1975.

H. J. Mund. *Das Petrusamt in der gegenwärtigen theologischen Diskussion.* Paderborn, 1976.

"Pro Oriente" Foundation. *Konziliarität und Kollegialität als Strukturprinzipien der Kirche. Das Petrusamt in ökumenischer Sicht. Christus und seine Kirche.* Innsbruck/Vienna/Munich, 1975.

R. E. Brown, ed. *Der Petrus in der Bibel. Eine ökumenische Untersuchung.* Stuttgart, 1976.

A. Brandenburg and H. J. Urban, eds. *Petrus und Papst. Evangelium, Einheit der Kirche, Papstdienst. Beiträge und Notizen.* Münster, 1976.

G. Schwaiger. *Päpstlicher Primat und Autorität der allgemeinen Konzilien im Spiegel der Geschichte.* Munich/Paderborn/Vienna, 1977.

V. Critiques of Ideology

H. Albert. *Traktat über kritische Vernunft.* Die Einheit der Gesellschaftwissenschaften: Studien in den Grenzbereichen der Wirtschafts- und Sozialwissenschaften, vol. 9. Tübingen, 1969.

———. *Plädoyer für kritischen Rationalismus.* Pieper Series, no. 310. Munich, 1971.

———. *Konstruktion und Kritik. Aufsätze zur Philosophie des kritischen Rationalismus.* Hamburg, 1972.

E. Topitsch and K. Salamun. *Ideologie. Herrschaft des Vorturteils.* Langen-Müller Stitchworte, no. 5. Munich and Vienna, 1972.

H. Barth. *Wahrheit und Ideologie.* Suhrkamp paperback, science, no. 68. Frankfurt am Main, 1974.

A. Stüttgen. *Kriterion einer Ideologiekritik. Ihre Anwendung auf Christentum und Marxismus.* Mainz, 1972.

M. Schmid. *Leerformeln und Ideologiekritik.* Heidelberger Sociologica, no. 11. Tübingen, 1972.

M. Gatzemeier. "Theologie als Wissenschaft," in *I: Die Sache der Theologie. II. Wissenschafts- und Institutionenkritik.* Problemata series, nos. 21 and 22. Stuttgart and Bad Cannstatt, 1974–75.

J. Nolte. *Dogma in Geschichte. Versuch einer Kritik des Dogmatismus in der Glaubensdarstellung.* Ökumenische Forschungen II, Soteriologische Abteilung, vol. 3. Freiburg/Basel/Vienna, 1971.

O. Köhler. *Bewusstseinsstörungen im Katholizismus.* Frankfurt am Main, 1972.

Index

Picture Credits

Archivio Fotografico Communale di Roma: 42, 44, 82, 93, 116, 119, 121, 124, 125, 186/187, 194

Archivio Segreto Vaticano, Spoglio Cardinale Bilio: 185

Archive of the English College in Rome, Talbot Papers: 118

Biblioteca Valicelliana, Rome: 109, 241

Pictorial Archive of the Papal Court Photographer, Giordani, Rome: 260

Pictorial Archive of the Jesuit Generalate, Rome: 73, 101

Bildarchiv des Süddeutschen Verlags: 257

Istituto per la Storia del Risorgimento Italiano, Rome: 47, 49, 51, 54, 84, 107, 189, 235, 239, 289, 291

Private archive of Professor Emile Poulat, Paris; a gift from Mrs. Guido Aureli, Rome: 249

Servizio Fotografico dell'*Osservatore Romano*, Rome: 284, 288, 293

R. Aubert and G. Martina, *Il Pontificato di Pio IX* (Turin, 1970): 59

A. Begey and A. Favero, S.E. Mons. arcivescovo L. Puecher-Passavalli: Ricordi e lettere (1870–1897) (Turin, 1911): 224

Berliner Wespen, June 25, 1875: 112

Gaëtan Bernoville, *Emmanuel d'Alzon* (Paris, 1957): 56

Lucien Christophe, *Louis Veuillot* (Paris, 1967): 62

Der industrielle Humorist, no. 7, 1870: 273

Ignaz von Döllinger/Lord Acton: Briefwechsel, 1850–1890, ed. by the Kommission für bayerische Landesgeschicht, rev. ed. by V. Conzemius, 3 vols. (Munich, 1963–71): 66, 87, 132, 180, 222

Ludovico Ferretti, *Il sepolcro di Pio IX in Roma nell'antico nartece della Basilica di S. Lorenzo fuori le mura* (Florence, 1915): 287

Victor Frond, *Actes et Histoire du Concile de Rome*, vols. I–VII (Paris, 1870–71): jacket illustration, 45, 58, 60, 65, 71, 75, 76, 79, 80, 85, 88, 90 (2), 94, 95, 96, 97, 98, 100, 102, 114, 138, 152, 167, 168, 172, 183, 191, 193, 195, 197, 201, 203, 205, 208, 209, 210, 212, 214, 216, 217, 219, 220, 226, 229, 231, 236

Francesco Biagioni Gazzoli, *Memorie de Mons. Tizzani. Con biografia e note* (Rome: Danesi, 1945): 227

Jean d'Hospital, *Drei Päpste. Pius XII, Johannes XXIII, und Paul VI* (Vienna and Hamburg: Zsolnay Verlag, 1971): 263

Le Concile oecumenique de 1869–1870 illustre (Lyon, 1870): 136

Ernst Nolte, *Der Faschismus von Mussolini zu Hitler. Texte, Bilder, Dokumente* (Munich, 1968): 256

Gaspare Pontrandolfi, S.P., *Pio IX e Volterra. Nel cinquantenario della morte di Pio IX* (Volterra [1928]): 105

Johann Friedrich Ritter von Schulte, *Lebenserinnerungen. Mein Wirken als Rechtslehrer, mein Anteil an der Politik in Kirche und Staat*, 3 vols. (Giessen, 1908–9), II: 143

John J. O'Shea, *The Two Kenricks: Most Rev. Francis Patrick, Archbishop of Baltimore. Most Rev. Peter Richard, Archbishop of St. Louis* (Philadelphia: John J. McVey, 1904): 204

Nino Valeri, *Storia d'Italia*, vol. IV (Turin, 1965), 332 (from *Il Fischietto*, Jan. 8, 1870): 161

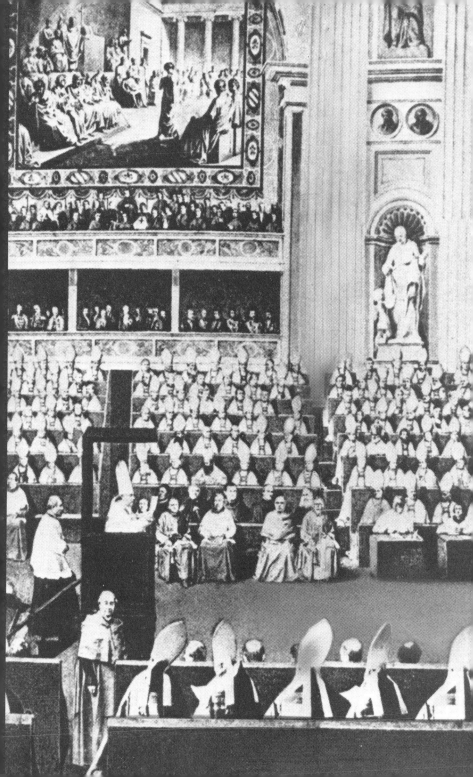